The Promise of Early Childhood Development in Latin America and the Caribbean

The Promise of Early Childhood Development in Latin America and the Caribbean

Emiliana Vegas and Lucrecia Santibáñez

with

Bénédicte Leroy de la Brière
Alejandro Caballero
Julien Alexis Hautier
and
Domenec Ruiz Devesa

1 2 3 4 12 11 10 09

This volume is a product of the staff of the International Bank for Reconstruction and Development / The World Bank. The findings, interpretations, and conclusions expressed in this volume do not necessarily reflect the views of the Executive Directors of The World Bank or the governments they represent.

The World Bank does not guarantee the accuracy of the data included in this work. The boundaries, colors, denominations, and other information shown on any map in this work do not imply any judgement on the part of The World Bank concerning the legal status of any territory or the endorsement or acceptance of such boundaries.

ISBN: 978-0-8213-7759-8   eISBN: 978-0-8213-8164-9
DOI: 10.1596/978-0-8213-7759-8

Library of Congress Cataloging-in-Publication Data
Vegas, Emiliana.
The promise of early childhood development in Latin America and the Caribbean / Emiliana Vegas and Lucrecia Santibáñez.

    p. cm.—(Latin American development forum series)
  Includes bibliographical references and index.
  ISBN 978-0-8213-7759-8—ISBN 978-0-8213-8164-9 (electronic)

  1. Children—Latin America—Social conditions. 2. Children—Caribbean Area—Social conditions. 3. Child development—Latin America. 4. Child development—Caribbean Area. 5. Child welfare—Latin America. 6. Child welfare—Caribbean Area. I. Santibáñez, Lucrecia. II. World Bank. III. Title.

  HQ792.L3V44 2011
  305.23109729—dc22

                                                                      2009040426

Cover design: ULTRAdesigns.
Printed in the United States.

Latin American Development Forum Series

This series was created in 2003 to promote debate, disseminate information and analysis, and convey the excitement and complexity of the most topical issues in economic and social development in Latin America and the Caribbean. It is sponsored by the Inter-American Development Bank, the United Nations Economic Commission for Latin America and the Caribbean, and the World Bank. The manuscripts chosen for publication represent the highest quality in each institution's research and activity output and have been selected for their relevance to the academic community, policy makers, researchers, and interested readers.

Advisory Committee Members

Titles in the Latin American Development Forum Series

Discrimination in Latin America: An Economic Perspective (2010) by Hugo Ñopo, Alberto Chong, and Andrea Moro, editors

The Promise of Early Childhood Development in Latin America and the Caribbean (2010) by Emiliana Vegas and Lucrecia Santibáñez

Job Creation in Latin America and the Caribbean: Trends and Policy Challenges (2009) by Carmen Pagés, Gaëlle Pierre, and Stefano Scarpetta

China's and India's Challenge to Latin America: Opportunity or Threat? (2009) by Daniel Lederman, Marcelo Olarreaga, and Guillermo E. Perry, editors

Does the Investment Climate Matter? Microeconomic Foundations of Growth in Latin America (2009) by Pablo Fajnzylber, Jose Luis Guasch, and J. Humberto López, editors

Measuring Inequality of Opportunities in Latin America and the Caribbean (2009) by Ricardo de Paes Barros, Francisco H. G. Ferreira, José R. Molinas Vega, and Jaime Saavedra Chanduvi

The Impact of Private Sector Participation in Infrastructure: Lights, Shadows, and the Road Ahead (2008) by Luis Andres, Jose Luis Guasch, Thomas Haven, and Vivien Foster

Remittances and Development: Lessons from Latin America (2008) by Pablo Fajnzylber and J. Humberto López, editors

Fiscal Policy, Stabilization, and Growth: Prudence or Abstinence? (2007) by Guillermo Perry, Luis Servén, and Rodrigo Suescún, editors

About the Authors

Emiliana Vegas is a Senior Education Economist at the Human Development Department of the World Bank. During 2003–08, she worked in the Bank's Latin America and Caribbean Region. In this capacity, she advised the Chilean and Uruguayan authorities on early childhood development policies and interventions to raise the quality of basic and secondary education. She is the author of several articles in peer-reviewed journals and institutional reports, many of them focusing on education quality, teacher labor markets, and teacher incentives. Her previous books include *Raising Student Learning in Latin America: The Challenge for the 21st Century* (2007, The World Bank Press, co-authored with Jenny Petrow) and *Incentives to Improve Teaching: Lessons from Latin America* (2005, The World Bank Press, Editor). She holds a Doctor of Education degree from Harvard University, an M.A. in Public Policy from Duke University, and a B.A. in Journalism from Andrés Bello Catholic University in Caracas, Venezuela.

Lucrecia Santibañez is a partner at Fundación IDEA in Mexico City, a non-profit, independent think tank focusing on education and public policy analysis. Until 2009, she was professor of public policy at the Centro de Investigación y Docencia Económicas (CIDE), where she began work on this book. Before that, she was a researcher at the RAND Corporation. She has published extensively on teacher incentives, teacher labor markets, educational evaluation, and school quality. She is a frequent consultant for The World Bank. She holds a Ph.D. in Education, an M.A. in Economics, and an M.A. in Latin American Studies, all from Stanford University.

Contents

TABLES

Acknowledgments

This book was prepared by a team of World Bank staff and consultants under the guidance of Evangeline Javier (Director for Human Development), Augusto de la Torre (Chief Economist, Latin America and the Caribbean Region), Keith Hansen (Health Sector Manager), Helena Ribe (Social Protection Sector Manager), Eduardo Vélez-Bustillo (Education Sector Manager), and Jennie Litvack (Lead Economist for Human Development). Jesko Hentschel (Sector Leader for Human Development) provided technical guidance in the initial stages of the book.

The team included Emiliana Vegas (Senior Education Economist, Task Team Leader, LCSHE), Lucrecia Santibáñez (Consultant, Fundación IDEA, Mexico), Bénédicte Leroy de la Brière (Senior Social Protection Economist, LCSHS), Alejandro Caballero (Young Professional, LCSHE), Domenec Ruiz-Devesa (JPA, LCSHD), and Julien Alexis Hautier (Consultant, LCSHE). Ada Rivera, Viviana A. Gonzalez, and Natalia Moncada (Program Assistants, LCSHD) provided support in the preparation and processing of the document. The book is based on several background papers authored by Erika Dunkelberg; the Mexican National Institute of Public Health; Emily Vargas Barón; and Hernán Winkler. The team also benefited from helpful comments and suggestions by Christine Lao Peña (Senior Human Development Economist, LCSHH), Alessandra Marini (Economist, LCSHS), Christel Vermeersch (Economist, LCSHE), and Norbert Schady (Senior Economist, DECRG). Nazumi Takeda (Consultant, LCSHD) and Peggy McInerny (Consultant, HDNED) helped in editing the manuscript for publication.

The team is most grateful to the peer reviewers—Hiro Yoshikawa (Professor of Education, Harvard Graduate School of Education), Vicente Paqueo (Country Sector Coordinator, EASHD), and Mary Eming Young (Lead Specialist, HDNCY)—whose valuable comments greatly contributed to improving early drafts of the book.

Abbreviations

BCG	Bacille Calmette Guerin (vaccine)
CCC	Chile Grows with You (Chile Crece Contigo)
CCF-I	Christian Children's Fund International
CEDLAS	Centro de Estudios Distributivos Laborales y Sociales, Universidad Nacional de La Plata, Argentina
CINDE	Centro Internacional de Educación y Desarrollo Humano
CMP	Community Mothers Program
DECRG	Development Research Group, the World Bank
DINETF	National Directorate for Initial and Primary Education
DPT	diptheria, pertussis, and tetanus (vaccine)
EASHD	Human Development Department, East Asia and the Pacific Region, the World Bank
ECCD	Early Childhood Care and Development
ECCE	Early Childhood Care and Education Centers
ECD	Early Childhood Development
ECI	Early Childhood Intervention
ECLS-K	Early Childhood Longitudinal Study–Kindergarten Class
EFA	Education for All
EHS	Early Head Start
EPPE	Effective Provision of Preschool Education Project
FA	Families in Action
FTI	Fast-Track Initiative
FUNDEB	Fundo da Educação Básica
GDP	gross domestic product
GED	general educational development
GER	gross enrollment rate
HDNCY	Children and Youth Unit, Human Development Department, the World Bank
HS	high school

HOME	Home Observation for Measurement of the Environment, a rating scale
IADB	Inter-American Development Bank
JPA	Junior Professional Associate
JSLC	Jamaica Survey of Living Conditions
JUNJI	Junta Nacional de Jardines Infantiles (National Council of Early Childcare Centers)
LAC	Latin America and the Caribbean Region, World Bank
LCSHE	Education Sector, Human Development Department, Latin America and the Caribbean Region, World Bank
LCSHH	Health Sector, Human Development Department, Latin America and the Caribbean Region, World Bank
LCSHS	Social Protection Sector, Human Development Department, Latin America and the Caribbean Region, World Bank
MDG	Millennium Development Goal
MMR	measles, mumps, and rubella (vaccine)
MOE	Ministry of Education
MOH	Ministry of Health
NGO	nongovernmental organization
NICHD	National Institute of Child Health and Human Development
OEA	Organization of American States
OECD	Organisation for Economic Co-operation and Development
PISA	Programme of International Student Assessment
PPVT	Peabody Picture Vocabulary Test
PRONOEI	Nonformal Program for Initial Education
SEDLAC	Socio-Economic Database for Latin America and the Caribbean, database maintained by World Bank
SERNAM	Chilean National Service for Women
SES	socioeconomic status
SISBEN	System for the Selection of Beneficiaries
UN	United Nations
UNESCO	United Nations Education, Science, and Culture Organization
UNICEF	United Nations Children's Fund
WDR	World Development Report, World Bank
WIC	Women's Infants and Children's Program

Introduction

This book aims to fill gaps in existing knowledge about early childhood development (ECD) efforts in Latin America and the Caribbean by reviewing a selection of ECD programs in the region—including those in early childhood education, health, and nutrition—and distilling lessons related to their design, implementation, and institutionalization. The book surveys existing evidence on the impact of programs worldwide that provide support to children during the period before birth through age six, including programs in developed and developing nations. It presents a compelling evidence-based argument for greater investment in ECD programs in Latin America and the Caribbean, while highlighting the need for both more rigorous evaluations and more accurate cost accounting of such programs. Improved evaluations and cost tracking will generate better data on how to effectively design, fund, and provide quality ECD programs to all children in the region, especially those from low-income families.

After developing an analytical framework for examining early childhood development outcomes, the study closely examines the macro and micro context of early childhood development in the countries of Latin America and the Caribbean. On this basis, it builds the case for increasing ECD investments in the region, particularly investments that target poor and disadvantaged children (and their parents) at very early ages. The book then surveys available evidence on ECD interventions around the world, presenting detailed findings on programs in the United States (the Perry Preschool, Carolina Abecedarian, Chicago Child-Parent, Head Start, and Early Head Start programs), OECD countries, the Philippines, Uganda, Turkey, and Vietnam.

Building on this survey of programs outside of the region, the study then examines contemporary ECD interventions and their impacts in Latin America and Caribbean. One major conclusion of this analysis is that individual countries in the region would benefit from developing national ECD policies to effectively scale up and sustain broader, integral investments in this area. The book accordingly devotes a chapter to reviewing the major components of a national ECD policy, and drawing on the policy experience of a number of OECD countries in building and implementing sustainable ECD policies. Finally, a concluding chapter summarizes the findings on early childhood development outcomes and interventions in the region, as well as the policy implications of these findings.

Analytical Framework

Existing research evidence indicates that three main ECD outcomes determine lifelong opportunities and outcomes: (i) cognitive development, which includes the acquisition of language and literacy; (ii) socioemotional development, which includes the ability to socialize with others; and (iii) physical well-being and growth, which encompasses height, weight, nutritional status, and other physical indicators. Although listed separately here, all three outcomes are considered interdependent, especially cognitive and socioemotional development.

The framework starts by recognizing that child development does not take place in a vacuum. In any given country, the macro context (that is, the economic, political, and social context) affects the nature and extent of social policies, which directly affect children's well-being, the type of programs made available to young children and their caregivers, and the organizations that operate these. Simultaneously, the micro context—the interaction between a child and her or his primary caregiver during the early years—sets a child on a trajectory that affects her or his future development. In addition, the availability of programs, services, and policies directed at children, their caregivers, or both, affects this interaction and trajectory.

Evidence on Early Childhood Development

Until fairly recently, it was widely believed that human beings were born with genetically predetermined abilities, as their brains were thought to be fully developed at birth. Recent scientific research has established that, to the contrary, the brain continues to develop and form neural connections during the early years of childhood. Research has also shown that nutrition, cognitive stimulation, and nurturing care during these early years strongly influence the extent to which a child's health, as well as her or his cognitive and socioemotional abilities, may develop to their fullest potential (Young 2002).

Children of families living in poverty face many developmental challenges during their early years that affect their opportunity to receive adequate nutrition, stimulation, and care. As a consequence, a high proportion of children of poor households are not able to reach their full development potential, impeding their physical, cognitive, and socioe-motional development. Early childhood development outcomes play an important role throughout life, affecting one's income-earning capacity and productivity, longevity, health, and cognitive ability. Importantly, the deleterious effects of poor ECD outcomes can be long lasting—affecting school attainment, employment, wages, criminality, and the social integration of adults. Indeed, differences in early childhood development across children from poor and nonpoor households have been shown to be related to important outcomes well into adulthood.

Investing in people has been long shown to be a good investment. In the mid-twentieth century, several researchers showed that investing in people—that is, in their skills and abilities—could be just as profitable as investing in physical capital. Schultz (1961, 1971) empirically showed the importance of education for productivity growth in the United States. At the individual level, Mincer (1958) was the first to empirically demonstrate that education differentials are related to differences in wages at later stages in life. Becker (1964) organized this work and that of others into what we now refer to as "human capital theory," the foundation of much recent work on the relationship between investments in people (including those made through education, health, and social protection) and the benefits (including both individual earnings and life outcomes, as well as multiple benefits for society as a whole).

Research has shown that early childhood interventions can act as an important policy lever to equalize opportunities for children and reduce the intergenerational grip of poverty and inequality. Recent work by Nobel Laureate James Heckman and colleagues builds on this previous literature and shows that human capital formation is a dynamic process that begins early in life and continues over the life cycle. Heckman and his colleagues have convincingly shown that factors operating during the early childhood years play an important role in the development of skills that determine outcomes later in life.[1]

Other recent research on early childhood development highlights that both cognitive such as language and mathematics skills) and noncognitive (such as social skills and self-discipline) skills are important for success in school and productivity in the labor market. One important finding is that a child's family environment is central to her or his development of skills and ability; hence, early interventions targeted at equalizing early family differences can contribute to reducing early inequalities. The parental environment and family income of a child are, moreover, far more decisive in promoting human capital and school success during early childhood than in later years.

This research has several important policy implications. First, all else being equal, returns to investments in early childhood will be higher than returns to investments made later in life simply because the beneficiaries have a longer time to reap the rewards from these investments. Second, investments in human capital have dynamic complementarities: improved

ECD outcomes result in improved educational attainment levels, health outcomes, and labor market outcomes. Third, while education policies are important, what happens in schools is not sufficient to equalize opportunities and reduce inequality. It is crucial to invest early in both children and their families, as the family environment plays an important role in the development of cognitive and noncognitive skills.

One important policy consideration of ECD investments is that they do not involve a trade-off between equity and efficiency. Currie (2001), for example, argues that it may be more effective to reduce inequality by equalizing initial endowments through ECD programs than to compensate for differences in outcomes later in life. Not only may ECD investments be more cost-effective because they have larger benefits relative to their costs; they avoid many of the moral hazard problems inherent in programs that seek to equalize outcomes in adulthood, such as tax and income transfers, which are often seen as inequitable.

Although there is strong evidence of the impact of ECD interventions, there is unfortunately little evidence on how to effectively design, fund, and provide quality ECD programs—including early childhood education, health, and nutrition programs—to all children, especially those from low-income families. In addition, few studies exist that analyze the cost-effectiveness of alternative ECD programs, which could help policy makers in choosing among competing policy alternatives.

The Argument for Investing in ECD in Latin America and the Caribbean

Ensuring that all individuals have equal opportunities to develop their full potential and lead a fulfilling life is fundamental for economic and social development. The 2006 *World Development Report: Equity and Development* (World Bank 2005) documented that many disparities can have irreversible consequences on individuals' opportunities and outcomes, outcomes that are then often transmitted across generations. In Latin America and the Caribbean, social and economic inequality is especially great. As *Inequality in Latin America and the Caribbean* argues:

> For as long as data on living standards have been available, Latin America and the Caribbean has been one of the regions of the world with the greatest inequality. With the exception of Sub-Saharan Africa, this is true with regard to almost every conceivable indicator, from income consumption expenditures to measures of political influence and voice and most health and education outcomes (De Ferranti and others 2003).

From a public policy perspective, inequality of circumstances, or opportunities, is of greatest concern. A recent attempt to empirically evaluate the extent of inequality of economic opportunity in Latin America (Ferreira and Gignoux 2007a) found that it accounts for a substantial share of observed economic inequality—between 20 percent and 50 percent (depending on the outcome variable used and the country).

Approximately 20 percent of the population in Latin America and the Caribbean live below the poverty line, with the proportion of poor children in some countries exceeding 40 percent. Overall, the region is second only to Sub-Saharan Africa in terms of the inequality of income distribution, political influence, voice, and most health and education outcomes (De Ferranti and others 2003).

Poverty and inequality in the region begin at birth: children who are born into poor families are much more likely to have parents who have low levels of education attainment, low-quality jobs, and low wages. They are also likely to have less access to public services, such as water and sanitation, health care, and education. Ferreira and Gignoux (2007), for example, estimate that the proportion of variation in student test scores in reading and mathematics on the 2000 Programme for International Student Assessment (PISA) that can be explained by the educational attainment of students' parents, their occupation, and place of residence (small town, rural, large city) is between 15 and 25 percent.

In many countries of the region, large numbers of children do not receive adequate nutrition, stimulation, or care. Many ECD indicators accordingly suggest that child development in the region is inadequate. For example, the average infant mortality rate in the region is 22 percent; in Bolivia, it exceeds 50 percent. Close to 50 percent of children in the region suffer from iron-deficiency anemia, high proportions suffer from other vitamin deficiencies, and 12 percent have stunted growth (in Guatemala, the rate is over 40 percent). With a few exceptions, access to health services and health care coverage is also limited and inequitable in the region. All of these conditions are exacerbated by poverty and inequality. Regional diversity is, moreover, extensive. In some countries very few children suffer from one or more of these conditions, while in other countries, most children do. All countries in the region, however, continue to face challenges in ensuring that all their young children receive equal opportunities to reach their highest potential.

Adequate ECD interventions can help equalize opportunities for low-income children, and thus hold particular promise for children in Latin America and the Caribbean. While ECD programs concern a well-defined population and have proven returns, countries in Latin America and the Caribbean have only recently begun moving towards a holistic approach to ECD implementation. Holistic approaches are useful because most ECD programs are multisectoral and involve interventions in health, hygiene and nutrition, education, and poverty alleviation. In addition, only a few countries (Chile, Jamaica, and Peru stand out) already have or are in the process of developing a national ECD policy championed by high-level political leaders. Most programs in the region are independent efforts that vary in scale, services offered, and mode of delivery. Moreover, the coverage of ECD services across Latin America remains low, as existing programs cover only a small fraction of potential beneficiary populations, especially among younger children.

Overview of ECD in Latin America and the Caribbean Today

Context

Even though Latin America and the Caribbean continues to lag behind developed countries in socioeconomic and ECD indicators, it fares much better, on average, than other, poorer regions in the world. Regional disparities, however, are large. Poverty rates among children and youth vary widely. In Costa Rica, Argentina, and Chile, for example, only a small share of the population under six years old lives in poverty. In El Salvador, Nicaragua, and Peru, by contrast, the situation is much more dire. In some countries in the region, most children have access to basic ECD services like education, health insurance, and vaccines, while in others, this is unfortunately not the case. In some countries, early childhood development indicators are closer to developed world standards, while in others (including Bolivia, El Salvador, Guatemala, and Nicaragua), young children—especially those in the lowest income quintiles and among indigenous peoples—are severely disadvantaged.

While ECD is an important concern for national populations in the region as a whole, mounting evidence on the benefits of ECD for disadvantaged populations make a compelling case for focusing on children living in poverty. (Slightly over 10 percent of children younger than five years old in Latin America today live on less than $1 per day, the benchmark for extreme poverty.) Empirical studies in Ecuador, Brazil, and Mexico, for example, show similar deficits in developmental outcomes among young children by socioeconomic category, with those of poor backgrounds being at the most disadvantage. Recent research also shows that indigenous groups in the region have the least access to social welfare programs, including those targeted at preprimary school-age children.

ECD Programs

Most programs that support early childhood development in the region are independent efforts that vary in scale, services offered, and mode of delivery. In addition, coverage of ECD services across Latin America remains low: existing programs reach only a small fraction of potential beneficiary populations, especially among younger children. Most of these programs pursue common goals, such as: (i) enhancement of a child's development early in life, including his or her cognitive and socioemotional development, physical growth, and well-being; (ii) enhancement of a mother's antenatal care with services and information to strengthen the probability of delivery of a healthy baby; and (iii) education of parents and/or caregivers in better parenting, health, and hygiene practices, as well as providing them the opportunity to participate in the labor force. ECD programs in the region thus affect children from birth to age six, their mothers, their caregivers, daycare centers, preschools, health centers, and communities.

ECD programs in the region have shown important benefits on a variety of outcomes. Conditional cash transfer (CCT) programs in Mexico have been shown to have large positive effects on the physical development of young children, although they do not appear to have improved cognitive outcomes for beneficiaries. Other evaluations of CCT programs in the region found that they improve the probability of young children attending preschool (Chile) and reduce developmental delays (Nicaragua).

Parenting programs in Jamaica, Bolivia, Honduras, Nicaragua, and elsewhere suggest that parents do improve their childrearing and child stimulation techniques, resulting in children with improved development of cognitive, language, motor, social, and other skills. In some cases, such as Jamaica, parenting programs that have been rigorously evaluated also show benefits for mothers, such as reduced maternal depression rates. Early education and preschool programs in Argentina and Uruguay suggest that children's language and math test scores, behavioral skills, as well as their long-term educational attainments, benefit from preschool attendance.

Nutrition and supplementation programs in the region appear to be especially important for improving children's physical well-being and growth, in addition to better cognitive outcomes. This finding held for subsidized milk and milk fortification programs for children and pregnant and lactating women in Mexico, nutrition and early child care programs in Colombia and Guatemala, and CCT programs in Mexico and Colombia. The evidence suggests that the nutrition component of ECD interventions targeted to low-income children is particularly beneficial. Several studies also found positive effects from programs that conditioned benefits on health controls and growth monitoring. In the case of CCT programs in Mexico, Colombia, and Honduras, for example, cash transfers were conditional on children's attendance at health centers and periodic physical monitoring. Even unconditional cash transfer programs, however, appear to have positive effects on the development of children's motor skills and other developmental indicators, due in part to better household nutrition (as in Ecuador).

Evidence from programs in Guatemala, Jamaica, Colombia, Nicaragua, and Bolivia suggest that interventions that offer nutrition supplements, together with those that combine several strategies (such as parenting practices, early childhood care, and nutrition) have positive effects on children's acquisition of language, reasoning, vocabulary, and schooling.

Overall, ECD programs in the Latin America and the Caribbean region show exceptional promise for improvements in cognitive and socioemotional development, as well as the physical well-being and growth of children. Notably, these effects appear to benefit mostly children from poorer backgrounds.

Policy Implications

Based on the ample evidence of the many benefits of ECD interventions in both developed and developing countries, early childhood development should be a national priority in Latin America and the Caribbean. ECD interventions offer a particularly important tool for reducing income and social gaps between poor and nonpoor populations in the region—gaps that are becoming exceedingly difficult to bridge. Moreover, such interventions appear to be more cost-effective than many interventions that attempt to improve conditions for poor people later in their lives. Finally, ECD programs are an important tool for removing the most glaring obstacles to children's development in the region, namely, malnutrition, illness, stunted growth, and illiteracy.

Countries in Latin America and the Caribbean are encouraged to develop national ECD policies to effectively scale up investments in ECD programs. Ideally, such policies create links among different policy areas that affect young children, including such services as health, nutrition, education, water, hygiene, sanitation, and legal protection. In other words, national policies are multidisciplinary and multisectoral, providing a framework that can coordinate the work of the various government sectors needed to deliver integrated ECD services.

Organization of the Volume

The organization of the rest of this volume is as follows. In Chapter 1, we discuss an analytical framework for early childhood development, which will be employed in our review of the evidence from developed and developing countries. In Chapter 2, we present the results from a comprehensive analysis of the most recent data to document the situation of early childhood development in Latin America and the Caribbean as well as an overview of ECD policies in the region. In Chapter 3, we summarize the evidence from rigorous evaluations of ECD interventions in developed and developing countries. Chapter 4 first presents an overall picture of investment in ECD programs in Latin America and the Caribbean; then, it examines individual interventions in the region in detail, with an eye toward their impact on the three major early childhood development outcomes: cognitive development, socioemotional development, and physical health and well-being. Chapter 5 presents a current snapshot of ECD policies in the Latin America and the Caribbean region, after which it outlines, using examples from the region as well as from OECD countries, some basic steps to develop a comprehensive ECD policy. The last chapter presents some conclusions and policy options to scale up ECD investments in Latin America and the Caribbean.

Notes

1. See Heckman 2006; Cunha and others 2005; Cunha, and Heckman 2007; Carneiro and Heckman 2003.

1

An Analytical Framework for Early Childhood Development

This chapter begins with a discussion of recent research on the development of the brain and its impact on early childhood development (ECD). It then develops an analytical framework that will be used throughout the book's investigation of ECD outcomes. The framework is intended to build the case for policy makers and others interested in improving these outcomes in the Latin America and the Caribbean region to adopt ECD interventions on a wider scale, particularly in support of poor and otherwise disadvantaged young children.

Early Development of the Brain

In the past, scientists thought the brain was fully formed by the time a child was born and, as a consequence, education or experience could do little to shape individual brain development. More recent research has revealed, however, that the brain keeps changing throughout life, with a great deal of brain formation taking place between birth and the age of three. Childhood experiences, moreover, shape the actual architecture and wiring of the brain (Young 2002). Thus, the care and stimulation that children receive in their earliest years is critical to their cognitive development and future lives.

Connections within the brain are made before birth and continue to be made more rapidly throughout childhood and well into adolescence. Indeed, early childhood is a period of incredibly rapid brain development. A newborn baby has approximately one hundred billion neurons—the building blocks of the brain's electrical system. At birth, approximately only 17 percent of neurons are linked through synaptic connections; these neurons have not yet differentiated and specialized by function.[1] The number of possible connections is, moreover, unlimited (OECD 2007). All animals with brains, however, must activate components of their genetic potential to produce a diversity of cells. Stimuli (experiences) have an effect on the formation of neural connections and the development of the sensory pathways (that is, vision, sound, speech, touch, smell, and perception). The sensing pathways are the core neuronal pathways and interact to influence and develop higher brain functions such as emotion, language, and behavior.

Brain development is the result of the interaction of nature (biological endowment or genetics) and nurture (or experiences). Genetics provide the hardwiring, or the blueprint, needed to build the brain. Experiences (the stimulation the brain receives from the environment) are responsible for the synaptic connections and pruning that take place within the brain—and therefore have a major effect on brain development, with far-reaching consequences. Rosenzweig and Bennett (1996) argue, for example, that all neurons (billions) have the same genetic potential.

During the early years of a child's life, brain plasticity is at its peak. Plasticity refers to the capacity of the brain to change in response to stimuli by creating and strengthening neuronal connections and weakening or eliminating others (OECD 2007). In addition, brain development goes through sensitive periods when its activity is focused on developing specific and important brain functions and structures.[2]

Impact of brain development on ECD outcomes

These sensitive periods constitute windows of opportunity for boosting a child's development. Experiences during these periods, more than at any other time, physically shape the structure of a child's brain because the brain is more malleable and more receptive to outside experiences. Unfortunately, the extreme plasticity of the brain during these periods is a double-edged sword that leads to both adaptation and vulnerability. Normal experiences (such as good nutrition and patterned visual information) during these sensitive periods support normal brain development. Abnormal experiences (such as prenatal alcohol exposure, occluded vision, or malnutrition) can cause both abnormal neural and behavioral development (Black and others 2008).

Both the family and the community (that is, the social environment) affect a child's development through the physical and social environment, experiences, socialization, and health behaviors (Duncan and Raudenbush 1999). The primary caregiver is the main source of brain stimulation in the first years of life and her or his interaction with a child heavily influences brain development. These early experiences are vital for the development of the capacity to regulate one's emotions, enjoy mental and physical health, and to develop perceptual, cognitive, and communication skills. When a young child's basic needs are met, she or he can go well beyond mastery of basic competencies; the child develops the ability to think critically, solve problems, cooperate with others, and builds greater self-confidence. These abilities also affect school performance and the life trajectory of the child (Young 2002).

As children grow, peers and other adults start to play a more prominent role in shaping and reinforcing their brain development. Approximately by 36 months, children begin to develop through social and play-based interactions with other children. By the time a child is three years old, the interactive stimulation of play with other children and early educators takes on a more prominent role, and the child increasingly becomes part of a social group.

Previous research did not address the interdependence of socioemotional and cognitive development. Rather, it emphasized the development of cognitive skills. New research on the brain, however, suggests that socioemotional and cognitive skill development are intertwined and benefit from a holistic approach to ECD (OECD 2007).

Research also shows that poor health in early childhood, as measured by low birth weight and nutritional status, is associated with poorer cognitive development and negative long-term schooling outcomes.[3]

Inadequate nutrition from before birth through the first two years of life, for example, can harm brain development (Black and others 2008; Grantham-McGregor 1995; Grantham-McGregor and Ani 2001). Indeed, birth weight is the single largest determinant of neonatal mortality. Two ECD outcomes of low birth weight—stunting and iodine deficiency anemia—also affect individuals later in life. Walker and others (2007) conclude that infants with iodine deficiency anemia are at developmental risk; these authors also note that children who experience intra-uterine growth retardation have been shown in several studies to have lower health, cognitive, and socioemotional development outcomes later in life.

When children's needs are not met, their development stalls. Poverty, therefore, can have deleterious effects on children's physical and emotional health, as well as their cognitive abilities and educational achievements.

The Case for ECD Interventions

As the preceding section makes clear, evidence on how the brain develops has important implications for policy making. First and most important, this evidence makes clear that the early years of a child's life matter. Experiences in early childhood have lasting impacts on a child's brain and physical development. Positive activities that promote healthy development have beneficial consequences for the entire life of a child. Conversely, experiences that affect or lead to underdevelopment can seriously hinder a child's potential. Second, nature and nurture both matter. Experience is crucial: it shapes both how (the quality) and how much (the quantity) the brain develops.

Much can be done to overcome socioeconomic disadvantages by facilitating positive experiences that promote brain development in the early childhood years, such as fostering positive interactions between a child and her or his environment and counteracting the negative effects of poor stimulation and care. In sum, early childhood presents a critical window of opportunity in which interventions can influence the healthy development of children and youth. Consequently, policies and programs targeted at early childhood development can have substantial and lasting impacts on human development. The importance of a child's earliest years for its long-term health, educational, and emotional outcomes makes a compelling case for expanding access to quality ECD interventions, especially for the most disadvantaged children.

An Analytical Framework for ECD Outcomes

Existing evidence indicates that three main ECD outcomes determine lifelong opportunities and results: (i) cognitive development, which includes the acquisition of language and literacy; (ii) socioemotional development, which includes the ability to socialize with others; and (iii) physical well-being and growth, which encompasses height, weight, nutritional status, and other physical indicators. Although listed separately here, all three outcomes are considered interdependent, especially cognitive and socioemotional development.

The analytical framework proposed here for analyzing ECD outcomes starts by recognizing that child development does not take place in a vacuum. In any given country, the macro context (that is, the economic, political, and social context) affects the nature and extent of social policies, which directly affect children's well-being, the type of programs made available to young children and their caregivers, and the organizations that translate these policies into programs for young children. The micro context—the interaction between a child and her or his primary caregiver during the early years—sets children on a trajectory that affects their future development. In addition, the availability of programs, services, and policies directed at children, their caregivers, or both, affects this interaction and trajectory.

Figure 1.1 shows the analytical framework. In the center oval are the three key ECD outcomes: cognitive development, socioemotional development, and physical well-being and growth. The context of ECD—at both the macro level of the country (economics, politics, and culture) and the micro level of the family—are depicted in the box at the upper left side of the figure. The box on the lower left side illustrates that ECD policies (including interventions in health, nutrition, education, and poverty alle-

Figure 1.1 Early Childhood Development: Analytical Framework

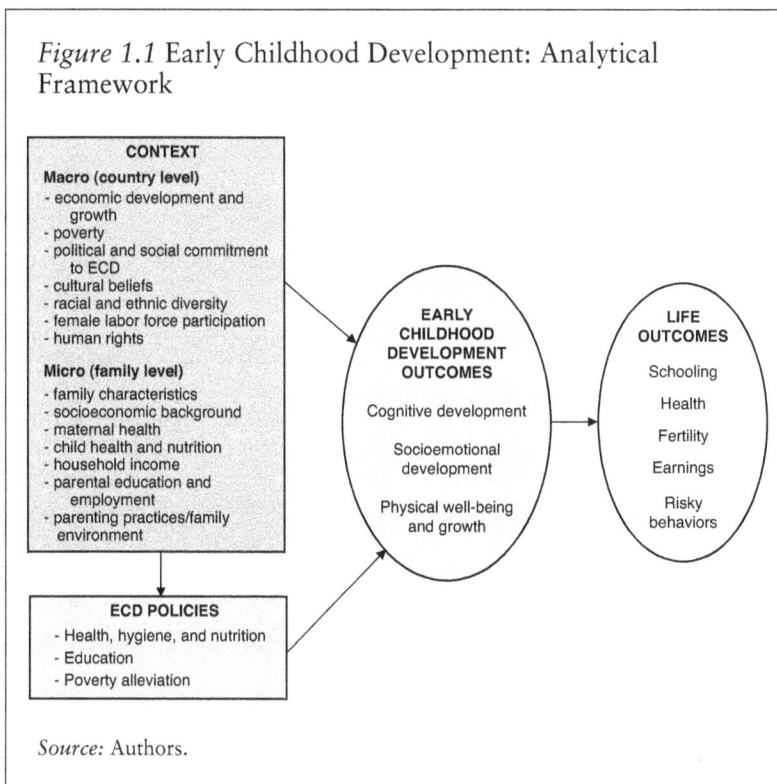

CONTEXT

Macro (country level)
- economic development and growth
- poverty
- political and social commitment to ECD
- cultural beliefs
- racial and ethnic diversity
- female labor force participation
- human rights

Micro (family level)
- family characteristics
- socioeconomic background
- maternal health
- child health and nutrition
- household income
- parental education and employment
- parenting practices/family environment

EARLY CHILDHOOD DEVELOPMENT OUTCOMES

Cognitive development

Socioemotional development

Physical well-being and growth

LIFE OUTCOMES

Schooling

Health

Fertility

Earnings

Risky behaviors

ECD POLICIES
- Health, hygiene, and nutrition
- Education
- Poverty alleviation

Source: Authors.

viation) also impact ECD outcomes. Finally, the oval at the far right of the figure shows the main life outcomes that, according to empirical research, are influenced by ECD outcomes. These outcomes include, among others, schooling levels, health, fertility, earnings and other labor market outcomes, as well as the probability of engaging in risky behaviors (for example, crime).

At the macro level, children born in developing countries are more likely to be malnourished, poor, and have less access to education and other services than are children born in developed nations. At the micro level, they are more likely to be born into families whose heads have less education and lower income. Not only does the context affect ECD directly, but it also affects it indirectly through its impact on ECD policies in a given country. These policies, which themselves are determined by the macro-level context, also affect children's early developmental outcomes. The arrow between the lower left box and the ECD outcomes oval in figure 1.1 illustrates this relationship. The amount of funding invested in early childhood development is thus related to the level of a country's economic development and growth.

Macro context: Economics, politics, and culture

Recent research documents that poverty adversely affects children's development, which can result in the intergenerational transmission of poverty (Grantham-McGregor and others 2007). A country that experiences continuous, *sustained economic growth* over long periods of time is in a better position to provide adequate and stable funding for ECD programs. As seen in chapter 2, while it is difficult to estimate total expenditure on ECD in Latin America and the Caribbean, countries in the region spend on average less than 1 percent of their gross domestic product (GDP) on early childhood education.

While a necessary condition for resource availability, economic growth alone does not translate into increased investment in young children. A *strong political and social commitment* to investing in early childhood development is also needed. The political context impacts both a country's investment in ECD and the type of policies and programs that it finances. Given that investment in young children has no immediate political return, it is atypical for political leaders to advocate investments in young children. Fortunately, this tendency is changing as political leaders become increasingly familiar with the latest evidence on the importance of early childhood and begin to implement major ECD reforms.

The *political commitment of international organizations* to early childhood development can play an important role in facilitating national political commitments to young children. Strong advocates of ECD investment include organizations such as UNESCO, UNICEF, the World Bank, the Inter-American Development Bank, the Organization of American States, and the Pan-American Health Organization; large, international, nongovernmental organizations (NGOs) such as Plan International, Save the Children, and the Christian Children's Fund; and foundations such as Van Leer. These large organizations offer both financial support and technical advice to leaders, including the latest evidence and best practices in the field.

Furthermore, international development agreements can support national and social policies that focus on the needs of children. International policies such as the Millennium Development Goals/Education For All (MDGs/EFA) offer developing nations both a challenge and an opportunity. Although highly sectoral in approach, the MDGs have a strong focus on children and create synergies in the international and national spheres that can be used to promote mainstream policies focused on children.

Cultural beliefs about childrearing, motherhood, and the role of women in society have implications for the public debate on childhood welfare. Such beliefs influence not only how children are raised, but also the degree to which the state is allowed to intervene to support them. That is, they shape whether childrearing is perceived as exclusively a family or state responsibility. Cultural beliefs also affect the investments that parents make in their children's futures. For example, these beliefs affect whether parents send their children to education and care programs outside the home to boost their development potential, or whether they are willing to receive guidance on parenting practices and education.

Cultural beliefs also affect perceptions of the role of women, especially whether women should remain at home or become active members of the labor force. The extent of *female labor force participation,* as well as the status of women as household heads, has consequences both for the kind of ECD interventions that are feasible in a country and whether such programs can benefit a high proportion of women. In addition, female labor force participation, in and of itself, affects ECD outcomes.

Whereas developed countries have experienced dramatic growth in female labor force participation among young women aged 25 to 34 years[4] (World Bank 2006a), labor force participation in Latin America among all women (not only those who are economically active) is moderate. In 2001, female participation in the labor force was 62 percent in France and 72 percent in the United States (Abramo and Valenzuela 2005). In Latin America, the rate is low but growing: the percentage of women in the workforce overall rose from 39 percent in 1990 to almost 60 percent in 2005–06.

It is well known that ECD policies can improve a mother's ability to participate in the labor force and contribute to household income. For example, maternity leave policies are designed to give working mothers the opportunity to remain at home and nurture a child during the early weeks, months, and in some countries, years, of life. Early child care policies are designed to give mothers the opportunity to return to the labor market after an interruption for the birth of their children. However, these policies often only benefit women who work in the formal sector, leaving maternity and child care programs unavailable to the large proportion of women in developing nations who are employed in the informal sector.

Racial and ethnic diversity also present unique challenges (and opportunities) for early childhood development. In fact, many ECD interventions strive to be culturally sensitive to minorities (see appendix 2), particularly in countries characterized by high racial and/or ethnic diversity. Unfortunately, countries with large indigenous populations, especially in Latin America and the Caribbean, often have less developed economies and therefore fewer resources to invest in ECD programs.

The *social recognition and prestige associated with early childhood professionals* also reflects cultural and social values regarding childhood. Early childhood workers are often paraprofessionals who earn low wages and receive few benefits, including social security or health insurance.

Lastly, it can be argued that early child care and child development are basic *human rights,* given the gradual expansion of the definition of human and child rights in international conventions over the past century.

The international community has specifically enshrined the obligation to protect infants and invest in their development in numerous declarations and treaties. A strong body of binding international law now supports the investment of public and private resources in child care and child development, indicating a consensus within the international community on the importance of securing a good upbringing for the next generations.

The concept of "child development" has, in fact, been a part of international declarations and treaties since the early twentieth century. As early as 1924, the League of Nations adopted the Geneva Declaration of the Rights of the Child, which states, "[T]he child must be given the means requisite for its normal development, both materially and spiritually" (United Nations 1924).

Thereafter, the U.N. General Assembly adopted the Universal Declaration of Human Rights in 1948. Formally a nonbinding resolution, this declaration has over time become customary international law due to its universal acceptance. The declaration does not refer to the rights of children specifically, but article 25 specifies, "[M]otherhood and childhood are entitled to special care and assistance. All children, whether born in or out of wedlock, shall enjoy the same social protection," and article 26 specifies, "...everyone has the right to education. Education shall be free, at least in the elementary and fundamental stages" (United Nations 1948). In light of the evidence presented in this book, there is reason to consider early childhood education a "fundamental stage" of education, as defined by the 1948 Declaration.

In 1959, the U.N. General Assembly passed a Declaration of the Rights of the Child, and in 1966, an International Covenant on Economic, Social, and Cultural Rights, which established direct obligations regarding child care and child development. The Covenant recognizes the "...right of everyone to be free from hunger" (article 11), and specifically mandates "provision for the reduction of the still-birth rate and of infant mortality and for the healthy development of the child" (article 12). The covenant also mandates that, "Special measures of protection and assistance should be taken on behalf of all children and young persons without any discrimination for reasons of parentage or other conditions. Children and young persons should be protected from economic and social exploitation. Their employment in work harmful to their morals or health or dangerous to life or likely to hamper their normal development should be punishable by law. States should also set age limits below which the paid employment of child labour should be prohibited and punishable by law" (United Nations 1966).

Finally, in 1989 the United Nations adopted the Convention on the Rights of the Child (United Nations 1989). This holistic convention covers all dimensions of child development, from birth to 18 years of age or other legally established threshold of adulthood. Article 6 establishes that "every child has the inherent right to life," and mandates the signatories to "ensure to the maximum extent possible the survival and development of the child." Along these lines, article 18.2 establishes that "children of working parents have the right to benefit from child care services and facilities" and article 23.2 recognizes the "right of the disabled child to special care." Regarding health outcomes, the Convention reiterates the principles of the 1966 Covenant by establishing (in article 24) "the right of the child to the enjoyment of the highest attainable standard of health" and the obligation of diminishing "infant and child mortality," combating "disease and malnutrition," and ensuring "appropriate prenatal and postnatal health care for mothers." Lastly, articles 27 and 28 recognize a child's right to a "standard of living adequate for the child's physical, mental, spiritual, moral and social development," as well as his or her right to education.

Micro context: Family characteristics and socioeconomic background

As noted in the introduction and illustrated in figure 1.1, child development is a cumulative process in which prior development affects future development. In terms of a child under the age of six, the cumulative development of the family affects his or her early development. Thus maternal health, the level of parental education (primarily, that of the mothers), socioeconomic status, household income, parental values and attitudes towards childrearing, and parental mental health all affect early childhood development outcomes.[5] The following subsections delve into these components of the "micro context" shown in figure 1.1.

Maternal health

A mother's' physical health, as measured by her current and past nutritional status, is an important determinant of whether she will deliver at term and whether her infant will have an adequate or low birth weight. Hoddinott and Quisimbing (2003) explain that maternal health and nutritional status are also related to the likelihood that a mother and her infant will survive complications during a delivery, as well as to the likelihood that breastfeeding will be successful. Maternal health and nutrition are therefore fundamental to infant and child health outcomes. Maternal mental health is also crucial, as depression and stress affect the childrearing behavior of mothers and their capacity to interact with their children. Walker and others (2007) report that in studies of children in Barbados, South Africa, and India, children of depressed mothers had lower levels of cognitive function and higher levels of behavioral problems than children whose mothers were not depressed.

Household income

The "accident of birth"[6] plays an important role in determining adult success. Children living with caregivers who are economically deprived are at higher risk of experiencing nutritional deficiencies that lead to stunting and malnourishment, as well as to childhood diseases, mortality, and morbidity. Children who are stunted are also more likely to develop weak cognitive skills and have poorer development overall. Caregivers of young children living in poverty are usually physically and mentally stressed, and thus often unable to engage in meaningful, enriching, and stimulating interactions with their children. Such children are more likely to receive poor care, which will negatively affect their cognitive and socioemotional development.

Understanding and distinguishing the effect of family income on child development outcomes continues to be a major area of interest to policy makers. A number of studies have explored the effects of income on children as young as 15 to 36 months, as well as older children aged 3 to 7 years (see Blau 1999; Aughinbaugh and Gittleman 2003; and Taylor, Dearing, and McCartney 2004). The evidence shows that income alone has small effects, with greater effects at lower income levels (Blau 1999). In fact, Blau notes that income effects diminish in magnitude when models control for unobserved child endowments or unobserved parental preferences regarding the allocation of resources to children. Some evidence does suggest, however, that family income appears to matter more in a child's early years than later in life (Duncan and others, 2004).

A study by Taylor, Dearing, and McCartney (2004) compares the effects of income on ECD outcomes to the effects of participating in the Early Head Start program in the United States. The authors conclude that the effects of family income on child outcomes are larger, in relative terms, than other determinants. Specifically, they find that income effects are larger for young children (aged 15 to 36 months) living in poor households with lower family income. They also find that the effect of income is comparable to, and sometimes larger than, the effect of other control variables such as maternal verbal intelligence. The authors note that redistributional policies designed to permanently increase the financial resources of poor families by approximately US$13,108 per year in the United States would likely generate similar effects to those associated with the Early Head Start program (the per-child cost of which is US$13,970).

The same study also examined the pathways through which income affects child development, finding that increased family and household income can be invested in opportunities that foster positive child development, such as the purchase of nutritional food, child care, development services, and books, among others. They also suggest that limited economic resources can affect maternal mental health (through depression) and create stress, which can lead to adverse mother and/or caregiver relationships and poor child stimulation.

Blau's 1999 study estimated the effects of parental income on children's cognitive, social, and emotional development, using data from the U.S. National Longitudinal Survey of Children and Youth. Although he found that the effect of current income was small, the effect of "permanent" income (defined as average income over the number of time periods available) was found to be substantially larger. The contribution of this study is to try and disentangle the effects of family income from that of other interventions on early childhood development. The author concluded that while the effect of permanent family income was large, it was not sufficiently large to substitute income transfers alone for early childhood interventions as a way of improving child development outcomes in the United States.

Parental education and employment

Research has demonstrated a strong correlation between maternal education and child outcomes in early infancy. Empirical evidence shows, for example, a strong link between a mother's education and her child's vocabulary and language skills. Mothers with higher levels of education are more likely to talk with their children and to use a broader range of vocabulary. The more language a child hears, the more likely she or he is to use language fluently. In Canada, data from the National Longitudinal Survey of Children and Youth showed that mothers with a college and/or university education were more likely to have children with average to advanced language skills, as measured by receptive vocabulary tests.

The effects of education and income are difficult to isolate, given that they are highly correlated. Yet studies show that the better parents' education and household income are, the less likely children are to suffer from malnutrition (Gragnolati 1999). As noted earlier, in addition to income, the education of a child's mother is an important predictor of a child's development of socioemotional skills.

The evidence on the effects of maternal employment on child development is mixed (Glick 2002). Some studies find that the timing of maternal employment is an important factor in determining its effects on ECD outcomes. In developed countries, Desai and others (1989) found that a mother's employment during a boy's infancy had adverse effects on the boy's language ability (as measured by the Peabody Picture Vocabulary scores). This pattern was not found among girls, children from low-income families, or among children whose mothers resumed employment after the first year of life.

Brooks-Gunn, Han, and Waldfogel (2002) explored the extent to which the negative associations between maternal employment and ECD found in some studies could be explained by the quality of the child care environment, the home environment, or parental sensitivity. They found that maternal employment by the ninth month was linked to lower school-readiness scores at 36 months, with the effects more pronounced when mothers were working 30 hours or more per week. The negative effects of working 30 hours or more per week in the first 9 months persisted, after controlling for child care quality, the quality of the home environment, and maternal sensitivity. In Haiti and Guatemala, maternal employment was associated with lower nutritional status for children under 1, but superior nutritional status for children aged 1 to 2 when the effect of income—via the purchase of nutritious food—was considered (Haggerty 1981; Engle and Pedersen 1989, as cited by Glick 2002).

The type of child care available is another important factor in determining mothers' decision to work, as well as the effect this decision will have on child development outcomes. Quisumbing, Hallman, and Ruel (2007) studied women's work in Guatemala City and Accra, Ghana, to explore linkages between maternal employment and the availability and cost of child care as a joint decision for employment. Their findings indicate that a woman's decision to enter the labor force and the use of formal child care are interrelated. In Guatemala and Accra, having children three years old and younger decreased the probability that a woman would work. Higher wealth also reduces the probability of being employed. In Guatemala, women were mostly employed in the manufacturing and industrial sectors, which are not usually compatible with parental day care. This employment resulted in increased utilization of formal day care, given the high cost of informal child care. In Ghana, where there are higher rates of informal female labor, the preferred child care arrangement was informal. This was also due to the fact that formal child care is not available to most women in Ghana, particularly low-income working mothers.

In his review of existing empirical research regarding the effects of maternal employment on children's health and schooling in developing countries, Glick (2002) argues that it is difficult to reach a conclusion on the impact of maternal employment on early childhood development outcomes. Both the wide range of methodologies used in various studies and the confounding variables that need to be analyzed (such as type of employment, hours spent [related to remuneration], and type of preferred alternative or substitute child care) make clear conclusions difficult.

Parenting practices and family environment

Parenting practices influence a range of childhood outcomes, including whether a child exhibits aggressive or prosocial behavior. In the United States, Benasich and Brooks-Gunn (1996) examined the effects of mothers' knowledge of child development and concepts of childrearing on the quality of the home environment and children's cognitive outcomes. They found that measures of maternal knowledge in these areas were significantly associated with the quality of the home environment and a number of child behavioral problems at 12 months. Another study (Ricketts and Anderson 2008) showed that poorer parents interacted with their children less often than higher-income parents. In addition, younger and more educated parents were more interactive with their children; that is, they monitored them to a greater degree and disciplined them in a more positive manner. Low-income parents were more likely to use physical punishment with their children, or to quarrel and shout.

Finally, if experienced at a young age, family violence increases the likelihood of mental problems for children later in life. Moreover, violence is transmitted intergenerationally. Daughters of mothers who have experienced abuse are more likely to be victims of violence in their own lives, and their sons more likely to become abusers. In addition, children born in violent homes are less likely to receive adequate care and more likely to die young (Heaton and Forste 2008).

ECD Policies

Health, hygiene, and nutrition

Healthy and well-nourished children are more likely to develop to their full physical, cognitive, and socioemotional potential than children who are frequently ill, suffer from vitamin or other deficiencies, and/or are stunted or underweight. To prevent these outcomes, particularly in the case of low-income children, ECD interventions can be designed to address areas of health, hygiene, and nutrition.

As noted earlier, the well-being of unborn children and their pregnant mothers is important for their future development. Prenatal care and lactation education and support can be crucial for ensuring that an unborn child develops adequately and, once born, is well nourished and receives the benefits of breast milk. Programs that support the nutritional intake of expectant and young mothers, as well as that of their young children, can counter the effects of low income on ECD outcomes in the early years. Similarly, state-supported programs to inoculate young children against common infectious childhood diseases are an ECD intervention used worldwide to assure the health of young generations.

Poverty alleviation

Poverty alleviation programs are specifically designed to help individuals, families, and communities. These programs can include such components as cash transfers, life and livelihood training, microfinance, and other mechanisms aimed at helping poor people exit poverty. Access to such programs, and the relative efficiency of their targeting, can provide children crucial support prior to birth through age six—the sensitive period during which development outcomes are generated that will affect their subsequent health, income, and well-being.

Measuring Early Childhood Development Outcomes

Because this book cites numerous studies of early child development worldwide, a brief overview of the methodological tools used in this research is in order. Child development outcomes are typically measured by a number of indicators and often use psychometric instruments, which help assess psychological constructs such as attitudes, behaviors, and intelligence. Language, cognition, and socioemotional outcomes are measured by psychometric tests, which are administered individually to children. These tests are used to measure a specific construct or domain (or subdomain) of language and cognition. Psychometric instruments are administered by psychologists, who generally use a battery of such tests to obtain a comprehensive picture of child development.

Physical well-being outcomes, on the other hand, are captured through anthropometrics (the measurement of human physical sizes and shapes), micronutrient status (such as iron, zinc, iodine, and Vitamin A levels), and the aggregate indicators of infant and child mortality and morbidity. Health outcomes are generally reported using measures of prevalence of childhood diseases, anemia, and underweight children, among other indicators. Long-term health outcomes generally are tracked by rates of morbidity, mortality, and under- and overweight births, among others. Long-term cognitive and language outcomes are generally captured by achievement and standardized tests, as well as aggregate output indicators such as repetition and dropout rates and high school completion rates. Long-term outcomes of socioemotional development are captured by rates of risky behaviors such as criminal activity, early pregnancy, and drug abuse.

Recently, the World Bank commissioned a review of psychometric instruments currently being used in developing countries in order to conduct cross-country impact evaluations of ECD programs (see table 1.1).

International donors and agencies are currently in the process of developing an instrument (or several instruments) that would provide a full picture of a child's development across different cultures, rather than data only from specific developmental domains (such as language or cognitive). The intended instrument will be population based, sufficiently robust to identify ECD vulnerabilities and risks, and generate data that could be collected regularly. Work toward such an instrument is an ongoing challenge for experts in early childhood development. Policy makers and experts agree that such an indicator or instrument could significantly contribute to evidence-based policy advocacy, decision making, and planning for early childhood development policies. It is hoped that such an instrument will become standardized and then used to monitor child development progress in any community, district, or nation in the world.

Table 1.1 Most Commonly Used Psychometric Tests in ECD Evaluations

Age range	Test name	Domain
Infants and toddlers	Bayley Scales of Infant Development	Comprehensive: gross and fine motor, social, emotional, and cognitive skills
	Ages and Stages Questionnaire	Comprehensive checklist of developmental milestones
Birth to 5 yrs	Denver Developmental Screening Test	Gross and fine motor, social, language, and social skills
3 to 5 yrs	MacArthur Communicative Development Inventories	Language and communication skills
2 to 5 yr olds	Woodcock-Johnson	Intelligence, cognitive skills
	Kaufman A-B-C	Intelligence, cognitive skills
	Stanford Binet	Intelligence, cognitive skills
	Leiter International Performance Scale	Intelligence, cognitive skills
	Weschler Preschool and Primary Scale of Intelligence	Intelligence, cognitive skills
	MacArthur Scale of Children's Abilities	Motor skills
	Leiter Examiner Scale	Executive function: self-regulation
	Strengthens and Difficulties	Social and behavioral development
	Achenbach Child Behavior Checklist	Social and behavioral development

Source: Fernald, Raikes, and Dean (2006).

Notes

1. Neurons connect through electrical impulses that travel from the neuron body downward to the axon and dendrites and pass out of the cell to neighboring neurons through connections called synapses. The neurons are wired together into circuits that perform specific simple to complex tasks and, one by one, constitute the structures and functions of the brain.

2. In the past it was debated whether these periods were critical, and if missed, whether the chance was lost for the brain to develop to its fullest potential. Today these time periods are better defined as "sensitive" rather than "critical," as some brain development can occur later on.

3. See Martorell 1995, 1999; Glewwe and King 2001; Grantham-McGregor 1995; Grantham-McGregor and Ani 2001.

4. An increase in female labor force participation obviously has repercussions on child care arrangements.

5. These characteristics affect parental decisions on and investments in children's development. As Hoddinott and Quisimbing (2003) explain, parents' assessments of the returns of the investments they make in their children are important. These assessments take into account the extent to which investments make sense for both them and their children in the future. Assessments involve parental knowledge about the returns to such potential investments, as well as related constraints. The ability of parents to undertake investments in their children are, moreover, constrained by the resources—including money and time—that are available to them and the costs associated with the investments.

6. Cunha and Heckman (2007) refer to the accident of birth as the place or situation in which a child is born. Those born in poor households are more likely to have fewer opportunities to develop their capabilities.

2

Overview of Early Childhood Development in Latin America and the Caribbean Today

Chapter 1 presented an analytical framework for examining early childhood development outcomes. It then reviewed recent evidence to support this framework, examining the contextual factors that affect childhood development. This chapter aims to provide a better understanding of the context of and opportunities for the development of young children in Latin America and the Caribbean. It begins with an examination of the macro context of this development by reviewing socioeconomic data, demographic indicators, and relevant cultural beliefs. The chapter then explores the micro context of children's development in detail, looking at a wealth of data on family characteristics, child health, and parental education and employment. Next, the text examines access to ECD programs in the region today, with a view toward understanding their beneficiaries and depth of outreach. To simplify the presentation of data, the chapter summarizes a number of detailed tables and figures that are found in appendix 1.

As this chapter will argue, the relationship between inequality and early childhood development is a dynamic process that feeds on itself. Inadequate or insufficient ECD interventions promote a negative cycle with important consequences for the populations involved. Because early childhood development interventions have been shown to be very effective in reducing gaps in young children's cognitive, socioemotional, and physical development, they also equalize opportunity. In this sense, ECD policies may be some of the most promising levers available to policy makers who are working to break the cycle of poverty and inequality in Latin America and the Caribbean.

The Macro Context: Poverty and Unequal ECD Outcomes

Although poverty in Latin America and the Caribbean is not as dire as that of other regions (particularly East Asia, South Asia, and Sub-Saharan Africa), a large proportion of the region's young children live below the national poverty line in poor housing, home, and family conditions. This reality makes these children vulnerable to poor ECD outcomes. Mounting evidence on the benefits of ECD for disadvantaged populations make a compelling case for focusing efforts in the region on children living in poverty.

Poverty rates

In 2005, the poverty headcount in Latin America and the Caribbean as a whole was 17 percent of the population, although only 8.2 percent lived in extreme poverty (World Bank, World Development Indicators).[1] In 2006, Chile at 2.4 percent, Mexico at 4.8 percent, and Uruguay at 4.2 percent had the lowest poverty headcounts in the Latin America and the Caribbean region (World Bank, World Development Indicators).

The region also has a sizeable proportion of children less than 5 years of age who live in poverty (less than $1 per day)—slightly over 10 percent in 2004 (see figure 2.1). Averages, however, mask wide disparities in the region. For example, using household surveys from 2005 and 2006, we estimate that fewer than 10 percent of children aged 0–6 live at or below the poverty line in Chile and Costa Rica, whereas this figure is close to 50 percent in Bolivia, El Salvador, Nicaragua, and Peru (World Bank estimates using CEDLAS data).

Many countries in Latin America and the Caribbean have relatively low poverty rates among the population as a whole, but much higher poverty rates among children aged 0 to 6 years. In Brazil, for example, the overall poverty rate is 16 percent, while the child poverty rate is 31 percent. When using GDP per capita to create a poverty trend line (see figure 2.2), it can be seen that Bolivia, Brazil, El Salvador, Guatemala, Mexico, Nicaragua, Peru, and República Bolivariana de Venezuela have more children living in poverty than their respective country GDP per capita would predict (World Bank and CEDLAS data).[2]

Poverty rates in Latin America are particularly acute in rural areas. Although the average poverty rate for the region as a whole was 17 percent in 2005, rural poverty rates are much higher, ranging in 2004 (the most recent year for which these data are available) from 28 percent in Mexico to 72 percent in Peru (World Bank, World Development Indicators).

Figure 2.1 Percentage of Children Less Than Five Years Old Who Are Poor, by Region, 2004

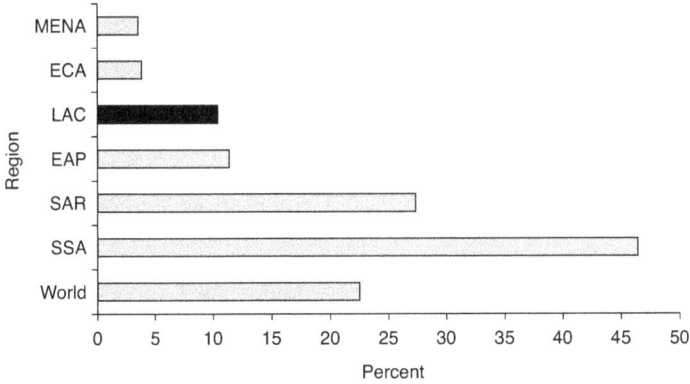

Source: Grantham-McGregor and others (2007).

Note: MENA = Middle East and North Africa; ECA = Europe and Central Asia; LAC = Latin America and the Caribbean; EAP = East Asia and the Pacific; SAR = South Asia; SSA = Sub-Saharan Africa.

Figure 2.2 Poverty Rates Measured by GDP per Capita, 2007

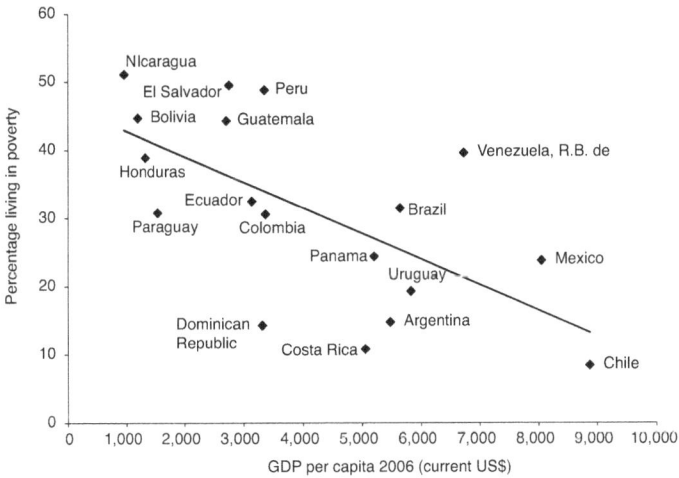

Source: World Bank calculations using SEDLAC household survey data (CEDLAS and World Bank, 2007). (See appendix 1.)

Income distribution and educational achievement

Most countries of Latin America and the Caribbean are characterized by highly skewed income distributions. In many nations, wealth is concentrated in the hands of a very small percentage of residents, with a large share of the population living in poverty. Unequal income distribution then leads to unequal educational achievement. Because early childhood development outcomes vary by socioeconomic status, ECD indicators in countries with highly unequal income distribution patterns tend to be lower than average.

In most countries in the region, nearly half of all children aged 0 to 6 years are concentrated in the bottom three deciles of the national income distribution. Very few children are in the top three deciles—in most cases, less than 20 percent. In 2005–06, individuals aged 25 years who came from poor families had on average 3.6 fewer years of schooling than their nonpoor counterparts. While only 16 percent of poor 25-year-olds had completed at least secondary school, 49 percent of their nonpoor peers had done so (World Bank using CEDLAS household surveys).

Similar patterns held for individuals aged 25–59 years, although the average years of schooling and the percentage who had completed secondary school were both lower (World Bank using CEDLAS household surveys). The lower educational achievements of the older group are unsurprising, given that younger generations tend to have more schooling on average. However, the fact that the difference in years of schooling between poor and nonpoor populations of varying ages remains roughly 3.5 years suggests that improvements in average schooling are not reducing this gap (World Bank using CEDLAS household surveys).

Figures 2.3 and 2.4 chart the respective percentage of nonpoor and poor 25-year-olds who have completed secondary school by country and national GDP per capita. Taken together, the figures demonstrate that the relationship between this education indicator and GDP per capita is increasing for the nonpoor population (figure 2.3), but is essentially flat for the poor population (figure 2.4). In short, a higher GDP per capita is associated with a larger share of the population completing secondary school, but this result appears to hold only for the nonpoor population. In other words, better-off individuals in the region appear to be disproportionately reaping the benefits of higher economic growth.

Given these facts, poor early childhood development outcomes may well be among the factors sustaining the unequal distribution of wealth and opportunity in the region. Even at an early age, socioeconomic differences are related to variations in early development outcomes. A well-known study by Hart and Risley (1995) on vocabulary differences among children in the United States, for example, showed that word accumulation, or vocabulary, begins very early in life. By 36 months, children from different socioeconomic backgrounds differ markedly in their verbal skills

Figure 2.3 Percentage of the Nonpoor Population Aged 25 Years That Has Completed Secondary School, by Country and GDP per Capita, 2005–06

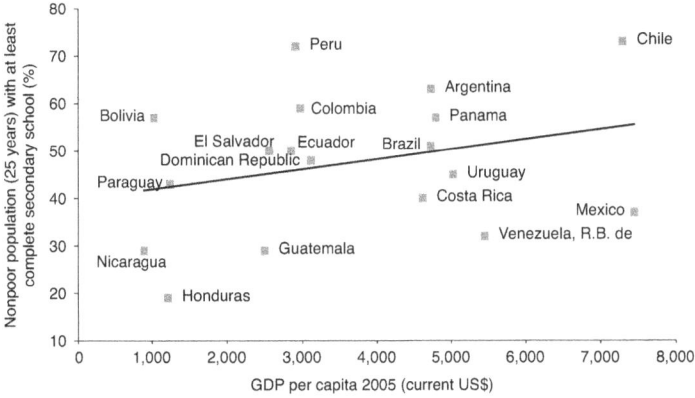

Source: World Bank calculations using SEDLAC household survey data (CEDLAS and World Bank, 2007).

Figure 2.4 Percentage of the Poor Population Aged 25 Years That Has Completed Secondary School, by Country and GDP per Capita, 2005–06

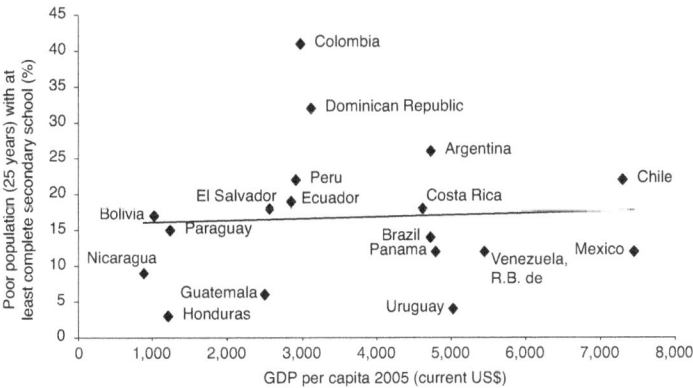

Source: World Bank calculations using SEDLAC household survey data (CEDLAS and World Bank, 2007).

(or trajectories for verbal skills), differences that remain present at age nine.[3] Evidence from Ecuador reveals a similar trend, with socioeconomic differences appearing to be associated with differences in cognitive skills at early ages (Paxson and Schady 2007).

Political and social commitment

As noted in the previous chapter, robust economic growth does not necessarily lead to increased investment in young children, particularly because children have no real voice in the political system. Broad-based interventions to support early child development therefore require a strong commitment on the part of political leaders. In the Latin American and Caribbean region, Chile and Jamaica are perhaps the two countries with the strongest political support for ECD. In both countries, high-level politicians have expressed a commitment to investing in young children.

In Chile, President Bachelet's strong political commitment to ECD has translated into increased financing for programs and an important reform of Chile's social protection system for children.[4] This reform included the consolidation of programs and services under the leadership of the Ministry of Planning and the technical supervision of a high-level advisory and technical council. Jamaica has embarked on a similar process, led by a national coordinating agency with support from high-level political figures, including the Minister of Finance.

Cultural beliefs

Cultural beliefs, including those about childrearing, motherhood, and the role of women in society, also directly affect government policies for early childhood interventions. These beliefs influence whether families perceive value in sending their children to preschool, support women's participation in the labor force, and their approach to childrearing (which can range from punitive to supportive). In a recent sample of poor Chilean families, for example, 90 percent of the self-reported reasons for not enrolling children aged 4 to 6 in preschool were related to the cultural perception that the children were too young or better cared for at home. Interestingly, a scarcity of preschools or financial constraints were not cited as reasons for the nonenrollment of these children (Galasso 2006).

Female labor force participation

As noted in chapter 1, ECD policies can facilitate a mother's ability to participate in the labor force and contribute to household income. Maternity leave policies, for example, are designed to give working mothers an opportunity to remain at home and nurture a child during the early weeks, months, and in some countries, years of life. Child care policies are similarly designed to give mothers the opportunity to return to the labor market after an interruption due to the birth of their children. However, these policies often only benefit women who work in the formal sector.

In 2005–06, the percentage of women in the workforce overall in Latin America and the Caribbean was almost 60 percent, ranging from a low of 46 percent in Honduras to a high of 73 percent in Uruguay. In urban areas, women comprise approximately 40 percent of the economically active population. Participation rates tend to be lower among women who are heads of household or spouses, and even lower among women who have children. Among economically active women, however, the employment rate hovers between 90 to 95 percent in most countries (World Bank estimates using CEDLAS household survey data).

A large proportion of these women, however, work in the informal sector and have no access to social security benefits. In Bolivia, Mexico, Paraguay, and Peru, for example, the share of women working informally is between 55 and 68 percent. These numbers are, moreover, higher than the level of GDP per capita in these countries would predict (see figure 2.5). In Uruguay, by contrast, the share is closer to 20 percent and lower than the general trend line, when controlling for GDP per capita.

Figure 2.5 Percentage of Employed Women in the Informal Sector, by Country and GDP per Capita

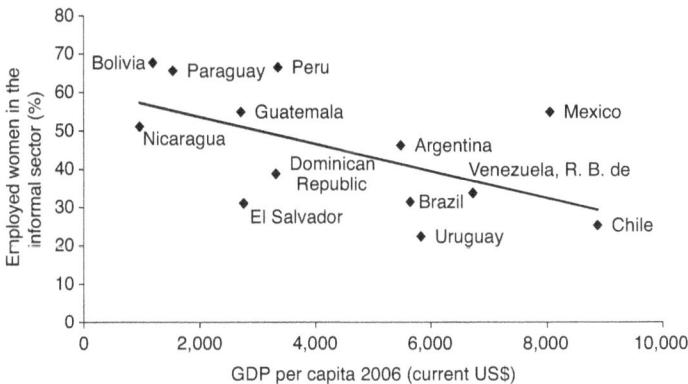

Source: World Bank calculations using SEDLAC household survey data (CEDLAS and World Bank, 2007).

Ethnic and racial diversity

Given the inequality of economic opportunity in Latin America and the Caribbean, it is unsurprising that inequality is apparent among ethnic and racial minorities. Countries with diverse populations in the region often have a pressing need for early childhood development efforts, as programs can be specifically designed to equalize the development opportunities and, consequently, life outcomes, of indigenous and nonindigenous populations. In Guatemala, for example, more than one-third of children aged 0 to 6 years are of indigenous ethnicity. In Bolivia, the figure is around 20 percent, and in Peru close to 8 percent. However, adapting ECD strategies to local and cultural needs often requires additional inputs and efforts, particularly in countries that have less-developed economies and fewer resources.

Status of early childhood professionals

The status of professionals who work in early childhood development is an important signal of both the level of ECD investment in a given country and cultural recognition of the importance of ECD interventions. At present, most people working in such programs in the region are paraprofessionals who don't receive health insurance or other benefits. One exception is Colombia, where the "madres comunitarias" or community mothers have been able to secure certain economic benefits, although they continue to struggle for recognition as civil servants with the accompanying higher salaries (Londoño and Romero 2005).

The Micro Context: Health, Family Characteristics, and Socioeconomic Background

Health and nutrition

As noted in chapter 1, adequate health and nutrition are very important for positive early childhood development outcomes. When young children are malnourished, both their physical and cognitive development are stunted. Malnutrition therefore limits a child's ability to reach her or his highest potential. ECD policies accordingly strive to improve nutrition among children as well as pregnant and lactating women. In some countries, however, the prevalence of malnutrition, underweight young children, and low birth weight for babies pose great challenges for adequate childhood development.

For example, studies of low-birth-weight children in Brazil, Guatemala, and Jamaica that compared these infants to babies with normal birth weights showed that these children had lower developmental levels—

including poorer problem-solving abilities at 7 months and lower cognitive scores at ages 2 and 3—and were more inhibited in their social interactions (Walker and others 2007). Even when controlling for other factors, such as parental education and race, low birth weight has been proven to have large and statistically significant negative effects on scores in cognitive ability and verbal tests at ages 2, 3, and 5 (Keating and Hertzman 1999).

As table 2.1 shows, about 10 percent of the infant population in Latin America and the Caribbean, on average, is characterized by low birth weight; about 5 percent of these infants are still underweight by age 4. In addition, close to 12 percent of the children in Latin America and the Caribbean are stunted. Although these indicators compare favorably to other developing regions, they nevertheless indicate that millions of children in the region experience some form of malnutrition.

Note that the regional averages shown in table 2.1 hide important country variations. In Chile, República Bolivariana de Venezuela, and Uruguay, for example, fewer than 5 percent of children are underweight,

Table 2.1 Comparative Nutrition Indicators for Developing Regions, 2005 (Percent)

Region	Prevalence of low birth weight infants (1)	Estimated prevalence of underweight children aged 0–4 years (2)	Estimated prevalence of stunted children aged 0–4 years (3)	Estimated prevalence of wasted children aged 0–4 years (4)
Latin America and the Caribbean	10	5.0	11.8	1.5
Developing countries	17	22.7	26.5	8.3
Africa	15	24.5	34.5	9.5
Asia	19	24.8	25.7	8.9

Source: Galiani (2007) using data from UN (2005).

Note: (1) Under 2,500 grams.

(2) "Underweight" is defined as z < 2 standard deviations of the weight-for-age median value of the NCHS/WHO international reference data. For further details, see annex 4 of UN (2005).

(3) "Stunted" is defined as z < 2 standard deviations of the height-for-age median value of the NCHS/WHO international reference data. For further details, see annex 4 of UN (2005).

(4) "Wasted" is defined as z < 2 standard deviations of the weight-for-age median value of the NCHS/WHO international reference data. For further details, see annex 4 of UN (2005).

whereas in Haiti and Guatemala, the numbers are close to and above 20 percent, respectively (see figure 2.6).

When the prevalence of underweight children in a country is charted against GDP per capita (see figure 2.6), it is interesting that countries like Chile and the Dominican Republic have lower percentages of underweight children in relation to the general trend line than their GDP per capita would predict. Conversely, countries like Argentina and Mexico, which have lower relative proportions of underweight children, actually have higher rates than their GDP per capita would predict. These charts thus suggest that the benefits of stronger economies are not always reaching vulnerable populations in the region.

Country disparities persist when the distribution of stunted children in Latin America and the Caribbean is charted against national GDP per capita (see figure 2.7). Fewer than five percent of children in Chile and Jamaica, for example, are stunted, whereas more than 25 percent are in Bolivia, Ecuador, Honduras, and Peru. The extreme case is Guatemala, where more than 45 percent of children are stunted (UNICEF ECLAC 2005). Even when controlling for GDP per capita, Guatemala is still a clear outlier, with a large proportion of stunted children (see figure 2.7). By contrast, Chile, the Dominican Republic, and Jamaica have much lower proportions of stunted children than their respective national GDP per capita would suggest.

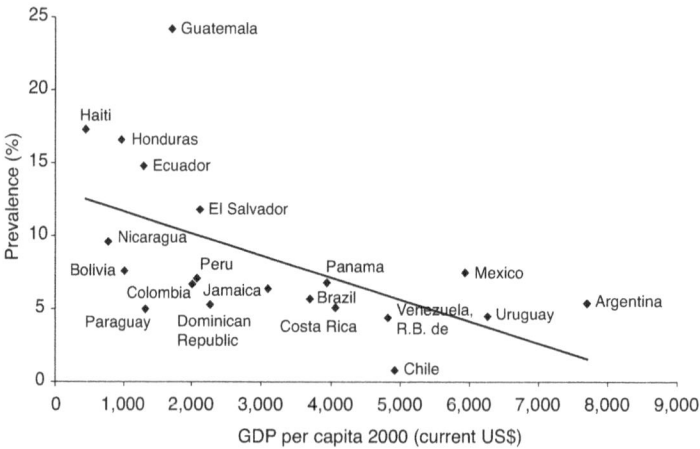

Figure 2.6 Prevalence of Underweight Children Aged 0 to 5 Years, by Country and GDP per Capita, 2002

Source: World Bank calculations using data from UNICEF ECLAC (2005).

Figure 2.7 Distribution of Stunted Children Aged 0 to 5 Years, by Country and GDP per Capita, 2002

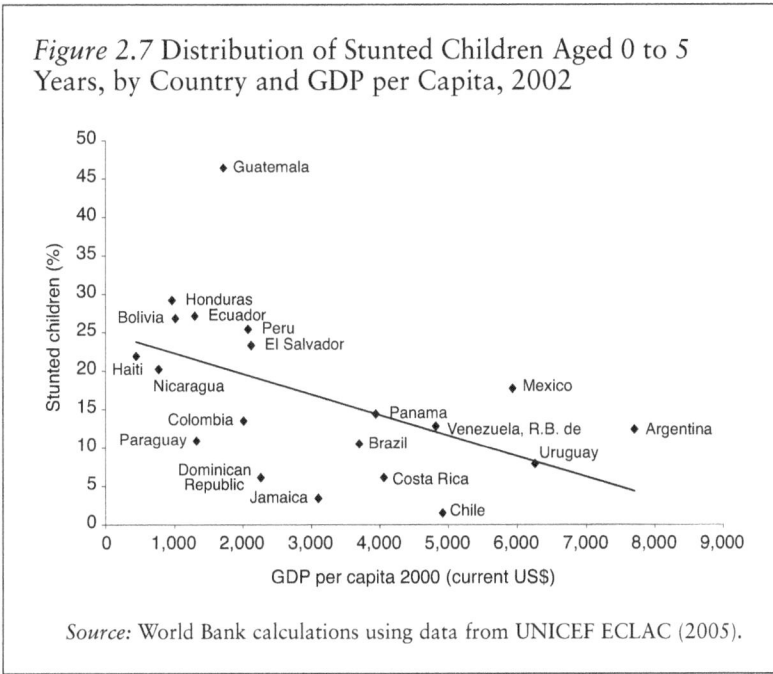

Source: World Bank calculations using data from UNICEF ECLAC (2005).

The region also has high proportions of children aged 0 to 4 years with vitamin A, iron, and zinc deficiencies. Iron deficiency (anemia) is particularly common in the region, with close to half of young children suffering from this condition (see Galiani 2007 and Caulfield and others 2006). Because anemia in children is tied to weakness, poor physical growth, a compromised immune system, and delayed cognitive and psychomotor development (see Galiani 2007), this statistic raises serious concerns about child development outcomes in Latin America.

Infant and child mortality rates represent additional causes of concern regarding ECD. Average improvements notwithstanding, infant and child mortality rates remain very high in many countries of the region. According to UNICEF (see table 2.2), around 48 infants in Bolivia died for every 1,000 live births in 2007, and 57 children under 5 years old died for every 1,000 live births. Although the Bolivian infant mortality rate is much lower than it was in 1990 (89 infants per 1,000 live births) and less than half what it was in 1980, it remains much higher than the Latin American average of 22 in 2007 (UNICEF 2009b).

In fact, when the infant mortality rate of each country is graphed against GDP per capita (see figure 2.8), most countries show numbers close to the general trend line, except for Bolivia, Brazil, and Mexico, whose rates are

Table 2.2 Infant and Child Mortality Rates by Country
(per Thousand Live Births), 1960–2007

Panel A. Infant mortality rate

Country	Infant mortality rate						
	1960	*1970*	*1980*	*1990*	*2000*	*2005*	*2007*
Antigua and Barbuda					13.0	10.5	9.5
Argentina	56.2	56.5	36.3	25.4	19.1	16.0	14.9
Bahamas	50.5	38.0	28.0	22.0	15.0	13.0	12.2
Barbados	74.0	39.5	22.0	15.0	12.0	11.0	10.6
Belize			52.2	35.0	24.0	22.2	21.6
Bolivia	152.0	147.0	115.0	89.0	63.0	52.0	47.6
Brazil	132.8	103.0	72.2	49.2	28.2	21.8	19.7
British Virgin Islands				28.0	20.0	16.0	14.4
Chile	118.0	78.0	35.0	17.6	9.7	8.4	7.9
Colombia	77.3	67.3	36.5	27.5	21.3	18.1	17.0
Costa Rica	87.0	62.0	26.0	16.0	12.5	11.0	10.4
Cuba	40.1	33.1	19.0	10.6	6.4	5.3	5.1
Dominica	79.8	40.5	10.1	14.4	13.4	10.1	9.0
Dominican Republic	102.3	92.1	69.7	53.5	33.8	32.1	31.4
Ecuador	107.0	87.0	64.0	43.0	27.0	22.0	20.0
El Salvador	129.0	111.0	84.0	47.0	29.0	23.0	20.6
Guatemala	136.0	115.0	97.0	60.0	39.0	32.0	29.2
Guyana			77.0	64.0	52.0	47.0	45.0
Haiti		148.7	140.1	104.9	78.0	62.2	56.9
Honduras	137.1	115.5	73.1	45.0	32.2	23.3	20.5
Jamaica	56.0	47.7	36.7	27.7	26.8	26.3	26.1
Mexico	93.2	79.0	57.9	41.5	31.6	29.5	28.8
Nicaragua	130.0	113.0	82.0	52.0	34.0	30.0	28.4
Panama	58.0	46.0	34.0	26.5	20.0	18.5	17.9
Paraguay	66.9	56.3	45.9	33.7	27.8	25.2	24.3
Peru	157.0	116.5	85.0	57.9	32.5	20.7	17.3
Saint Lucia		49	28.2	16.4	13.4	13.7	13.7
Saint Vincent and the Grenadines		50.9	43.7	17.9	20.5	16.6	16.6
St. Kitts and Nevis				30.0	21.0	17.5	16.1
Suriname			50.5	40.6	32.2	28.7	27.4
Trinidad and Tobago	60.4	46.4	35.5	30.4	30.3	31.1	31.1
Uruguay	51.3	46.9	36.8	21.3	14.8	13.1	12.4
Venezuela, R. B. de		47.7	37.1	27.0	20.5	17.8	16.8

Panel B. Under-5 mortality rate

Country	Under-5 mortality rate						
	1960	1970	1980	1990	2000	2005	2007
Antigua and Barbuda					15.0	12.0	10.8
Argentina	67.5	67.9	42.0	28.6	21.1	17.5	16.3
Bahamas	67.7	49.0	35.0	29.0	19.0	15.0	13.4
Barbados	90.3	54.1	28.8	17.0	13.0	12.0	11.6
Belize			68.6	43.0	28.5	26.2	25.4
Bolivia	255.0	243.0	175.0	125.0	84.0	65.0	57.4
Brazil	176.3	133.7	89.5	57.9	31.8	24.2	21.7
British Virgin Islands				34.0	23.0	18.0	16.0
Chile	155.0	98.0	45.0	21.0	10.7	9.5	9.0
Colombia	122.5	104.8	50.8	35.0	26.1	21.8	20.3
Costa Rica	123.0	83.0	31.0	18.0	14.0	12.2	11.5
Cuba	51.3	39.4	22.9	13.4	8.4	6.9	6.5
Dominica	127.1	60.0	12.9	18.2	15.5	12.5	11.4
Dominican Republic	153.3	130.6	88.1	65.8	36.9	37.4	37.6
Ecuador	178.0	140.0	98.0	57.0	32.0	25.0	22.2
El Salvador	191.0	162.0	118.0	60.0	35.0	27.0	23.8
Guatemala	202.0	168.0	139.0	82.0	53.0	43.0	39.0
Guyana			106.0	88.0	70.0	63.0	60.2
Haiti		222.3	209.0	151.7	109.0	84.2	76.0
Honduras	204.1	168.7	101.3	57.5	39.2	27.5	23.9
Jamaica	74.6	61.5	45.3	33.2	32.0	31.4	31.1
Mexico	133.0	110.6	77.6	52.4	38.5	35.7	34.7
Nicaragua	193.0	165.0	113.0	68.0	43.0	37.0	34.6
Panama	88.0	68.0	46.0	34.0	25.5	23.5	22.7
Paraguay	91.6	75.0	58.8	41.3	33.4	30.0	28.8
Peru	234.9	170.4	120.1	77.6	39.7	24.2	19.9
Saint Lucia		66	35.3	20.7	16.0	18.1	18.1
Saint Vincent and the Grenadines		71.5	56.7	22.4	24.0	19.1	19.1
St. Kitts and Nevis				36.0	25.0	20.0	18.0
Suriname			60.2	51.1	38.1	31.0	28.5
Trinidad and Tobago	72.5	54.3	40.7	34.4	34.3	35.3	35.3
Uruguay	67.2	60.3	45.5	25.0	16.9	14.8	14.0
Venezuela, R. B. de		61.5	46.0	32.3	23.9	20.5	19.3

Source: UNICEF 2009b (also available at http://www.childinfo.org/statistical_tables.html).
Note: The under-5 mortality rate is the number of deaths of children under age 5 per 1,000 live births; infant mortality is the number of deaths of infants (one year of age or younger) per 1,000 live births.

Figure 2.8 Infant Mortality Rates (Deaths per 1,000 Live Births) by Country and GDP per Capita, 2005

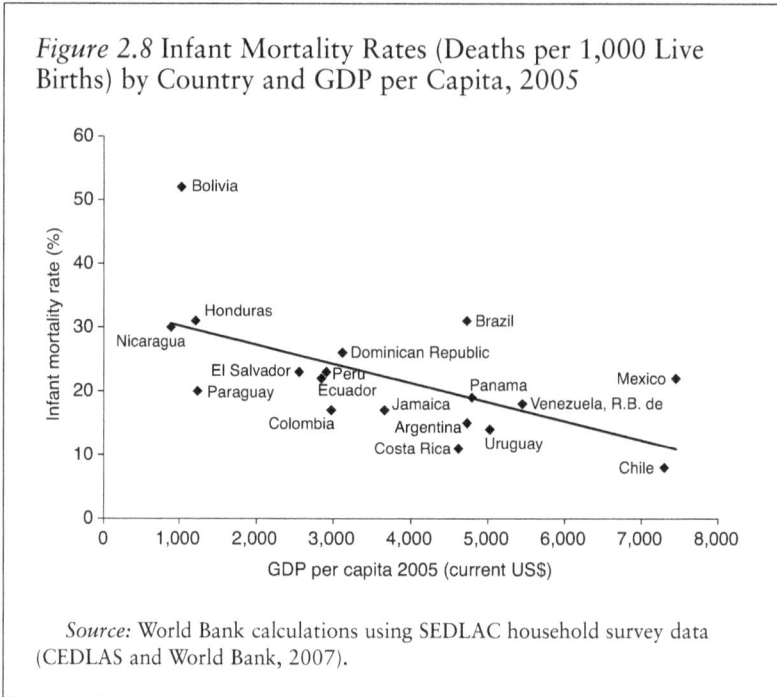

Source: World Bank calculations using SEDLAC household survey data (CEDLAS and World Bank, 2007).

conspicuously higher than their respective levels of GDP per capita would predict. By contrast, Costa Rica and Colombia appear to fare better than their respective levels of GDP would predict.

Family characteristics

Home environment

As noted in chapter 1, a child's home environment, including the physical home and family characteristics, are important factors that affect her or his development (see Duncan and Raudenbush 1999). In many countries in Latin America, a large proportion of children live in poor housing conditions such as in a house or dwelling located in a shantytown, a clearly identifiable poor neighborhood, or the street. More than 60 percent of children under 6 years of age in Bolivia, for example, live in these conditions. In El Salvador, over 35 percent of children live in poor housing conditions. In Uruguay, by contrast, only one percent of children live in poor housing conditions. The figures are also low in Argentina, Brazil, and Costa Rica (see figure 2.9).

Figure 2.9 Percentage of Children Aged 0 to 6 Years Living in Poor Housing Conditions

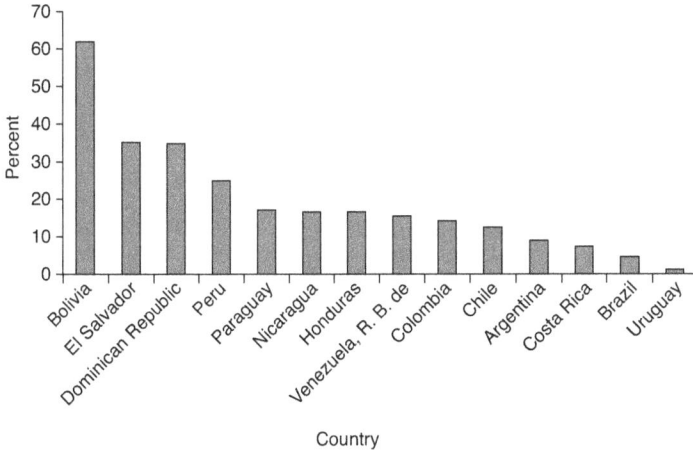

Source: World Bank calculations using SEDLAC household survey data (CEDLAS and World Bank, 2007).

Parental education and socioeconomic status

The strong correlation between maternal education and early child development outcomes is apparent among poor families in the region. Preliminary data from St. Lucia (Janssens 2006), for example, corroborates that poor children whose mothers had little or no education had even lower development outcomes than poor children whose mothers had some education.

In general, little evidence exists on the cognitive development and cognitive outcomes of young children in the region. However, evidence from specific countries suggests that, indeed, cognitive development in the region is low and related to children's socioeconomic status and poverty status. In Ecuador, Paxson and Schady (2007) found that socioeconomic status (mainly, maternal education) was positively related to cognitive development and that the effects of this status were cumulative. The authors estimated that a child in Ecuador whose family is in the ninetieth percentile for wealth, maternal education, and paternal education is associated with a language score that is approximately 33 points (about two standard deviations in test scores) higher than a child whose family is in the tenth percentile for each of these variables. As a result, they concluded that "poorer children in Ecuador arrive at the threshold of formal schooling at a significant disadvantage" (Paxson and Schady 2007, p. 52).

The Ecuador study also found strong evidence that parenting quality is associated with child cognitive development. Children who are read to or who live in households with fewer siblings have higher test scores, as do children whose parents receive better scores on an index of the quality of the home environment. In Guatemala, Khandke and others (1997) similarly found that maternal education influenced children's performance on cognitive tests and health status, starting from birth through age 7.

Parent income, parenting practices, and family environment

As noted in the introduction, a recent study found that inequality of economic opportunity in Latin America accounted for between 20 and 50 percent of economic inequality overall in the region (Ferreira and Gignoux 2007a). Another study by the same authors (2007b, see figure 2.10) concluded that in Argentina, Brazil, Chile, Mexico, and Peru, between 15 and 25 percent of the variation in children's reading and mathematics scores on the 2000 Programme for International Student Assessment (PISA) could be explained by the educational attainment of the students' parents, their occupation, and place of residence (for example, small town, rural area, or large city).

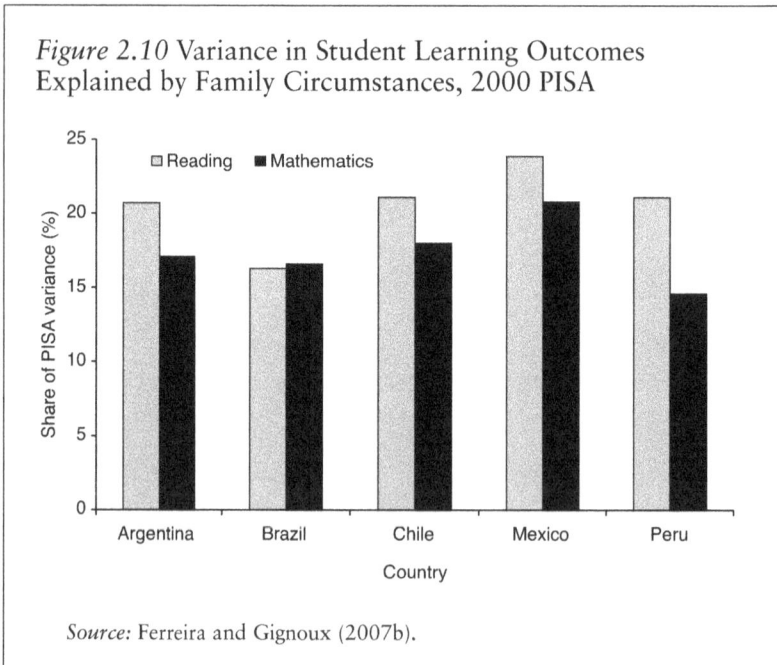

Figure 2.10 Variance in Student Learning Outcomes Explained by Family Circumstances, 2000 PISA

Source: Ferreira and Gignoux (2007b).

In Mexico, Gertler and Fernald (2004) found that poorer children in their sample appeared to have serious cognitive deficits (including deficits in long- and short-term memory, vocabulary, and visual integration, as measured by the Woodcock-Johnston-Munoz and Picture Vocabulary Peabody tests), compared to the population used to norm the tests. Likewise, another recent study documented differences by socioeconomic status (known as socioeconomic gradients) in children's developmental outcomes of gross and fine motor skills, language, and socialization among a sample of children born in Pelotas, in the state of Rio Grande do Sul, Brazil (Halpern and others 1996, as cited by Schady 2006).

As is true worldwide, parenting practices in Latin America and the Caribbean also have a direct impact on early childhood outcomes, particularly the socioemotional development of young children. As noted in chapter 1, poorer parents tend to interact less with their children and in a more punitive manner than do higher-income parents.

A recent study of parenting in Chile, Colombia, India, and South Africa found that higher levels of maternal responsiveness were associated with increased cognitive ability and fewer behavioral problems in preschool children (Walker and others 2007). In Jamaica, Ricketts and Anderson (2008) reported that poverty, consumption status, and the number of children in the care of parents significantly impacted the fulfillment of parenting responsibilities in Jamaica. Using the Jamaica Survey of Living Conditions (JSLC),[5] the study noted that, compared to nonpoor parents, poor parents were almost three times more likely to report that they always or often felt that they were not coping with their parenting duties.

Countries in Latin America and the Caribbean also exhibit one of the highest rates of both family violence—more than double the global rate—and domestic violence towards women and children (Cohen and Rubio Pardo 2007), both of which have serious adverse impacts on childhood development. A study by UNICEF (2000) documented that in a sample of women in Chile, Colombia, Mexico, and Nicaragua, 26 to 30 percent reported having experienced at least one episode of violence from their partner.

ECD Policies in the Region: An Overview

As the analytical framework and the studies reviewed in preceding sections demonstrate, both the macro and micro context impact ECD policies in individual countries. National investment in ECD interventions is affected by the level of economic development and growth, political and social commitment, cultural attitudes toward childrearing, the perceived benefit of early childhood development programs, and other factors such as women's participation in the workforce. Most such interventions are aimed at improving the health, hygiene, and nutrition of very young children and their mothers, although education and poverty alleviation interventions can also contribute greatly to improving early childhood development outcomes.

As discussed in the previous section, a substantial share of children in Latin America are malnourished; suffer from iron, vitamin, and other deficiencies; are stunted; or face other developmental challenges. All of these conditions are exacerbated by poverty and inequality. Regional diversity is, moreover, great. In some countries very few children exhibit one or more of these conditions, while in other countries the majority do. All countries in Latin America, however, continue to face challenges in ensuring that all their young children receive adequate development services and thus have equal opportunities to reach their highest potential.

This section presents an overview of current ECD programming in Latin America. Access to ECD services varies widely across the region, as do indicators that track this development. Whereas children in some countries appear to be receiving adequate ECD services and have very positive ECD indicators, children in other countries face great challenges, with the result that their development is severely compromised.

This chapter presents only a high-level overview of ECD programs, leaving chapter 4 to explore the ECD policies and programs implemented in various countries in more depth. This section accordingly concentrates on early childhood indicators, including those that track access to health care and nutrition, early education enrollment, and poverty alleviation.

Health, hygiene, and nutrition policies

As noted earlier, many nations worldwide are seeking to improve the health of pregnant and lactating women. In Argentina, Ecuador, Guatemala, Nicaragua, and Panama, the share of pregnant women receiving prenatal care, and the share who breastfed their babies for at least three months in 2005–06, surpassed 80 percent.[6] Unfortunately, little data is available for other countries in the region to determine whether these figures are representative of the region as a whole.

Vaccines are another important way to prevent illness and promote good health in children. Children who receive all recommended vaccines are less likely either to fall ill or spread disease to others. Again, comparable data are not available for all countries in the region. Vaccination rates for children younger than 6 years are available for Argentina, Ecuador, Guatemala, and Nicaragua. The BCG vaccine is practically universal in Argentina and Nicaragua, where a large proportion of young children also receive the Triple and the Triple Viral vaccines (World Bank calculations using data from CEDLAS and World Bank 2007).[7]

Available data on access to health insurance and health care also indicate wide regional variations (see figure 2.11). In Chile and Costa Rica, for example, the majority of young children have access to health insurance.

Figure 2.11 Percentage of Children under Six Years in the Region with Access to Health Insurance, by Country and GDP Per Capita

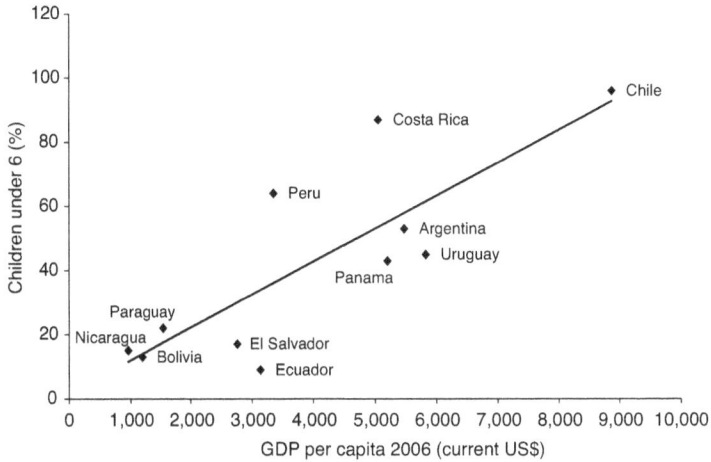

Source: World Bank calculations using SEDLAC household survey data (CEDLAS and World Bank, 2007).

In other countries, such as Bolivia and El Salvador, only about one-sixth of young children have access to health insurance. The case of Costa Rica is interesting, given that it has a GDP per capita in the middle range, but a much higher percentage of children with access to health insurance than other countries with similar GDP per capita levels (World Bank calculations using data from CEDLAS and World Bank 2007).

Health insurance coverage ratios also vary by income quintile, with few countries able to achieve equal coverage regardless of their income status. Again, Chile and Peru are very equitable with respect to health insurance coverage for children under 6 years, with the ratio of coverage rates of the first to the fifth income quintiles being close to one. In Argentina, Bolivia, El Salvador, Nicaragua, and Uruguay, however, this ratio does not exceed 0.20—indicating inequitable health insurance coverage for children by income quintile (World Bank calculations using SEDLAC household survey data [CEDLAS and World Bank 2007]).

Education and child care

The proportion of children enrolled in Early Childhood Care and Education Centers (ECCE) is another basic indicator of how well ECD objectives are being achieved. When compared to other regions and other developing

Figure 2.12 Gross Enrollment in Preprimary Education
Worldwide, 1999–2004

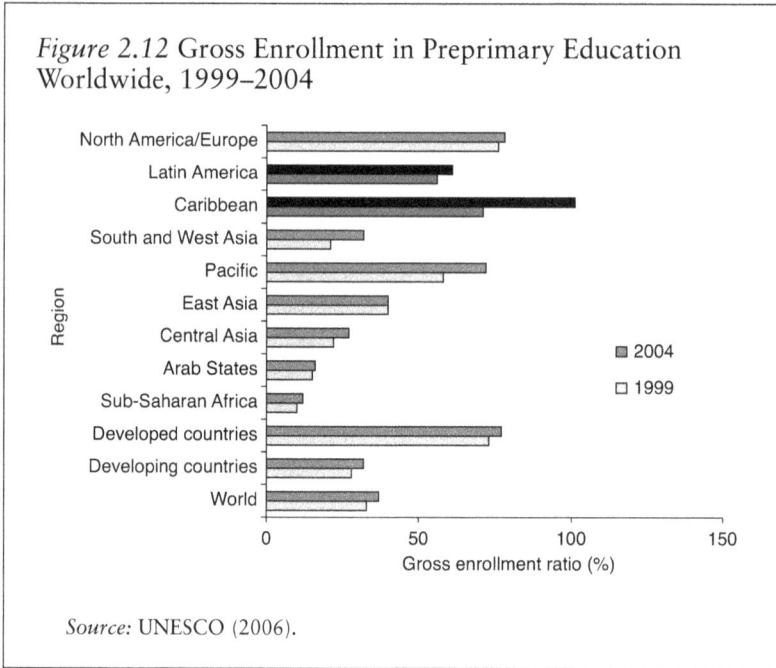

Source: UNESCO (2006).

countries, the Latin American and the Caribbean region has, on average, relatively good ECCE indicators. Figure 2.12 shows that preprimary gross enrollment rates (GER[8]) in the region are slightly above 60 percent. In recent years, the region has improved children's participation in ECCE. Countries in the Caribbean, for example, have recently experienced a spectacular increase in preprimary GER, which rose from 70 percent in 1999 to universal coverage (100 percent) in 2004. In most countries in the region, compulsory preschool lasts only one year and is publicly provided, making this service more accessible to lower-income populations.

As is true for other childhood development services, regional preprimary enrollment rate averages mask important variations. In Cuba, Guyana, and Jamaica, for example, the preprimary GER is close to or exceeds 100 percent.[9] In other countries, however, including Colombia, the Dominican Republic, Guatemala, and Paraguay, the comparable GER is below 40 percent. In these countries, GER is below what the general trend line, when controlling for GDP per capita, would predict (see figure 2.13). Conversely, in Ecuador, Guyana, and Jamaica, GER is much larger than would be expected. These findings suggest that the latter three countries have made a greater relative effort to expand preprimary enrollments than countries with comparable levels of GDP per capita.

Figure 2.13 Gross Preprimary Education Enrollment by Country and GDP per Capita, 2004

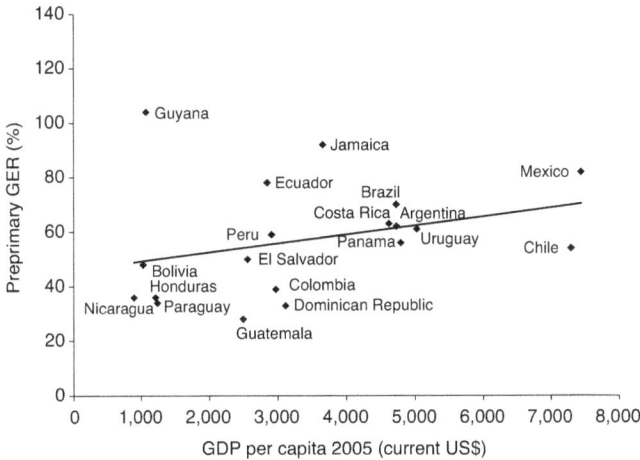

Source: World Bank calculations using SEDLAC household survey data (CEDLAS and World Bank, 2007).

In 2004, a child in most countries in the region could expect to complete, on average, less than two years of preprimary education. The exceptions were Cuba and Jamaica, where children could expect to complete approximately three or more years. By contrast, children in Ecuador and Paraguay were not expected to complete even one year of preprimary education (UNESCO 2006). A comparative graph of preprimary duration can be seen in figure 2.14.

As children progress to primary school, many are behind. In the region as a whole, slightly over 80 percent of children who enter the first grade are expected to finish the fifth grade. This proportion is higher than in other, poorer regions, such as South Asia and Sub-Saharan Africa. Nevertheless, it implies a substantial primary school dropout rate of close to 20 percent (UNESCO 2008).

With respect to income inequality and enrollment in preprimary education programs overall, rates are not uniform across income quintiles, suggesting that socioeconomic differences account for at least some of the variation in enrollment rates within countries. The latter is especially true in Bolivia, Brazil, El Salvador, Nicaragua, Panama, and Paraguay, where children in the first (lowest) quintile are enrolled in early education programs at almost half the rate of children in the fifth (highest) income

Figure 2.14 Expected Years of Preprimary Education by Country, 2004

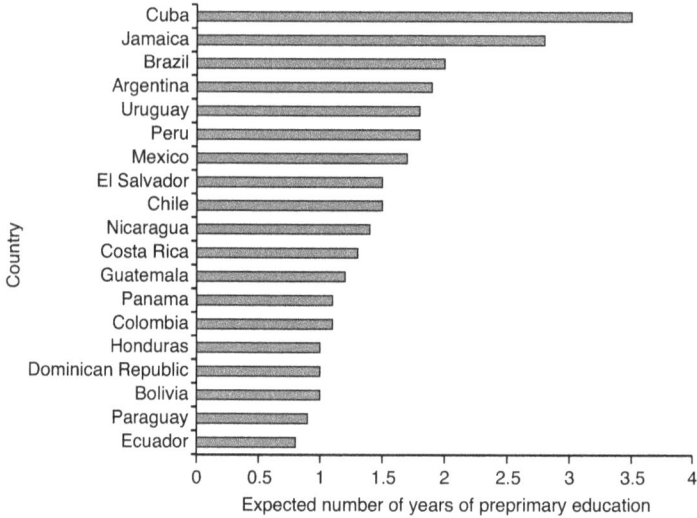

Source: UNESCO 2006.

quintile. Enrollment rates are more homogeneous across the income distribution in Mexico, Colombia, and Ecuador. In fact, the ratio of enrollment rates of the first to the fifth quintile (that is, the number of enrolled children whose families are in the lowest quintile to the number of enrolled children whose families are in the highest quintile) is not equal to one in any country in the region with available household data (World Bank calculations using SEDLAC household survey data [CEDLAS and World Bank 2007]).

When the enrollment ratio of the first to fifth quintile is used for children aged 5 and 6 only, the ratios are over 80 percent in many countries, including Argentina, Chile, Colombia, Ecuador, Mexico, and República Bolivariana de Venezuela (World Bank calculations using SEDLAC household survey data [CEDLAS and World Bank 2007]). The fact that enrollment heterogeneity is lower in most countries when the group under consideration includes only children aged 5 to 6 years suggests that inequality in education access decreases with age. The explanation probably has to do with the fact that children in this age group are most likely to be enrolled in compulsory preschool.

Indeed, household survey data suggest that, as expected, public sector enrollment increases among lower income quintiles. In most countries, the

highest share of public sector enrollments occurs in the first income quintile. By contrast, in most cases fewer than 12 percent of the children in the
fifth quintile are enrolled in public sector preprimary schools.

Sociocultural differences in Latin American are intrinsically associated
with economic differences and with access to services. Data on participation in ECD educational programs show that indigenous groups have the
least access to social welfare programs, including preprimary schools. A
recent study commissioned by the Inter-American Development Bank,
for example, found that there was a wide gap in enrollment between
indigenous and nonindigenous children in ECD programs in Colombia,
Ecuador, and Peru (Reveco and Cruz 2006). In Ecuador, the enrollment
gap between indigenous and nonindigenous groups is particularly wide
for children aged 1 to 5. While Ecuadorian nonindigenous children, not of
African descent, who are 5 years old enroll in early childhood education at
rates close to 80 percent, indigenous children's enrollment is closer to 50
percent, and Afro-descendent children's enrollment, closer to 70 percent
(Reveco and Cruz 2006).

Poverty alleviation

There is enormous variation in the prevalence of poverty alleviation programs in Latin America and the Caribbean, even among households in the
lowest income quintiles. According to 2007 data of the Socio-Economic
Database for Latin America and the Caribbean (SEDLAC), produced by
Centro de Estudios Distributivos Laborales y Sociales (CEDLAS) and the
World Bank, fewer than 3 percent of households with young children in
Argentina, Bolivia, and Nicaragua and participate in poverty alleviation
programs.[10] (See appendix 1 for detailed tables.) Only 2 to 5 percent of
households with young children in the lowest income quintile in these
countries receive some kind of poverty alleviation assistance. The low
percentage of beneficiaries in this income bracket is particularly surprising
in the cases of Bolivia and Nicaragua, which are among the poorest countries in the region. Other countries, such as Chile and Peru, have a higher
proportion of households with children in such programs (CEDLAS and
World Bank 2007). As one would expect, the highest share of children
who receive poverty alleviation assistance in both of these countries are in
households in the first and second income quintiles.

Summary

This chapter reviewed the context of early childhood development in Latin
America and the Caribbean, including the macro and micro environment
and the general ECD indicators. Both socioeconomic and ECD indicators
show that the region continues to lag behind developed regions, but fares

far better than other, poorer regions of the world. The striking characteristic of the region is the wide disparity in many childhood development indicators.

While certain countries in the region have ECD indicators closer to the standards of developed nations, the indicators for Bolivia, El Salvador, Guatemala, and Nicaragua reveal that young children, particularly those in the lowest income quintiles, are at a severe disadvantage. Table 2.3 summarizes the key contextual and ECD features that have been discussed in the chapter, country by country.

As the table shows, only a small share of the population under 6 years of age in Argentina, Chile, and Costa Rica lives in poverty. By contrast, the situation is much more dire in El Salvador, Nicaragua, and Peru. Similar contrasts are found with respect to access to basic ECD services, such as education, health insurance, and vaccines. The indicators shown above may reflect low historic levels of investment in ECD. Unfortunately, few countries in the world break down public investment figures by ECD activities. In Latin America and the Caribbean, moreover, no such figures exist. The estimate of investment in ECD shown in table 2.3 was obtained by looking at each country's expenditures (as a share of GDP) on preprimary education. While this number does not include expenditures on health, nutrition, or other ECD services, it can nevertheless be used as a rough measure of a country's effort on ECD activities. The percentages shown in the table suggest that few countries spend more than 0.2 percent of GDP on preprimary services, a figure that compares unfavorably with developed Organisation for Economic Co-operation and Development (OECD) countries, whose average is close to 0.4 percent.

Notes

1. The poverty rate is defined as the percentage of the population living with less than US$2.00 per day in purchasing power parity (PPP). The extreme poverty rate is defined as the percentage of the population living with less than US$1.26 per day in PPP (World Bank, World Development Indicators).

2. Note that whenever a trend line is estimated, cases will always fall above and below it. If instead of charting poverty rates by GDP per capita, another indicator were used, such as the logarithm of GDP, a different picture would likely emerge. Thus points that are only slightly above or below a trend line should probably not be overemphasized. The authors thank one anonymous reviewer for making this point, and note that this chapter focuses only on more extreme cases revealed by estimated trend lines.

3. Carneiro and Heckman (2003) found that cognitive skills among young children differed by socioeconomic class as early as age six. Heckman (2006), using data from the U.S. National Longitudinal Survey and math tests administered at ages 6, 8, 10, and 12 for children from different socioeconomic groups, showed substantial gaps between income groups. His study showed that these socioeconomic gradients in outcomes persisted and widened with time.

Table 2.3 Summary of Contextual and ECD Features in Latin America and the Caribbean, by Country (2005, 2006, or Latest Available Year)

| | Socioeconomic and demographic indicators | | | Access to ECD services | | | | Investment in ECD |
| | Percentage of children living in… | | | Percentage of children who… | | | | |
	Poverty	Poor housing conditions	HH in bottom 3 income deciles	Attend preprimary education	Have health insurance	Receive BCG vaccine	Receive triple vaccine	Preprimary education as % of GDP
Argentina	15	9	46.7	72	53	100	80	0.3
Bolivia	45	62	35.4	76	13	n.a.	n.a.	0.2
Brazil	32	5	51.8	40	n.a.	n.a.	n.a.	n.a.
Chile	8	12	41.4	41	96	n.a.	n.a.	0.4
Colombia	31	14	35.4	91	n.a.	n.a.	n.a.	0.1
Costa Rica	11	7	39.4	71	87	n.a.	n.a.	0.4
Dominican Republic	14	35	41.3	76	n.a.	n.a.	n.a.	n.a.
Ecuador	32	n.a.	41.5	91	9	90	90	n.a.
El Salvador	49	35	39.2	41	17	n.a.	n.a.	0.2
Guatemala	44	n.a.	37.8	n.a.	n.a.	90	90	0.1
Honduras	39	17	37.9	43	n.a.	n.a.	n.a.	n.a.
Mexico	24	n.a.	39.1	94	n.a.	n.a.	n.a.	0.5
Nicaragua	51	17	38.4	26	15	100	70	0.02
Panama	24	n.a.	43.2	79	43	100	60	n.a.
Paraguay	31	17	39.5	74	22	n.a.	n.a.	0.3
Peru	49	25	40.1	60	64	n.a.	n.a.	0.2
Uruguay	19	1	52.6	55	45	n.a.	n.a.	n.a.
Venezuela, R. B. de	40	15	38.9	68	n.a.	n.a.	n.a.	n.a.

Source: Data for socioeconomic, demographic, and ECD access indicators come from SEDLAC household surveys for the latest year available (in most countries, 2005 or 2006). Preprimary enrollments figures refer to children of different ages, depending on the country. In Argentina, El Salvador, Honduras, Peru, and Republica Bolivariana de Venezuela, preprimary enrollment rates are for children ages 3 through 6; in Bolivia, Colombia, Costa Rica, Mexico, Panama, and Paraguay, the figures are for children ages 5 through 6; and in the Dominican Republic and Nicaragua, they refer to children ages 4 through 6. In all other countries, the rates are for children ages 0 through 6. Preprimary education is defined here to include preschool and early education services.

Note: Certain countries are omitted from the table because data on most indicators were unavailable.

n.a. = Not available.

4. Another important driver for building a social protection system for children in Chile is a growing economy in need of increased female labor participation.

5. The Jamaica Survey of Living Conditions (JSLC) is fielded annually to monitor the impact of structural adjustment and stabilization programs on household welfare. The survey regularly features a special module that focuses on topics of national importance. In 2004, the JSLC featured a parenting module. The justification for this module was that parenting and the functioning of the family are critical to social cohesion, as high levels of crime and violence are associated with poor family functioning and ineffective parenting.

6. Data for breastfeeding and prenatal care practices, as well as for child vaccination rates and poverty alleviation programs, come from SEDLAC household survey data from 2003–2006 (CEDLAS and World Bank), and were calculated by the World Bank.

7. The Bacille Calmette Guerin (BCG) vaccine, which is given to protect infants and young children against tuberculosis), is practically universal in Argentina and Nicaragua; it is one of the most widely used vaccinations in the world. A large proportion of children in both these countries also receive the triple vaccine (against diptheria, pertussis, and tetanus, or DPT) and triple viral vaccine (against measles, mumps, and rubella), both of which are highly recommended (in some cases, even mandatory) for infants and young children in the developed and developing world.

8. Gross enrollment rates are calculated by dividing the number of children of any age enrolled in school over the total number of children in the official school-age group.

9. It is possible for GER to exceed 100 percent because of the enrollment of overage children.

10. The Socio-Economic Database for Latin America and the Caribbean (SEDLAC) categorizes safety net and other poverty alleviation programs. In Latin America, these programs include Programas Jefes de Hogar in Argentina; Pasis, Asignaciones Familiares, Subsidio único Familiar, Subsidio de Cesantía, and Subsidio de Agua Potable in Chile; Comedores Escolares in Colombia; a wide range of social programs in Guatemala; food stamps in Jamaica; Procampo and Progresa (Oportunidades) in Mexico; Programa de Empleo and Programa de Donación de Alimentos in Nicaragua; food, health, and education assistance programs in Peru; and Asignaciones Familiares in Uruguay (CEDLAS and the World Bank 2007).

3

Evidence on Early Childhood Development Interventions from around the World

This chapter addresses existing evidence that early childhood development interventions—including interventions in health, nutrition, education, and poverty alleviation—are among the best policy levers available to governments to lift young children out of poverty and enable them to enjoy more productive, happier lives. As noted in earlier chapters, ECD policies range from the provision of early childhood care and education services, to health, hygiene, and nutrition programs for parents and children, to poverty reduction interventions. Figure 3.1 shows the various sectoral policies that can improve ECD outcomes. These policies can be targeted to the child, parent, and/or primary caregiver. Interventions can take place in the home, school, or child care center; a hospital, clinic, or community health center; or at a community gathering space. Often, ECD policies are targeted to a number of groups and take place at a variety of locations.

Numerous studies document that ECD programs benefit children and their parents well beyond the years of an intervention. However, the rigor and comparative basis of such studies differ markedly. Nevertheless, it can be safely stated that research on both small- and large-scale programs has shown positive results, in developed as well as developing countries. Despite the varied quality of existing studies, the collective body of evidence supports the notion that ECD programs can foster children's development and mitigate the negative effects of disadvantaged circumstances. The following sections review some of the major research studies that have contributed to this body of work. It begins with a discussion of programs in developed countries and then turns to studies of programs in developing countries outside of Latin America and the Caribbean. Chapter 4 then explores the evidence on programs in that region.

Figure 3.1 Diverse Multisectoral Policies That Can Affect ECD

ECD Policies   **Target Groups**

Health, hygiene,
and nutrition
Maternal care
Water and sanitation
Preventive care
Mental health
Food and supplements

Child (prenatal)

0–2
3–4
5–6

Education
Parenting practices
Child care
Preschool

Mother (prenatal)

Parent or Caregiver

Poverty alleviation
Income support
Family or maternal leave
Female labor force participation
Household infrastructure

Source: Authors.

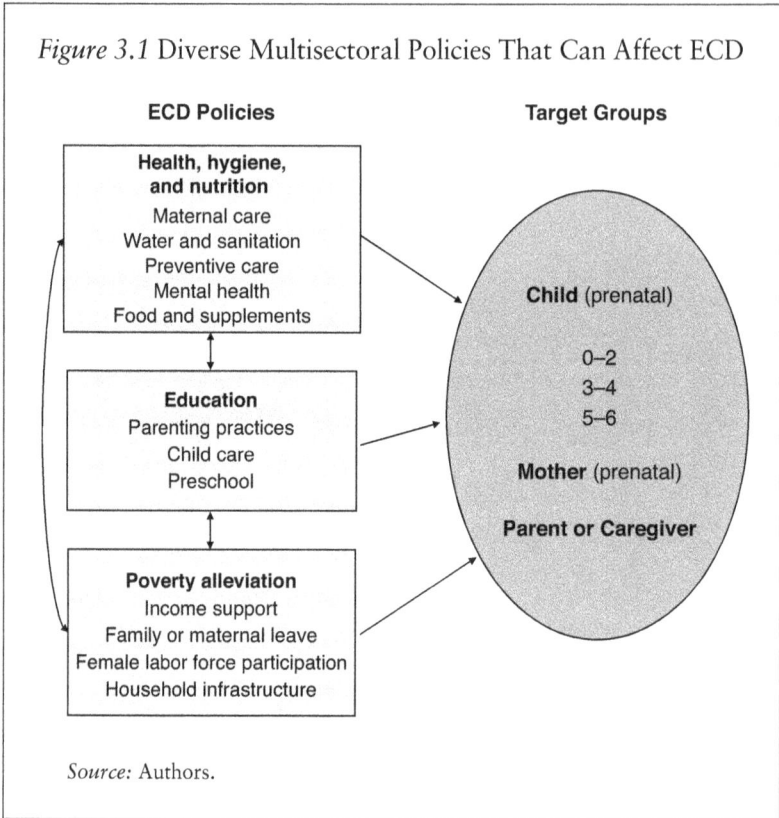

Interventions in Developed Countries

Perhaps the three most studied ECD programs in the developed world are the Carolina Abecedarian Program, the Chicago Child Parent Program, and the HighScope/Perry Preschool Program in the United States. Extensive research has been written about their impressive short- and long-term results.

Small-scale programs

The Perry Preschool Program in Ypsilanti, Michigan, was initiated in 1962 and ran through 1967. The program provided a half-day of preschool to 123 children aged 3 and 4 years, plus a one-and-a-half hour weekly home visit with the mother and the child for two years. The beneficiary group was at-risk children from disadvantaged neighborhoods.

Box 3.1 Interpreting Existing Studies of ECD Interventions

The results of impact evaluation studies of ECD programs must be interpreted with a number of caveats, which collectively argue for a nuanced, and sometimes conditional, use of their findings. The numerous methodological challenges of these studies include the following:

- Impact and longitudinal studies of the subject vary in rigor, including the size of the sample, the rigor of the study design, and whether the estimated effects result from a randomized trial in which children are randomly assigned into treatment and control groups.
- The long-term impacts of ECD interventions on later life outcomes are difficult to discern. Numerous studies indicate only "associations" between the two that do not necessarily imply causality because of the process used to select program participants (see, for example, Behrman and others 2008 and World Bank 2007).
- It remains unclear how important the starting age of children in ECD programs, as well as the duration of their participation, is to the overall effectiveness of such programs.
- The different dimensions of early childhood development—cognitive, socioemotional, and physical—may differ in importance in different contexts and may also have important synergies.
- Interpreting evaluations of the impact of parental education levels on ECD outcomes is difficult because more educated parents are also more likely to have higher cognitive ability. Therefore, the associations between parental schooling and child outcomes may be overestimated given the underlying association between parental ability and schooling.

Source: Authors.

Note: Randomly assigning children into treatment and control groups allows researchers to correctly identify program effects, and separate them from preexisting, unobserved, and uncontrolled differences between the treatments and controls.

Children were randomly assigned to a treatment and control group at the start of the program. Program evaluations were performed annually until the children were 11 years old, and then again at ages 14, 15, 19, 27, and 40. Each time the children were assessed, important benefits were documented. Participation in the treatment group resulted in better performance on cognitive and language tests up to age 7; in school achievement tests at ages 9, 10, and 14; and in literacy tests at ages 19 and 27. At age 40, the median earnings of the adults who had participated in the program were more than one-third higher than the mean earnings of adults who had not participated in the program. In addition, participants had lower incarceration rates and were more likely to be employed than nonparticipants (Schweinhart 2005, as cited by Schady 2006).

The Carolina Abecedarian Program is another small-scale intervention that showed similar positive results. Implemented in North Carolina in the United States, the program offered particularly intensive services from birth to age 5 to approximately 100 disadvantaged children. Children were randomly assigned to a treatment or control group. The treatment group received enriched center-based child care 8 hours per day, 5 days a week, for 50 weeks a year. By the time the children entered primary school, those who had been in the early education program were again randomized into two groups, one of which received no further intervention. The other group received continued intervention in the form of a home-school resource teacher. Data on children were collected at ages 3, 5, 12, 15, and 21. The data showed that children who participated in the early education program from birth to age 5 had higher scores on achievement tests and fewer grade repetitions and special education than children who did not participate in the program (Campbell and others 2001). At age 21, individuals who had participated in the early education program had higher average test scores and were twice as likely to remain in school or to have attended a four-year college than young adults who had not benefited from the program (Campbell and others 2002).

Another small-scale program that demonstrated positive impacts on childhood development outcomes was the Chicago Child Parent Program. The program offered preschool and family support services to low-income children aged 3 or 4 years in 22 centers located in Chicago public schools. The centers offered teaching basic language and readings skills, as well as social and psychological development programs, and encouraged parental involvement in classroom activities, field trips, and adult education classes. The centers also provided health services and free breakfast and lunch. Thirteen of these centers provided additional educational services through the third grade. Data on children in treatment and control groups were collected periodically, with some studies collecting data until the children where 22 years old (Lynch 2004). These data showed that participation in the program was associated with positive behavioral outcomes, including higher cognitive skills, greater educational attainment and achievement, lower use of remedial services, higher school completion rates by age 20, and lower rates of juvenile arrest at age 18 (Reynolds and others 2002).

The Chicago Longitudinal Study followed nearly 1,150 students who attended the Child Parent centers from 1983 to 1986, and compared them to a control group of 389 children of the same age who met the eligibility criteria for participation in the program. The study found that children who participated in the program had higher achievement test scores at ages 5, 6, 9, and 14, and spent less time on special education through age 18. They also had lower grade repetition rates than children who did not participate in the program. Moreover, delinquency rates among participants were significantly lower, and high school graduation rates were higher than for nonbeneficiary children.

Large-scale programs

The Perry Preschool, Carolina Abecedarian, and Chicago Child Parent programs were implemented at specific sites (Ypsilanti, Michigan; North Carolina; and Chicago, Illinois, respectively), which could make their context and program features difficult to replicate on a larger scale. However, there is evidence that national ECD programs in the United States achieved similar effects operating on a large scale in very different contexts and situations. Two of the most studied of these programs are Head Start and Early Head Start.

The Head Start Program was introduced in 1965 to provide children aged 3 to 5 years with comprehensive support services, including early childhood education, development, health, and nutrition services. The program also offered educational services for the parents of these children. Between 2001 and 2007 the program covered over 900,000 children every year; they were serviced in 2007 by over 18,000 local centers.[1] Although the program is large, it serves only approximately 35 percent of all eligible children aged 3 to 4 years (Currie 2000). Local programs can opt for center- or home-based delivery, or a combination of both. There is tremendous variation in how the program has been implemented across time and sites. Yet all programs must comply with specific performance standards that ensure a minimum level of quality. Compliance is assessed every three years by federal monitors.

Although a randomized large-scale longitudinal evaluation of the Head Start Program has not been performed, nonrandomized studies using relevant comparison groups report positive results. Several studies (Currie and Thomas 1995, 2000; Currie 2000, 2001; Barnett 2002; Garces and others 2002; Oden, Schweinhart, and Weikart 2000) have found positive long-lasting effects of Head Start on participating children, as documented by test scores, high school completion rates, and college attendance. These studies also found that participants had a higher probability of obtaining a General Educational Development high school diploma and a lower probability of being arrested. However, the impact of Head Start throughout childhood and adolescent years is an issue of contentious debate. Some studies have found that the positive effects fade as participants reached ages 7 through 11. Currie and Thomas (2000) found that the fading effect is the result of subsequent low-quality schooling for African-American children participating in the Head Start Program. Other researchers, including Barnett (2002), have argued that no such fade-out effect exists, attributing it to flawed evaluation designs.

Evaluation of the Early Head Start (EHS) Program, an offspring of Head Start, has attempted to respond to the criticisms of previous Head Start evaluations. The EHS program targets children from birth to 3 years of age, together with pregnant and lactating women. Like Head Start, local program implementation is highly varied. A carefully controlled randomized evaluation (Love and others 2005) was carried out from 1996 to 2001 in which 3,001 families were randomly assigned to 17 EHS programs. Interviews with primary caregivers, child assessments, and observations of parent-child interactions were conducted at the time of participant registration in the program and again when the children were 3 years old. The study aimed to determine (i) if a federally financed, national-scale, community-implemented program could impact children's developmental trajectory (as single site demonstration programs had been shown to do); (ii) whether the quality of key services (as measured by compliance with EHS performance standards) mattered; and (iii) whether the intervention should target parents, children, or both. Findings showed that 3-year-old participant children performed significantly better than children in the control group in cognitive and language development.[2] In addition, 3-year-old participants displayed lower levels of aggressive behavior, as reported by their parents, and rated higher on evaluations of their ability to engage their parents in a semi-structured play situation. Further, EHS parents were more emotionally supportive, provided their children more stimulation at home, read more often to them, and spanked them less than parents in the control group. The evaluation found no impact on cognitive and language development of participants in home-based programs, but the center-based and mixed approaches both yielded positive effects. On the other hand, significant impacts were found on socioemotional development in the home-based and mixed models.

A similar program was implemented in Ireland under the name Community Mothers Programme (CMP). Launched at the beginning of the 1980s, the CMP helps mothers who are giving birth to their first child get off to a good start. It operates mainly in less-privileged areas of cities and is offered to all first-time mothers; participation is voluntary. In 2005, more than 50 percent of the women enrolled in the program were single mothers; close to 10 percent were teenagers (Bardon 2006).

CMP provides support services until participating children are 1 year of age. To evaluate its effectiveness, a randomized controlled trial was carried out in 1990, at a time when participating children (and those in the control group) were 1 year old. The evaluation documented a strong association between mothers in the treatment group and positive parenting behavior. Mothers who participated in the program were more likely to read to their children daily and play games that promoted cognitive development. Eight years after the program was first launched, a follow-up study assessed whether the benefits demonstrated at age 1 were sustained at age 8. Evaluators found that the program resulted in sustained beneficial effects on parenting skills and maternal self-esteem, with benefits extending to subsequent children. Mothers who participated in the intervention were significantly more likely to check homework and disagree with punitive discipline methods than mothers in the control group (Johnson and others 2000).

Longitudinal studies

Studies based on longitudinal surveys of children and youth in developed countries also provide an important resource for documenting the long-term outcomes of early childhood interventions. For example, the Study of Early Child Care in the United States by the National Institute of Child Health and Human Development (NICHD) is a longitudinal study that began in 1991 using a national sample of 1,300 newborn children. The survey has showed that children who participated in higher-quality child care programs performed better on cognitive and language skills than children in low-quality programs. It also found that children who spent longer hours in lower-quality care displayed more behavioral problems linked to aggression (Waldfogel 1999).

A similar study of preschool effectiveness in the United Kingdom sought to establish whether positive trends could be observed among participants later in life. The Early Childhood Longitudinal Study—Kindergarten Class of 1998–99 (ECLS-K) collected data on a nationally representative sample of children and found that prekindergarten attendance increased math and reading skills at school entry (Magnuson, Ruhm, and Waldfogel 2004).[3] Data from the 1958 British Cohort Study, which followed 8,500 children through childhood to age 33, also found that, after controlling for important factors such as child, parental, family, and neighborhood characteristics, adults who had participated in some form of ECD program had higher wages than those who were cared for at home. The study found that the effects of compulsory preschool on cognitive tests were highly significant at ages 7, 11, and 16, but that these gains diminished in size over time (from an increase of 9 percent of a standard deviation in average test scores at age 7 to just over half this size by age 16). The effects of socialization were mixed, with some smaller but positive effects at age 7, yet ECD participation also negatively affected particular types of social skills such as self-control skills (including irritability and difficulty concentrating). Finally, adults who had attended precompulsory education were found to be more likely to have obtained qualifications and be employed at age 33 (Goodman and Sianesi 2005).

Another longitudinal study in the United Kingdom, the Effective Provision of Preschool Education Project (EPPE), followed over 3,000 children ages 3 through 11 years who attended a variety of preschools. The study found that both the quality and quantity of preschool attendance had positive effects on cognitive and social and/or behavioral development.

Children who attended integrated programs that combined education and child care, as well as nursery schools with more highly qualified staff, made more developmental gains. Additionally, the study found that attending a high-quality preschool had benefits for mathematics and reading skills that persisted through age 10, even after controlling for socioeconomic differences (Samons and others 2007).

Interventions in Developing Countries outside Latin America

Developed countries are not alone in recognizing that ECD interventions can have lasting positive results. Evidence on the effectiveness of ECD programs in the developing world is growing. In 1999, for example, the Philippine government launched a five-year ECD project in three southern regions that encompassed roughly 2.2 million households. In 2002, the project became part of a broader governmental program that was formally established by the Early Childhood Care and Development Act (Republic Act 8980).

The Philippines

The ECD program's overarching goal is to improve the survival and developmental potential of children, particularly the most vulnerable and disadvantaged, by (i) minimizing the health risks of very young children; (ii) contributing to the knowledge of parents and the community about child development and encouraging their active involvement in the program; (iii) advocating for child-friendly policies and legislation; (iv) improving the ability and attitude of child-related service providers; and (v) mobilizing resources and establishing viable financing mechanisms for ECD projects (Armecin and others 2006).

Longitudinal data were collected over three years for approximately 6,700 children in randomly selected households in both the treatment and control regions. Participation in the program was not, however, randomly assigned.[4] The study measured intention to treat (the effect of having the program for all children in a given age range in a community, whether or not all children attended), and found positive effects on a range of development outcomes. Positive results were documented on children's cognitive, motor, language, and social development skills, as well as their short-term nutritional status. Children in treatment areas also showed substantial improvement in all seven domains of child development compared to children in control areas. The study also documented that the duration of participation increased program impacts, with larger impacts found for participation longer than 12 months. Finally, the study found that the effects of program participation were larger for children under 4 years old at the time of the last survey: z-scores for children ages 2 and 3 were higher by 0.5 to 1.8 standard deviations for motor and language development (Armecin and others 2006).

Uganda

A recent study in Uganda tracked the progress of participants in the Uganda Nutrition and Early Child Development Program. Initiated in 1998, the program consisted of pilot ECD services in selected sub-counties in more than 30 districts of the country. Activities included child health fairs organized at the parish level every six months, together with community growth promotion activities[5] and community-based grants for food security or ECD programs. The evaluation included a randomized trial with baseline survey data and follow-up survey data for children in 50 parishes in the eastern part of the country. Treatment parishes were randomly assigned to receive all project services or all project services plus deworming medicine.

The project was found to have had a positive impact on the nutritional status of children under 1 year old, with effects of one-half of a standard deviation. The project also had positive, albeit not statistically significant, effects on caregiving practices at project sites. In terms of the impact on cognitive development, the project only had a positive effect for children aged 3 with regard to their facility with number concepts (Alderman 2007). The services in the Uganda project were neither as intensive nor comprehensive as those in the Philippines project, which may perhaps explain why it had smaller estimated effects on child developmental outcomes.

Turkey

The Turkish Early Enrichment Project set out to assess the impact of an optimal combination of educational preschool care and home intervention on the overall development of socioeconomically disadvantaged urban children in Istanbul. The program offered both early childhood enrichment and training of mothers in low-income areas of the city. Both center- and home-based enrichment services were studied separately and in combination (Kagitcibasi, Sunar, and Bekman 1988). The study followed 255 low-income children aged 3 to 5 and their mothers. Some families participated in center-based and some in home-based enrichment interventions. A third group received a combination of both interventions for a period of two years.

Mothers attended group meetings to enhance parenting practices, which trained them to promote child language development and problem-solving skills. In a 10-year follow-up study, Kagitcibasi (1992) showed that 86 percent of the children in the program were still in school, compared to 67 percent of the children in the control group. Child participants also had higher school grades and greater self-confidence.

Vietnam

In Vietnam, Watanabe and others (2005) sought to assess whether an early childhood education intervention, which included adding a nutritional intervention during preschool ages, had lasting effects on the cognitive development of school-aged children in rural Vietnam. The study focused on a total of 313 children aged 6½ to 8½ (grades 1 and 2 in primary school) in two communes who participated in either the nutritional intervention or both the nutritional and early childhood education interventions from 1999 to 2003.

Measurements of the children's height and cognitive test scores were collected, and household characteristics were determined by interviews with their mothers. A longitudinal data set was constructed by integrating these data with previously collected information from the same children in past surveys. The analysis detected significant effects of the preschool intervention, compared with the nutritional intervention. The beneficial effect of the program on cognitive test scores, for example, was large for the most nutritionally challenged children, whose height-for-age z-scores either declined or remained in the stunted range.

Summary

Evidence from developed and developing countries outside Latin America shows that ECD programs can have positive effects and enable governments to offset some of the consequences associated with inequality of opportunity (such as children born into poverty or raised in nonstimulating environments). If children from poor families are offered positive and enriching childhood development services through programs that are especially geared to them and their caregivers, it is very likely that their developmental outcomes will be improved. The chapter that follows builds on the analysis begun here with an examination of ECD interventions in the countries of Latin America and the Caribbean.

Notes

1. Data from the U.S. Department of Health and Human Services, Administration for Children and Families, http://www.acf.hhs.gov/programs/ohs/about/fy2008.html.

2. Cognitive development was measured by the Bayley Scales of Infant Development and language development was measured by the Peabody Picture Vocabulary Test.

3. To control for potential selection bias based on unobservable variables, the researchers used fixed effects, propensity score matching, and instrumental variable methods. The study found significant effects of prekindergarten attendance on mathematics and language skills (with an effect size of 0.10 to 0.12), but noted that such attendance increased aggression and behavioral problems. The effects of attendance lasted longer among children from poor families.

4. The Armecin study (2006) uses differences-in-differences estimation propensity score matching techniques to evaluate the program's impact, while controlling for a variety of observed characteristics measured at the municipal, household, and child levels, as well as for unobserved fixed characteristics (such as child health and home environment).

5. Community Growth Promotion is one widely advocated approach to promoting recommended practices for child care that actively engages families of small children and their community in maintaining the adequate growth of young children.

4

Early Childhood Development Programs in Latin America and the Caribbean

This chapter builds on the evidence presented in chapter 3 on ECD interventions in countries outside of the region. The chapter first presents an overall picture of investment in ECD programs in Latin America and the Caribbean. It then examines individual interventions in the region in detail, with an eye toward their impact on the three major early childhood development outcomes: cognitive development, socioemotional development, and physical health and well-being.

Regional Investment in ECD

Estimating total expenditure on children from birth through age 6 in the region is not an easy task. Few public finance indicators in Latin America and the Caribbean deal specifically with ECD investments, making it impossible to determine an accurate picture of each country's efforts. Better accounting that resulted in detailed ECD public finance indicators would generate improved information, which could then be used to justify public investments in the sector.

Although public spending on ECD as a share of GDP is a rough measure for comparing various countries' relative efforts to promote and implement ECD programs, it is very difficult to calculate national ECD investments for two main reasons. First, investment funds for ECD are derived from multiple sectors, including education, health, and social welfare. Second, the share of investment in ECD programs within a given sector is not usually earmarked. Given that figures for overall investment are unavailable, most rough estimates rely on investments in preprimary education.

Preprimary education: a working indicator

It is common for countries in Latin America and the Caribbean to refer to the share of the education budget spent on preprimary education as an ECD indicator. Unlike OECD countries, coverage of social protection and assistance services and transfers is limited in most countries in the region. Investment in health services is, moreover, usually not considered when calculating youth investments. Looking at expenditures on preprimary education in the region (see figure 4.1), it is apparent that ECD investments range from less than 1 percent to slightly over 12 percent of total educational expenditures of individual countries.

Investment in preprimary education can also be analyzed as a share of gross national product (GNP). When measured in this way, regional public expenditure on ECD is extremely low. With the exception of Guyana,

Figure 4.1 Preprimary Education Expenditure as Share of Total Educational Expenditure, 2004 (Percent)

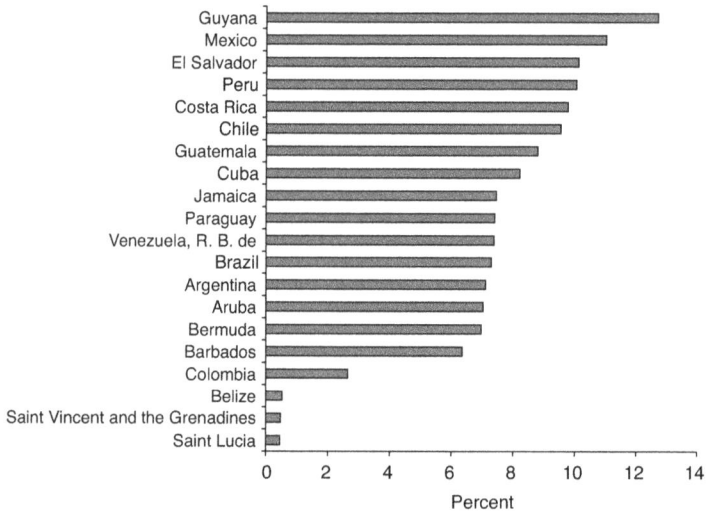

Source: UIS Data Centre, UNESCO Institute for Statistics (http://data.un.org/).
Notes: Data come from the most recent year available, as follows: Guyana, 2007; Mexico, 2005; Chile, 2006; El Salvador, 2007; Peru, 2004; Costa Rica, 2006; Guatemala, 2007; Cuba, 2007; Jamaica, 2007; Paraguay, 2007; Venezuela, R. B. de, 2004; Brazil, 2005; Argentina, 2004; Aruba, 2007; Bermuda, 2006; Barbados, 2005; Colombia, 2004; Belize, 2005; Saint Vincent and the Grenadines, 2005; Saint Lucia, 2006.

Figure 4.2 Public Expenditure on Preprimary Education as a Share of GNP, 2004 (Percent)

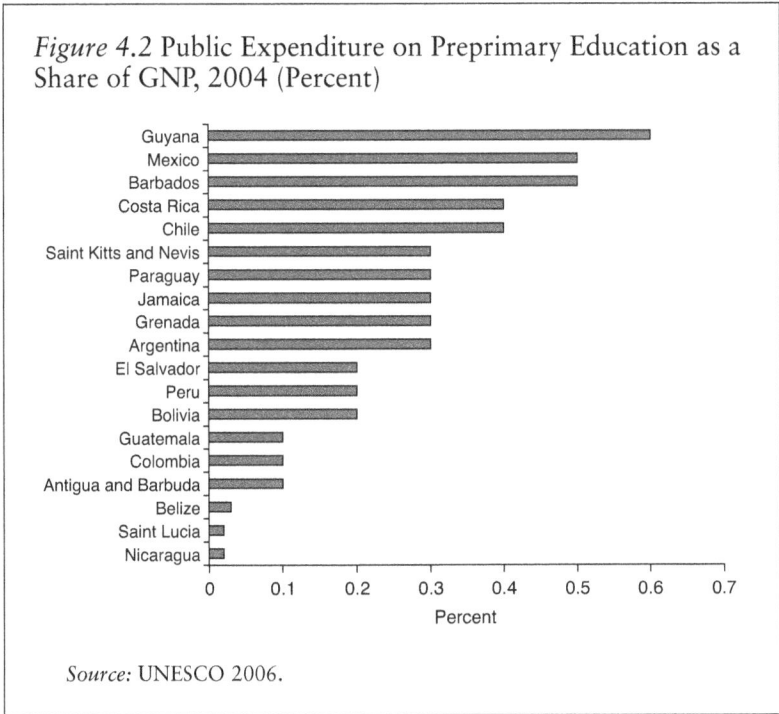

Source: UNESCO 2006.

Mexico, and Barbados, individual countries spend less than 0.5 percent of GNP on preprimary education (see figure 4.2).

A comparison with OECD countries (see figure 4.3) reveals just how small the level of ECD investment is in Latin America and the Caribbean, particularly given that most OECD countries have larger economies. Because few countries classify all childhood investments in one category, it is hard to gain a better comparative measure than those shown in figure 4.3. Sweden is one of the few countries in the world that reports public expenditures on young children, together with the allocation of these expenditures. The majority of Swedish investment in children is targeted at the early years in the form of cash transfers, preschool (for children aged 1 to 6), and health care. In fact, Sweden's public investment in early childhood as a percentage of the GDP is one of the highest in the OECD. It spends approximately 1.3 percent of GDP on services for children ages 1 through 6 in the form of child care and preprimary education, both of which fall under the category of preschool. Adding these investments to cash transfers and tax breaks, Sweden spends approximately 3.5 percent of GDP on total family benefits for young children. Only Norway and Finland invest more than Sweden in early childhood. In comparison with the United States, which spends roughly 0.6 percent of GDP on early child-

Figure 4.3 Public Investment in ECD as a Percentage of GDP in OECD Countries, 2007

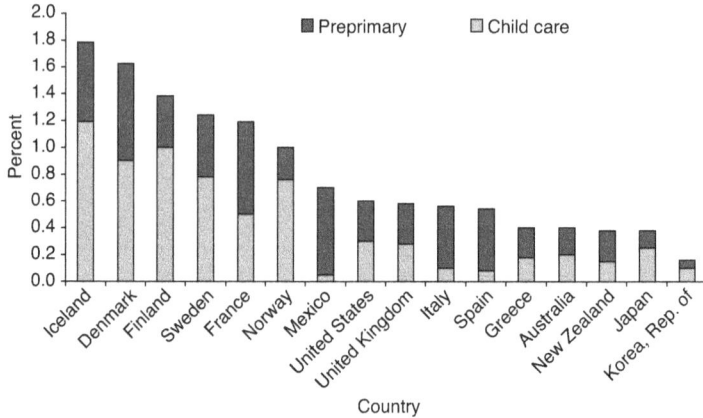

Source: OECD Family Database 2007 (www.oecd.org/els/social/family/database).

hood development, the Scandinavian level of investment is impressive. Even Mexico invests a higher relative share of its GDP in this sector than does the United States—approximately 0.8 percent.

Overview of ECD Programs in Latin America and the Caribbean

As previously mentioned, most programs that support early childhood development in the region are independent efforts that vary in scale, services offered, and mode of delivery. In addition, coverage of ECD services across Latin America remains limited: existing programs reach only a small fraction of potential beneficiary populations, especially among younger children. Most programs pursue common goals, including (i) enhancement of a child's development early in life, including his or her cognitive and socioemotional development, physical growth, and well-being; (ii) enhancement of antenatal care with services and information to strengthen the probability of the delivery of a healthy baby; and (iii) education of parents and/or caregivers in better parenting, health, and hygiene practices, as well as providing them the opportunity to participate in the labor force. ECD programs in the region thus affect children from birth to age 6, their mothers, their caregivers, daycare centers, preschools, health centers, and communities.

As discussed in chapter 1 (see figure 1.1), most ECD policies are multi-sectoral and include interventions in health, hygiene and nutrition, education, and poverty alleviation, often through the use of conditional cash transfers. A wide variety of small-, medium-, and large-scale ECD programs have been implemented in Latin America and the Caribbean. This section focuses on the most important interventions implemented in the region since the 1970s. Most of these interventions have explicit physical development, health, and well-being objectives. In fact, most evidence on the impact of ECD interventions focuses on this area. Certain programs have explicit objectives to influence early childhood development by improving parenting practices, antenatal care, maternal health, lactation, and maternal employment. Many programs also include additional strategies aimed at child development, including nutrition and cognitive development, making it difficult to disentangle the impact of different components on children.

In keeping with the analytical framework established in chapter 1, this chapter examines the impacts that various programs have had on the three major ECD outcomes of cognitive development, socioemotional development, and physical well-being and growth (including height, weight, nutritional status, and so forth). To review, cognitive development outcomes include language development and literacy, school attainment and grade progression, and standardized test scores. Socioemotional outcomes include a child's ability to socialize with others as well as other behavioral components. Physical outcomes encompass weight, height, and various nutritional measures. The discussion highlights a wide variety of programs, 10 of which were studied in depth for this book.[1] For each intervention, program evaluation results, as well as operational and organizational characteristics recorded in surveys that were completed by program administrators in each country (Vargas-Barón 2007b), are examined.[2] The seven programs that were specifically chosen for in-depth analysis were:

1. *Conozca a su Hijo* (CASH), Chile
2. *Hogares Comunitarios de Bienestar Familiar* (HCBF) and *Familias en Acción*, Colombia
3. *Proyecto de Atención Integral a Niños y Niñas Menores de Seis Años de la Sierra Rural* (PAIN), Peru
4. *Atención Integral a la Niñez Comunitaria* (AIN-C), Honduras
5. *Proyecto Nutrición y Protección Social* (AIN-C for Nutrition and Social Protection), Honduras
6. *Madres Guías*, Honduras
7. *Oportunidades*, Mexico

Some of the programs listed above are discussed in this chapter, and others in appendix 2.

In addition, some programs are mentioned due to their scale or relevance, although no evaluations of their impact have been carried out. These include:

- PROMIN and *Plan Nacer*, Argentina
- *Junta Nacional de Jardines Infantiles* (JUNJI), Chile
- *Fundación Educacional para el Desarrollo Integral del Menor* (INTEGRA), Chile
- *Educación Inicial no Escolarizada* (CONAFE), Mexico

This chapter organizes interventions in the region according to their most prominent goals, such as nutrition, child and maternal health, or parenting support. However, it should be noted that many programs offered multiple services, even though they are discussed only under one category to avoid repetition. Throughout the chapter, program results are reported beginning with the most rigorous evaluations, followed by less rigorous evaluations. Rigorous impact evaluations allow for causal inferences or, at the very least, produce strong associations between factors. These kinds of evaluations are often based on data collected from representative samples (in the statistical sense), which include enough information to adequately model the relationships between program inputs and outputs.

For the most part, the data examined in the chapter is recent (that is, the programs were implemented within the last decade) and comply with at least some of the following criteria:

- data were derived from either a program evaluation or an efficacy trial[3]
- evaluations included a randomized controlled trial or consisted of a quasi-experimental evaluation with a control and comparison group, using rigorous techniques to control for observable and unobservable characteristics
- evaluations reported on child development outcomes in early infancy.

In some instances, evaluations had certain methodological flaws or offered only preliminary results. These less rigorous evaluations are included in the discussion when relevant to the topic or when they highlight particularly interesting program results.

Nutrition Programs

INCAP, Guatemala

During the mid 1960s, protein deficiency was seen as one of the most important problems in developing nations since many believed it could affect children's ability to learn (Maluccio and others 2006). To address these concerns, INCAP (the Institute of Nutrition of Central America and Panama) began a series of programs to carry out community-based nutrition interventions in Guatemala from 1969 to 1977. The program provided children in rural areas with a nutritional supplement (a protein drink) and preventive health services such as immunizations and deworming. The protein supplement was also offered to pregnant and lactating women in the targeted regions.

A long-term impact study of the program (Maluccio and others 2006) used longitudinal panel data to track the effects of the program on children from birth through 36 months. In the original sample, two sets of village pairs were matched and selected based on their similarities. Of these, one pair was randomly assigned to receive the high-protein energy drink, Atole. The other pair received a non-protein, low-energy drink (Fresco). All children younger than 7 and pregnant and lactating women in these villages were included in the study. Data were collected until a participating child turned 7 years of age or the program ended, whichever came first. The length of program exposure and timing at entry varied among children. A second survey was conducted in 2002–04 that collected data from 61 percent of the original sample, representing 1,469 adults.

Using an intent-to-treat model, the Maluccio study assessed the impact of the nutrition program on children's school attainment, grade progression, and cognitive ability (using Raven's Progressive Matrices and a reading comprehension test). It found a positive impact on the education outcomes of participants 25 years after their participation ended; the impacts were particularly significant for women who received the high-protein nutritional supplement in early childhood. Grade attainment by these women increased by one full grade, increasing their likelihood of completing primary and some secondary school. These women also showed speedier grade progression. With respect to cognitive skills, the study showed that both men and women in the treatment group scored 14 percentage points higher than the comparison group's average score on a reading comprehension test (nearly one-and-a quarter statistical deviations) and 9 percentage points higher than the comparison group's average score on nonverbal (Raven's) cognitive tests (one-quarter of a statistical deviation).

The long-term impact of the INCAP program on participants' labor market outcomes also appears to be positive and significant. Hoddinott and Bassett (2008) conducted a follow-up study of the original INCAP study cohort and concluded that exposure to Atole before 3 years of age significantly increased hourly wage rates by between US$0.62 and US$0.67. The effects were greater for those who received Atole supplementation between birth and the age of 24 months. For this group, the corresponding increase in the hourly wage rate was US$0.67, representing an increase of over 46 percent over average wages in the study sample. This later study, however, had several limitations.[4]

PASL, Mexico

In Mexico, the *Programa de Abasto Social de Leche* (PASL) aims to improve the nutrition of low-income families, pregnant and lactating women, and older adults. PASL is a government-subsidized program administered through Liconsa, a public company that began to distribute liquid and powder milk at low prices to poor families in 1944 (Villalpando and others 2006).

In 1999, a nationwide survey in Mexico revealed a high prevalence of iron deficiency among children in the country (Villalpando and others 2003). In response, PASL milk began to be fortified with iron and other micronutrients in 2000 to improve growth and reduce the prevalence of anemia among children under 5 years old (Villalpando and others 2006). Poor families with children between 6 months and 12 years old, girls 12 to 15 years old, pregnant and lactating women, women 45 to 59 years old, and adults above 60 years of age can currently buy up to 24 liters of the iron-fortified subsidized milk every week.

In 2003, a randomized control trial was designed to evaluate the efficacy of fortified milk distributed by PASL in reducing anemia (Villalpando and others 2006). A group of children living in a poor community outside the city of Puebla was randomly chosen and assigned to drink 400 milliliters of fortified milk each day for two years.[5] A second group was given nonfortified milk for a year and fortified milk the next year. A third group never consumed any milk and was used as the control. Results showed a reduction in the prevalence of anemia in the intervention group from 41 percent to 12 percent: a reduction of 29 percentage points.

Shamah and others (2007) summarize results from a second PASL evaluation. This time it was an effectiveness evaluation (as opposed to the efficacy trial evaluated by Villalpando and others 2006 and discussed in the previous paragraph). The effectiveness evaluation assesses program impact not under controlled circumstances, but under the "real world" circumstances on which the program operates. As was the case with the Villalpando study, this evaluation randomly assigned 17 villages in four Mexican states to receive fortified or nonfortified milk. The study compared a sample of 702 children in these villages; half received fortified Liconsa milk for two years, and half received nonfortified Liconsa milk during the first year and fortified Liconsa milk the second year. A third group of 370 children, the control group, never received any milk. Twenty-four months after the evaluation began both groups receiving milk had decreased the prevalence of anemia to less than 3 percent, much lower than the control groups' prevalence of 9 percent. Iron deficiency was also lower in both the fortified and nonfortified milk groups than in the control group. Children in both treatment groups grew 1.2 centimeters more per year than those in the control group (Shamah and others 2007).

Bolsa Alimentação, Brazil

A study of a nutrition program (*Bolsa Alimentação*) in Northeast Brazil that used conditional cash transfers found that the program had no effect on children's nutritional status (Morris and others 2004a).[6] These findings must be interpreted with caution, however, because the study did not collect baseline data and the families in the control group were beneficiaries of a similar program with an educational component. The authors of the study suggest that the lack of nutritional impact might be due to a perception of participants' parents that children had to remain malnourished and underweight in order to maintain their eligibility for the program.

Nutritional and Parenting Programs

Jamaica Program on Cognitive Development, Jamaica

Many ECD programs in the region have a strong parenting component, in addition to health and nutrition elements. The best-evaluated parenting programs in the region have been implemented in Jamaica. Eight parenting programs there that target malnourished, low-birth, or undernourished children have been evaluated, generating data on their short- and long-term impacts. One of the most rigorously evaluated of these programs was an intervention designed in the mid-1980s to test the effects of nutrition and stimulation on the development of stunted children. In 1986, a group of researchers designed a randomized trial to compare the effects of providing nutritional supplementation, psychological stimulation, or both to a group of stunted children aged 9 months to 24 months. Follow-up surveys were carried out two years after the program, and again when participants were 7 to 8, 11 to 12, and 17 to 18 years old (Walker and others 2005; Walker and others 2000).[7]

The psychological stimulation consisted of one-hour home visits once a week by a community health worker. The objective of the visit was to improve mother-child interactions through demonstrated play techniques, using homemade toys and a semi-structured curriculum that emphasized increasing verbal interaction between them.

The supplementation component of the program consisted of one kilogram of milk-based formula per week. Children were followed up at different times throughout the lifespan of the program, using a combination of psychometric instruments. Two years after the program was launched, findings showed that both stimulation and nutritional supplement interventions had positive impacts on child development, with the largest effect on the group that received both interventions. By ages 11 to 12, the benefits of the nutritional supplementation (seen last at age 7), seem to have disappeared. Children who had received stimulation, however, showed higher scores on the Weschler Intelligence Scales for Children—Revised (WISC-R) Full Scale (IQ), verbal scale, and tests of vocabulary and reasoning[8] than did the control group or the group that received only the supplementation (Walker and others 2000).

The long-term benefits of this intervention on children's adult cognitive and education outcomes were measured 17 to 18 years later, with the last follow-up study conducted in 2002–03 (Walker and others 2005). This later study found sustained cognitive benefits and positive impacts on program participants' school achievement (as measured by reading comprehension and achievement tests) and dropout rate.[9] The tools used to measure cognitive outcomes included the Wechsler Adult Intelligence Scale (WAIS), Raven's Progressive Matrices, the Corsi Block Test, the Peabody Picture Vocabulary Test (PPVT), and a reading and math test. Results showed that stunted children who received psychosocial stimulation had sustained cognitive and educational benefits at ages 17–18 years (effect sizes of 0.4 to 0.6 standard deviation). Stunted children who did not receive stimulation had significantly poorer scores than the non-stunted group on all cognitive and educational measures (Walker and others 2005).

A study of Jamaican children tested the effects of a parenting program. This intervention was designed by researchers to test the effects of integrating early stimulation into primary care for undernourished children in Jamaica (Powell and others 2004) (see box 4.1). This study found that children from the intervention group showed significant improvements in development, as evidenced by greater points in the Griffiths Mental Development Scales. In addition, mothers in the intervention group showed improvements in the knowledge and practices of childrearing, measured by their responses to questionnaires.

Another study of Jamaica parenting programs (Baker-Henningham and others 2005) found that parenting programs targeted to mothers of undernourished children had positive effects on the reduction of maternal depression. Mothers of 139 undernourished children aged 9–30 months were recruited from government health centers in Jamaica and received weekly home visits by community health aides for one year. These mothers were shown play activities to do with their child using homemade materials, and parenting issues were discussed. A final evaluation was conducted at the end of the intervention on 125 mothers (90 percent follow-up). Mothers in the intervention group reported a significant reduction in the frequency of depressive symptoms (an equivalent to 0.43 standard deviation). The number of home visits that participants received ranged from 5 to 48, with the data clearly showing that the intervention worked best when women received a substantial number of home visits. Mothers receiving more than 40 visits and mothers receiving between 25 and 39 visits benefited significantly from the intervention, while mothers receiving less than 25 visits did not benefit. A final evaluation also showed that

---

Box 4.1 Curriculum of an Early Stimulation Program in Jamaica

This intervention was designed by researchers to test the effects of integrating early stimulation into primary care for undernourished children in Jamaica (Powell and others 2004).

The core elements of the parenting curriculum of this program were as follows:

- Weekly half-hour visits by community health agents over a period of one year. The health agent follows a structured curriculum involving development of homemade toys and books, which are left at the home each week and exchanged at the next visit. Parenting issues are also discussed with the mother.
- Demonstration by the health agent of play activities involving the mother and child.
- Specially trained community health aides implement the intervention. These aides are trained paraprofessionals who assist the work of clinics involved in the program by visiting homes to give advice on health and nutrition. These aides receive six to eight weeks of training in maternal and child health. For this particular intervention, aides attended two additional one-week workshops on child development and the intervention.
- Continuous supervision of program implementation. Once a month, a supervisor observed each community health aide during visits and visited the clinics every two weeks to discuss the program and review the records of the visits.

Source: Powell and others (2004).

---

maternal depression was negatively correlated with the childhood development outcomes of boys.

Roving caregivers, other Caribbean nations

The Roving Caregivers Program (RCP) has a long tradition in the Caribbean region. RCP provides nonformal, integrated child development and parenting education through a home-visiting service, which targets at-risk households with children from infancy through 3 years old. The objective is to change inappropriate childrearing practices and facilitate the development of young children to their fullest potential.

After successful implementation of RCP in Jamaica,[10] the intervention is currently being piloted in four Eastern Caribbean countries. In 2006–09, the Amsterdam Institute for International Development (AIID) is carrying out a longitudinal impact evaluation of RCP in the Caribbean island of St. Lucia. Preliminary baseline evaluation data showed that the cognitive development of children living in the poorest families, even very young children (less than 2 years old), was significantly lower than that of their more affluent peers (see figure 4.4). These associations were not, however, found for socioemotional development (Janssens 2006). Child development was measured along multiple dimensions, including cognitive ability, motor skills, hearing and speech development, socioemotional development, and anthropometrics, which were summarized in development scores.

Maternal and Child Health Programs

PROMIN and Plan Nacer, Argentina

In Argentina, the first and second Maternal and Child Health and Nutrition Projects were implemented between 1993 and 2003 (PROMIN I ran from 1993 to 2000, PROMIN IIk from 1997 to 2003). PROMIN I had maternal, child health, and nutrition components: delivery of a basic package of services to promote women's reproductive health and child health care; food supplementation for undernourished pregnant and lactating women, as well as children under 6 years of age; and health and nutrition education and promotion. PROMIN I also included an early

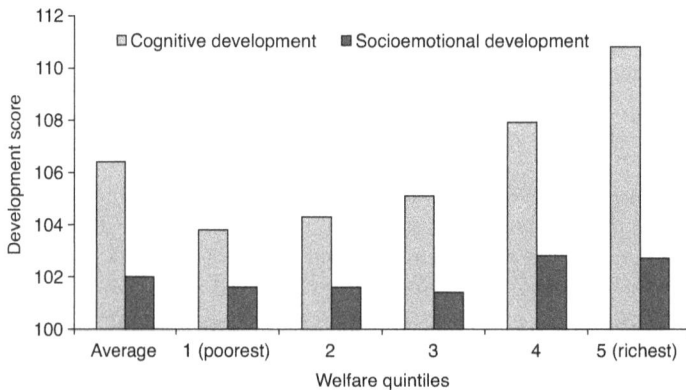

Figure 4.4 Baseline Measurements for Roving Caregivers Program in St. Lucia

Source: Janssens (2006).

childhood development component that transformed existing feeding programs for children and kindergartens into child development centers, or *Centros de Desarrollo Infantil* (CDIs), for children ages 2 through 5 years in urban slum areas.[11] It is difficult to provide definitive statements about the health impact of PROMIN I due to the lack of baseline data, difficulty in identifying appropriate control groups, the overlap between PROMIN I and PROMIN II, and varying utilization rates of the CDIs.

Data from the PROMIN II program is also derived from nonrigorous evaluations (World Bank 2006b). Although the evaluation cannot establish a causal link between project activities and changes in desired outcomes, these data suggest that the infant mortality rate of young children who participated in the program decreased by 23.4 percent in PROMIN provinces from 1997 to 2004, compared with a 14.8 percent decline in non-PROMIN provinces. However, non-PROMIN provinces were more economically and socially developed areas than those in which PROMIN II was implemented. These areas also had their own health services model, raising doubts about their comparability with the PROMIN provinces. PROMIN provinces also reported that the percentage of malnourished, poor pregnant women decreased from 28 percent in 2001 to 13 percent in 2005, and the percentage of malnourished children aged 0 to 5 years, from 3 percent in 1995 to 2 percent in 2004 (World Bank 2006b).

The number of participating children's medical checkups was used to ascertain the linkages between the health service referral service and attendance of children at the CDIs. The evaluation found that approximately 87 percent of children attending ECD centers received at least one medical checkup a year. The percentage of ECD centers that were functionally linked with a primary health center increased from almost zero at the start of the project to 87 percent in 2005 (World Bank 2006b). As previously mentioned, these results must be interpreted carefully, as the evaluation did not have a proper experimental design with treatment and control groups.

Argentina also implemented a Maternal and Child Health Insurance program called *Plan Nacer* in nine of its poorest provinces. The objectives of the program are to improve access to basic health services for poor pregnant women and children up to age six, as well as to improve the performance-based contracting within the public health sector.[12] The program offers pregnant women comprehensive pre- and postnatal care, including immunizations; controls such as pre- and postnatal checkups; and education on breastfeeding, healthy delivery, and other health-related aspects of pregnancy and delivery. The program also offers child-oriented activities: children from birth to 6 years old benefit from baby well-being controls (during the first year of life, one control per month; from month 18 to age 3 years, one control every six months, and from age 3 to age 6, one control per year), including immunization and counseling to parents on child health and nutrition.

Atención Integral a la Niñez Comunitaria (AIN-C), Honduras

The *Atención Integral a la Niñez Comunitaria* (AIN-C) program in Honduras was launched in 1990, in response to the high level of malnutrition among young children, and has evolved as a national, community-based, public health and nutrition program that addresses critical health issues of poor young children under age two. It connects the government's public health system with families through a child growth promotion program run by *monitoras* (community volunteers), who provide monthly, tailored counseling to parents on child feeding, home care of common illnesses, and appropriate use of health services.[13] A midterm evaluation was carried out in 2000 (Van Roekel and others 2002), and a final impact survey was carried out in 2002 (Plowman and others 2004). The midterm evaluation showed positive impacts on participating mothers' knowledge of, attitudes toward, and behavioral practices related to child nutrition, childrearing, and family demand for health care, as well as on children's nutritional status (Van Roekel and others 2002). The impact evaluation of 2002 used the same indicators of program performance, and added a measurement for nutritional status. This study, however, suffered from control group contamination. By 2002, 24 percent of children in the control group were participating in the program's growth-promotion activities (Griffiths and McGuire 2005). This intervention on the control group confounded the evaluation's results (see Plowman and others 2004; Van Roekel and others 2002).

Specifically, the midterm evaluation found that the program had positive effects on mothers' knowledge and application of childrearing practices, including breastfeeding practices, appropriate caregiving, and seeking care for children with diarrhea. It also documented that the program was reaching 92 percent of children under 2 years of age in the treatment regions. In treatment households, exclusive breastfeeding increased from 21 to 39 percent (while declining in control areas); oral rehydration in cases of diarrhea increased from 32 to 50 percent (while increasing by only 2 percentage points in control areas); continuing to feed and giving children fluids during a bout of diarrhea increased from 21 to 33 percent in project households (while decreasing in control areas); and timely introduction of complementary feeding increased from 70 to 76 percent (while declining from 70 to 63 percent in control areas).

A final evaluation was published in 2008, which re-analyzed the AIN-C 2002 data to address the issues of group contamination. In this study, the pre/post, intervention/control community comparison was replaced with an analysis based on individual, community-level participation in AIN-C. Using the follow-up data, children who participated in AIN-C were compared with children who did not, regardless of the community in which they lived. Thus, the original "intent-to-treat" model was replaced with a model estimating the effects on the treated. The results of this evaluation suggest that AIN-C had a significant, positive impact on young child feeding and care practices and on nutritional status, especially among poorer households and children who participated more regularly in the program. Mothers participating in AIN-C practiced exclusive breastfeeding longer than those who did not (1.5 months longer). Also, children participating in AIN-C had higher rates of complete immunization coverage than nonparticipating children. The percentage of children through 23 months receiving iron and vitamin A supplementation was also significantly higher for AIN-C. Results also suggest positive effects on nutritional status, particularly in poorer households (Schaetzel and others 2008).

Hogares Comunitarios de Bienestar Familiar, Colombia

In Colombia, *Hogares Comunitarios de Bienestar Familiar* (HCBF) is a large-scale childcare and nursery program with a nutrition component that uses local mothers to provide program services in home-based "centers" (see box 4.2). Launched between 1984 and 1986, the program seeks to serve pregnant women, mothers, and children living in poverty. Hogares Comunitarios offers combined parental education and child services. Children at HCBF centers receive lunch and two snacks that include a nutritional beverage called *bienestarina*. Other services include parent education and support; early stimulation; feeding services; health education and preventive health care; height and weight measurements; and daycare centers that offer child care and preschool education. Feeding and child care services are provided by a mother in the local community, who is called a *madre comunitaria*, or community mother.

An evaluation of the program in 2004 (Attanasio and Vera-Hernandez 2004a) found a statistically significant effect on the probability of children who had been in the program of being in school and progressing a grade when they reached the ages of 13 through 17 years. While effects were not significant for children aged 8–12 years,[14] results for children aged 13–17 years showed that attending HCBF before age 6 increased the probability of a child being in school by 0.198 percentage points. Since the average attendance rate for children aged 13–17 in the sample is 0.63, this effect is significant. Attendance over 29 months increased the probability of attending school by 0.208 percentage points.

The 2004 evaluation by Attanasio and Vera-Hernandez used data from an impact evaluation of another conditional cash transfer (CCT) program in Colombia—*Familias en Acción,* which was implemented in some of the same localities—to evaluate the impact of HCBF on nutrition outcomes, specifically height for age.[15] Data included information on children's current and past attendance at an HCBF center, primarily in rural areas. The evaluation employed an instrumental variable approach to compare participating and nonparticipating children, using distance from the child's

Box 4.2 Program Evaluation: *Hogares Comunitarios de Bienestar Familiar*, Colombia

Implemented in the mid 1980s, the *Hogares Comunitarios de Bienestar Familiar* (HCBF, or Community Welfare Homes) Program has been providing assistance to families with young children in Colombia. The program, which is implemented by the *Instituto de Bienestar Familiar* (ICBF, or Colombia Family Welfare Institute), reaches approximately 1 million boys and girls under the age of 7 in 1,098 municipalities.

Community mothers (*madres comunitarias*) are the frontline workers, or "executors," of the HCBF program, and provide services in "centers" from four to eight hours a day. Approximately 53 percent of these mothers serve full time, and 23 percent, part time. Mothers between the ages of 31 and 40 represent 39 percent of the group and about 35 percent of all mothers working in the program hold a high school diploma. Community mothers with the least education are usually located in rural areas, where only 27 percent have completed high school, compared to 39 percent of community mothers in urban areas. The rate of turnover among community mothers is low. Data from 1987 to 2004 show that 50 percent of the mothers then working in the program had joined it before 1996. The average tenure of these women in the program is 8.2 years, and the maximum tenure, 17 years. Approximately 74 percent of them have participated in the program for almost 4 years.

The government evaluated the program in 1997, which led to a series of measures designed to improve quality. Overall, the impact evaluation suggested that HCBF has positive effects on child growth and school enrollment. Although the home centers were found to be achieving the goal of reaching and protecting the poorest sectors of the population, they did not comply satisfactorily with ICBF norms. Specifically, the evaluation pointed out inadequacies related to the (i) infrastructure of home centers; (ii) educational materials, toys, and food-preparation equipment; (iii) the training and knowledge of community mothers regarding children's nutrition, health, and psychosocial development; and (iv) the community-level administration of the program. The study concluded that administration and management of the program at the community and executive levels was deficient, with a low level of training, follow-up, and monitoring of program quality and performance. Unreliable accounting and tracking of invoices was of particular concern.

Source: Londoño and Romero Rey (2005).

household to the HCBF center and the median fee in the municipalities as instruments. The findings showed that the program had positive effects on children's height,[16] with an effect of 0.59 standard deviations on the z-scores, corresponding to a height gain of 2.86 centimeters among boys and 2.90 centimeters among girls aged 72 months (Attanasio and Vera-Hernandez 2004a, revised 2007).

Hogares Comunitarios, Guatemala

The Guatemala *Hogares Comunitarios* program (HCP), similar to the program in Colombia, provides child care for children of working parents aged 7 or younger (see box 4.3). Ruel and others (2006) found that HCP had positive effects on nutritional outcomes, including a significantly better diet at the place of care among children participating in HCP compared to those using other child care facilities. The authors used two empirical strategies to estimate program effects: beneficiary/control matching (also called matching by design) and propensity score matching. The matching method suggests that participants consumed on average 20 percent more energy, protein, and iron, and 50 percent more vitamin A, than nonparticipants. These positive effects were robust when estimated using propensity-score matching methods, although the significance levels of the effects observed with these methods were slightly weaker. The study also found the program provided a good work opportunity for caretaker mothers, who tended to be older than the average beneficiary mother.[17] In addition, the evaluation revealed additional information on the quality of the program (see box 4.3), which complemented the evidence on its impact on nutrition and is a good example of the type of program information that can be collected in a process evaluation.

Other programs (non-rigorous studies)

Conozca a su Hijo, Chile

Conozca a su Hijo (Know Your Child Program, known by the Spanish acronym CASH) was developed in the 1980s to help develop poverty-stricken rural areas of Chile. CASH targets rural mothers, preferably those who belong to *Sistema Chile Solidario*[18] and/or indigenous mothers living under the poverty line who have children from infancy to the age of 5, and live in areas that lack preschool education centers. Services include early child stimulation; parent education and support; nutrition services; social protection; preschool education; early childhood intervention services for children with developmental delays or disabilities; and participatory activities with communities. An evaluation of CASH commissioned by the Ministry of Education of Chile reported that the program had positive effects on the language development of participating children aged 2 to 5 and led to higher language development scores compared to children who did not participate in the program. Participating children also had higher cognitive development scores than the control group when they entered the first grade of basic education. These differences, however, disappeared upon completion of first grade. Similar findings were obtained for children who, at the time of the evaluation, were entering the second grade (Ministerio de Educación de Chile, 1998). The findings need to be taken with caution, however, because of the methodological problems of the evaluation design.[19]

Box 4.3 Program Quality of *Hogares Comunitarios*, Guatemala

The *Hogares Comunitarios* (HCP, or Community Day Care Program) is an urban, community-based child care program, conceived in the 1990s to ensure care for children of working women in poor communities. The program operates Monday to Friday from 6 am to 6 pm. Each caretaker is responsible for up to 10 children from birth to age 6 at her home (*hogar*).

An operational (process) evaluation of the program showed that, in general, it operates quite effectively. The initial provision of material, furniture, and equipment reaches the newly opened hogar in a timely manner. The furniture and equipment, however, tend to break and caretakers then find it difficult to replace them. The program also provides monthly cash transfers to the caretaker for the purchase of nutritious food.

Data collected in the evaluation pointed to some areas of concern. First, it showed that the size of the cash transfer needs to be sufficient to match increases in the prices of food, and to allow for purchasing renewable materials for the children. Second, it takes a long time for caretakers to collect the cash transfer. This process takes them away from the hogar for long periods of time. Third, parents are expected to pay a monthly fee, or quota, and contribute with resources and materials. Before a hogar is opened, for example, parents are expected to become involved by contributing money or in-kind labor and support. The evaluation showed that parents encountered difficulties contributing monthly inputs and quotas. In addition, their overall involvement and participation in the program was limited. Fourth, with respect to the quality of services, observers rated the hygiene and safety of the hogar and daily routine based on an eight-hour, semi-structured observation. On average, the general condition of the hogar was good, but additional work on safety and hygiene was deemed necessary.

In terms of the daily schedule, most caretakers followed the suggested time allocation for various activities: domestic work, child care, food preparation, food serving, early stimulation, and so forth. The proposed schedule, however, underestimated time spent on general child care chores such as hygiene and taking care of children's general needs. Time spent on psycho-pedagogical activities was the main weakness, absorbing only 6 percent of daily activities.

Overall, caretakers expressed the need for additional support to improve the quality of their services, which requires the provision of health supplies. Caretakers also reported not having any links to health services. Another of their concerns was the expectation that they act as teachers when they had only limited training and support. Parents, on the other hand, expressed a need for expanding services to Saturday, providing assistance when a child was sick, and linking the hogars (through referral services) to health services, as well as allowing them to take more than one infant to each hogar.

Source: Ruel and others (2006).

Kallpa Wawa, Bolivia

The *Kallpa Wawa* ("strengthening the child") program is a nonformal parenting, community-based program that supports indigenous Quechua women in Bolivia. The program offers literacy sessions to these women in order to improve their practical ability to care for their children at home; other program components include health, nutrition, psychosocial development, and child protection. Parents are trained through workshops and home visits by community promoters, under the supervision of municipal technical workers.[20]

Morenza and others (2005) evaluated the Kallpa Wawa pilot, which was supported by UNICEF, in Cochabamba, Potosí, and Sucre. The evaluation compared children in Kallpa Wawa with a control group of children who did not receive the program as well as with a similar parenting program called Wawa Wasi (this program also includes community child care). Children participating in Kallpa Wawa scored higher than those in the control group on cognitive tests controlling for age.[21] These results need to be interpreted with caution, however, as the Morenza report provided limited information on the strategy used to identify beneficiaries for the programs. It is possible that differences in outcomes are attributable to both unobservable or observable differences between participants.

Madres Guías, Honduras

The *Madres Guías* (Mother Guides) program in Honduras seeks to improve overall child development outcomes. Founded in 1992 by the Christian Children's Fund of Honduras (CCF-H), Madres Guías provides continuous parent education, health, and nutrition services for pregnant women and children from infancy through four or six years of age. Services are delivered by community mothers. A baseline study of Madres Guías was conducted before the program was designed and implemented. Evaluation results suggest the program has been successful in expanding child literacy and building the self-esteem of women participants. Moreover, men in the treatment areas recognize and accept the importance of the program activities for women, and that these activities also benefit children and the community at large (Vargas-Barón, 2007b). These evaluation results must be taken with caution, as many details, including methodologies and data, are unclear.

Programa Familias en Acción, Colombia

Founded in 1999, the *Programa Familias en Acción* (FA, or Families in Action Program) is a CCT program, based on *Oportunidades* in Mexico. FA is a parent-oriented program that targets pregnant women and mothers with children less than 7 years of age. The program provides direct services to mothers, including cash transfers and nutritional supplements, which are conditioned on the use of health services for children (such as immunizations and growth and development controls). Older children in a family are required to be enrolled in school in order to receive subsidies.

By December 2008, the program had reached 1,857,760 families (Acción Social 2008). The cash nutrition subsidy amounts to US$16 per family per month (for families with children under 7); this subsidy is conditioned on children participating in a nationwide growth and development program that schedules preventive health care visits for measuring and weighing them, as well as assessing their nutritional status. Frequency of visits varies by age. In addition, a school subsidy is awarded to children in grades 2 through 11 (the size of the transfer is doubled for high school students), conditioned on school attendance.

An evaluation documented positive effects of the FA program on the height and nutritional status of participating children (Attanasio and others 2005). Using propensity score matching methods, the authors show that for children under 24 months of age, height-for-age standardized scores or z-scores increased by 0.16. For a 12-month-old child, this is the equivalent of 0.43 centimeters. This in turn translates into a lower probability of chronic malnourishment. No effects were found for children 24 months and older. Another finding of the Attanasio study was that FA reduced the probability of reported diarrhea symptoms by approximately 10 percentage points among participating children less than 48 months old in rural areas. Finally, the program increased the probability that participating children complied with the national growth and development program (by 23 percent) and with vaccination schedules (by 9 percent).

PATH, Jamaica

In Jamaica, the *Program of Advancement through Health and Education* (PATH) required children from infancy through 1 year to visit a health center five times per year, and children from 1 to 5 years of age, to visit a center twice per year. A recent study of the program (Levy and Ohls 2007) found that it had positive and significant effects on child participation in health controls, with impact estimates calculated for the marginal participant. Impacts were captured using a regression discontinuity technique that compared eligible households that participated in the program with near-eligible households that were used as a comparison group. According to Levy and Ohls, PATH had a significant and positive impact on health center attendance by participating children under 5. The magnitude of the impact was about 0.3 visits during the preceding six months, the equivalent of a 30 percent increase in the mean of the number of visits.

PRAF, Honduras

In Honduras, the *Family Allowances Program* (PRAF) is a CCT and health program that conditions subsidies on children's participation in preventive child health consultations. Four different packages were randomly allocated to four groups, which included, respectively, money transfers to households, resources provided to local health teams (combined with community-based nutrition), both packages together, and neither package. PRAF had positive effects on growth monitoring and increased the percentage of participating children who were vaccinated. Data was collected at baseline and two years afterward, based on a mother's questionnaire. An evaluation (Morris and others 2004b) found that the household-level intervention had a large impact on reported coverage of antenatal care and well-child checkups (which increased by 15 to 20 percentage points), but not on prenatal checkups. These findings, however, must be treated with care, given the limitations of the impact study.[22]

Red de Protección Social, Nicaragua

In Nicaragua, the *Red de Protección Social* program provided support to children living in extreme poverty[23] via a combination of cash transfers for education and health, health controls, and nutritional supplements. The program was implemented in two stages, with stage I beneficiaries receiving one set of benefits for three years and a second, reduced set for two years. The program covered a total of 46,000 households, which received a school bonus of US$90 per family per year for children ages 7 through 13 enrolled in grades 1 to 4, and a school backpack bonus of US$21 per year, as well as a per student bonus. The health component consisted of an initial household transfer of US$207 for the first eligibility period, and a decreasing bonus in the second phase. Mothers were required to participate in health prevention talks and to guarantee the regular participation of children under 6 in growth monitoring controls.

An impact evaluation of the program (Maluccio and Flores 2005) documented a range of positive effects on child health measures, including a significant increase in the percentage of children younger than 3 years who were taken to health visits (controls) and weighed during the preceding 6 months, as well as in the percentage of children aged 0 to 3 who were given iron supplements in the preceding 12 months. The evaluation used an experimental randomized design with a difference-in-difference approach used to calculate the net impact of the program between control and treatment groups. Positive significant effects were found for up-to-date vaccinations of children aged 12 to 23 months, which increased by 18 percentage points. Further, the program resulted in an average net increase of 16.3 percentage points in the participation of children younger than 3 years old in the growth and monitoring controls for the period 2000–01. However, after two years of program implementation, this percentage remained positive (only 8.4 percent in 2002) but not significant, since participation by the control group increased substantially.

A similar pattern was seen for attendance of children younger than 3 years in health controls to record their growth, development, and weight every six months. The percentage of children attending these controls rose 29 percentage points at the end of the program's first year. In addition, the program had a net effect on the stunting of children under five years of age, which declined by 5.5 percentage points from 2000 to 2002 (at a 10 percent significance level). This decline was 17 times faster than the annual percentage decline from 1998 to 2001. Beneficiary children also experienced a positive and significant reduction of 6.2 percentage points in prevalence of being underweight (Maluccio and Flores 2005).

Preschool Programs

National preschool program, Argentina

There are a number of preschool programs in Latin America and the Caribbean, but only in a few cases has their impact on early childhood development outcomes been rigorously evaluated. Two of the first evaluations of the impact of preprimary education on the life outcomes of participants were those of Berlinski and Galiani (2005) and Berlinski, Galiani, and Gertler (2006). These authors took advantage of Argentina's dramatic preschool construction program[24] to study its effects on primary school achievement, using data from the program and the country's National Education Assessment to test the benefits of a national, publicly funded, early childhood education program.

The authors used a difference-in-difference strategy and combined differences in the number of facilities built across regions with differences in exposure across cohorts induced by the expansion of the program over time. The expansion of preschool facilities had a positive impact on attendance, with an average increase in the probability of preprimary school attendance of approximately 7.5 percentage points. The construction program thus explained half of the 15 percentage point increase in gross enrollment rates from 1991 to 2001 (Berlinksi and Galiani 2005).

Berlinski, Galiani, and Gertler (2006) then examined the effect of preschool attendance on medium-term learning outcomes, using standardized test scores for grades 3, 6, and 7. The authors found that preschool attendance at ages 3 to 5 increased performance in language and mathematics by 6 to 4.5 percentage points, respectively, or 0.3 to 0.2 of a standard deviation, with similar gains for boys and girls. The effect of having attended preschool on third grade test scores was, moreover, twice as large for students from poor backgrounds than for students from non-poor backgrounds. One year of preschool increased average third grade math and Spanish test scores by 8 percent of a mean, or by 23 percent of the standard deviation of the distribution of test scores. Further, preschool participation positively affected students' behavioral skills, including attention, effort, class participation, and discipline, as measured by teacher responses.[25] The gains realized from preschool education were again bigger for students living in more disadvantaged municipalities.

National preschool program, Uruguay

A similar analysis was carried out by Berlinski, Galiani, and Manacorda (2007) on preschool attendees in Uruguay. The study found positive long-term effects of participation in preschool on their subsequent school outcomes. Using a Uruguayan household survey that collected retrospective information on preschool attendance, the authors were able to isolate the effect of a rapid expansion of preschool places by comparing differences between treated and untreated siblings. The authors used a variety of approaches to control for selection bias (both observable and unobservable characteristics may lead parents to enroll children in preschool).[26] The study captured differences in school progression for students ages 7 through 15 years based on one, two, or three years of preschool participation.

Among the findings of the study was that preschool attendance had a significant and positive effect on school enrollment as a child grows. At age 7, the difference in enrollment rates between children in the program and control groups was 3 percentage points; by age 15, this difference was 20 to 28 percentage points. By age 15, participating students had roughly 0.8 additional years of education compared to students who did not participate in the preschool program. This finding represents an overall increase in the average level of education of 15-year-olds of around one-tenth of one year, and a rise in the school participation rate of around 3 percentage points. The analysis also showed a small additional effect of having attended two years of preprimary school, as compared to none, an effect discernible after the age of 12. There were no additional gains due to a third year of preschool participation. Results also showed differential effects of preschool exposure for children whose mothers were less educated, those living outside of the capital, and boys. These results are similar to previous findings by la Administración Nacional de Educación Pública (ANEP) (2001 and 2005).

Proyecto Integral de Desarrollo Infantil, Bolivia

Bolivia's *Proyecto Integral de Desarrollo Infantil* (PIDI, or Integrated Child Development Project) was implemented in the 1990s and offered full-time daycare, plus nutritional and educational services, to children between the ages of 6 months and 72 months in poor urban areas. Behrman, Cheng, and Todd (2004) used propensity score matching (selection on observables) to construct a comparison group and estimate program impacts by comparing a group of participant and nonparticipant children. Three groups were compared: beneficiary children, children in the matched comparison group, and children who received the treatment for a shorter period of time.

The study found that the program was successful in reaching the poorest children in the poorer neighborhoods; had positive impacts on participants' gross and fine motor skills, psychosocial skills, and language acquisition, compared to nonparticipants and children who participated in the program for just over two months; and had a larger positive impact on anthropometrics for children from better-off families. Impacts were found to be cumulative, with greater impacts associated with longer program exposure, particularly longer than seven months.[27] Program impacts were, moreover, concentrated among children aged 37 months and older. When the length of exposure to the program was considered, effects were most clearly observed in children who were exposed to the program for more than a year.

Preschool program, Mexico

Mexico provides an opportunity to evaluate the impact of preschool attendance among very young children. In 2001, the Mexican government enacted a law that made preschool compulsory for children aged 3 to 5 years. The law was the first ever to mandate preschool for 3-year-old children. Between 2003 and 2005, the enrollment of children 4–5 years old increased significantly, with virtual universal enrollment of children aged 5 and 81 percent enrollment of children aged 4. The expansion of enrollment was accomplished by increasing the number of classrooms, the number of children in the classrooms, and the number of teachers.

However, a recent study by Yoshikawa and others (2006) shows that the policy did not have such a positive effect on the enrollment of 3-year-olds. In fact, there appears to have been a trade-off: as preschool enrollment of children aged 4 and 5 years was expanding, enrollment of 3-year-olds was decreasing in half of the participating states. The expansion also had a direct impact on teacher-student ratios, with an increase in the proportion of preschools with ratios greater than 30:1. The implications of the increased enrollments on the quality and size of participants' ECD outcomes are not yet known (Yoshikawa and others 2006).

Preschool program, Brazil

A recent study in Brazil (Curi and Menezes-Filho 2006) examines the effect of daycare and preschool on the educational attainment, school performance, and wages of participants. The study uses retrospective data, data from the *Pesquisa de Padrão de Vida* (PPV, or Survey of Life Patterns) of the Brazilian Institute of Geography and Statistics (IBGE) carried out in 1996–97, and data from the *Sistema Nacional de Avaliação da Educaçãco Basica* (SAEB, or National Basic Education Evaluation System) in 2003. The authors conclude that daycare and preschool had a positive impact on the probability of participating students' completion of schooling cycles, performance on tests scores, and earnings.

Preschool program, Peru (small sample)

In Peru, Cueto and Diaz (1999), using retrospective data from a small sample of children who attended formal preschools (*Centro de Educación Inicial,* or CEI) and nonformal preschool programs (*Programa no Formal de Educación Inicial,* or PRONOEI) reported differences in the language and mathematics outcomes of the two groups of children. The sample was taken from nine schools in the urban metropolitan area of Lima. In each school, a first-grade classroom was selected at random. In total, 304 children who entered first grade for the first time were included in the sample.

Using teachers' reports on math and Spanish language performance, the study showed that the probability of higher achievement by children with CEI preschool experience increased by 25 percent in language and 22 percent in mathematics. For children with PRONOEI experience, the respective probabilities increased by 15 and 17 percent, as compared to children with no experience. Compared to children with no ECD experience, students who attended both formal and nonformal preschool performed better in both areas. These results need to be interpreted with care, however, as the study had certain important caveats. More importantly, perhaps, it was not designed as an impact evaluation study.[28]

Integrated Multiservice Programs

Oportunidades, Mexico

The Mexican *Oportunidades* program is the most studied of all CCT programs in the Latin American and Caribbean region. It began in 1997 and currently targets five million extremely poor families (25 percent of the Mexican population). Originally designed as a cash transfer program for families living in poverty who could demonstrate compliance with program education and health conditions, Oportunidades has increasingly become a combined parent-child strategy via cooperative agreements with health, nutrition, and educational service providers.

In addition to providing cash payments to families, program services include prenatal education and health care; childbirth support; services for newborns; nutritional supplements for pregnant women and children from infancy through 24 months; child screening and assessments; parent education and support; and primary health care services.[29] Malnourished children aged 2 to 5 also receive nutritional supplements. Target beneficiaries include pregnant and lactating women and their children from birth through secondary school (approximately 15 years of age), with a major emphasis on children from birth through 24 months of age.

Evaluations of Oportunidades have benefited from the random assign-
ment of beneficiaries to control and treatment groups during the expansion of the program. Households identified as the original control group
were enrolled in the program at later stages, allowing researchers to take
advantage of the phased expansion of the program. The comprehensive-
ness of the data collected has allowed for multiple studies. A midterm
survey in rural areas (six years after the program was launched) and a
short-term evaluation (one year of enrollment) in urban areas are the
primary sources of data. As the following paragraphs illustrate, the program has been highly successful in enhancing the physical growth and
well-being outcomes of participating children, particularly in rural areas.
However, it has not been found to significantly impact cognitive development outcomes.

An early program evaluation (Gertler 2000) showed that the program
had a positive impact on children's attendance at health centers, as seen in
a 12 percent decline in illness among participating children under 5 compared to nonparticipating children. The evaluation also showed a positive
impact on the height and probability of being stunted of participating
children aged 12 to 36 months.

Another early study (Behrman and Hoddinott 2001) used fixed-effects
estimates to control for observed and unobserved differences between
beneficiary and nonbeneficiary children (administration of the nutritional
supplement was not randomized). The study estimated improvements of
one-sixth of the mean growth rate per year among participating children
aged 12 to 36 months as compared to nonparticiating children. Children
in the program experienced growth of about one centimeter per year
greater than nonbeneficiary children. The impact was larger for poorer
children from poorer communities and among children whose parents
had more education. A study by Neufeld and others (2006) found that
Oportunidades also had positive impacts on stunting, height, and weight.
Children from beneficiary households who at the baseline were younger
than six months were on average one centimeter taller and weighed about
0.5 kilograms more than children from nonbeneficiary households.[30]

Gertler and Fernald (2004) used a battery of psychometric instruments
to capture the impact of Oportunidades on a range of child development
outcomes.[31] The authors calculated the program's impact by comparing
its effects on three different groups of children: a group that received benefits for five-and-a-half years (the treatment group), a group that received
benefits for a year and a half (the original control group), and a group
that never received benefits (the new control group). Gertler and Fernald compared the results of the first two groups with those of the third
group. Using multivariate regression and matching methods to control
for observed differences between the treatment and new control groups
(and to prevent biased estimates of true program impacts), the researchers

reconstructed a control group that matched the treatment group in terms of individual, household, and community characteristics.

The study found that the program had no impact on cognitive development, but did have a positive impact on participants' motor skills and socioemotional development. Findings showed average increases of 15 percent and 10 percent, respectively, on the scores of boys and girls across eight motor skills tests. Using the Achenbach Child Behavior Checklist, the study also found an improvement of about 9 percent in the socioemotional development of girl participants and a positive but nonsignificant improvement among boy participants. Interestingly, no differentiated impact of Oportunidades was found on the development of children who started in the prenatal period, as compared to those who started in the first two years of life.

Another study focused on cognitive development (Behrman, Parker, and Todd 2004) and found few medium-term effects of Oportunidades on the educational outcomes of participants. The authors assessed the impact of the nutrition package (which consisted of infant nutritional supplements) on the educational performance of children from birth to age 8. The study compared the schooling rates of children aged 0 to 8 in 1997 (before the intervention began) and aged 6 to 14 at the time of the rural evaluation survey with children in the original control group.

The evaluation compared children who participated in the program and received infant nutrition supplementation and health checkups (although they might have benefitted indirectly from other aspects of the program such as income transfers to other household members) with children who did not. The authors used two different approaches to capture impact. First, they used the difference-in-difference technique to estimate the impact of differential program exposure of about one-and-a-half years in a group of children who were randomly selected to receive program benefits in 1997 (treatment group) and a group who started receiving benefits in 2000 (the original control group). The second approach used a matched comparison group (that was to be incorporated into the program in 2004). Through this method the researchers were able to estimate the differences between exposure to the program for five-and-a-half years and no exposure. Data was derived from a baseline survey in 1997 and a follow-up survey in 2003. Education performance was captured by age when starting school, grade progression, educational attainment, and enrollment in secondary school.

The study found that Oportunidades had positive effects for participating children ages 0 through 2, but few significant effects for children ages 3 through 5. For children aged 2 and under, the study found weak evidence that children were likely to enter school at a slightly earlier age and stronger evidence that they were more likely to progress through schooling levels on time and complete more years of schooling. The program had particularly strong impacts on children who were 1 year old in 1997, increasing their schooling and probability of progressing through schooling levels on time. The study did not find significant impacts on age at school entry. For children aged 3 to 5, the study found a reduction in the probability of failing a grade for boys aged 5 in 1997 (11 in 2003) and an increased likelihood of grade progression for boys aged 4 in 1997. There were no significant effects for girls or boys of other ages. It is worth noting that this group of children benefitted only from the health checkup component of the program. The authors argue that it is not surprising to see few positive impacts given that this group of children neither benefited from the nutrition component nor the educational scholarships because they were either too old or too young to qualify (Behrman, Parker, and Todd 2004).

Programa de Atención Integral a la Niñez Nicaragüense, Nicaragua

In 1996, the Nicaraguan government introduced the *Programa de Atención Integral a la Niñez Nicaragüense* (PAININ). PAININ consolidated previously existing services (preschool education, weighing, and referrals) to provide an integrated program of early childhood stimulation, health, nutrition, and daycare services for children from birth through the age of 7. Services are targeted to children under the age of 6 in the poorest 35 municipalities in the country and provided through networks of community centers or via a home-based model. (PAININ has since expanded to 66 municipalities.)[32] The Ministry of the Family is responsible for overall program operations, and outsources the provision of services to qualified providers.[33]

Macours and Vakis (2007) analyzed data from a sample of children from six municipalities in a poor border region of Nicaragua, where migration to other Central American countries is widespread. Using an instrumental variables approach to estimate the impact of parents' migration on early childhood development, the authors compared the outcomes of children who participated in the program with those who did not.[34] Their analysis showed that PAININ had a substantial impact on the language scores (captured with the PPVT) of participants as compared to nonparticipant children. Unlike other studies, the effects were larger for children in the two highest consumption quintiles in the sample, as compared to households in the lowest two quintiles. The authors hypothesized that a nutrition constraint might exist and that the stimulus (that is, PAININ) might not be as beneficial for children who have severe nutritional problems. The program also seems to have a larger impact on the language scores of children of migrant mothers versus nonmigrant mothers.[35]

Chile Solidario, Chile

In 2002, Chile implemented the *Chile Solidario* social assistance program, which aims at reaching the poorest households with an innovative
approach that combines cash assistance with psychosocial support. The
long-term objective of Chile Solidario is to move away from an approach
based on single programs towards a "system" of social protection, where
the government provides a cash transfer combined with social programs
that are tailored to meet the specific needs of households living in extreme
poverty. An evaluation (Galasso 2006b) of the program demonstrated that
it had a positive impact on the likelihood of enrollment in preschool for
beneficiary households with young children. The evaluation looked at the
effect of Chile Solidario during its first two years of operation. Using two
different methods, matching control and regression discontinuity, Galasso
found an increased likelihood that participating children aged 4 and 5 years
would be in preschool. The effect ranged from 4 to 6 percentage points in
urban and rural areas and was present regardless of the method used.

Atención a Crisis, Nicaragua

Atención a Crisis is a randomized CCT program in rural Nicaragua. The
program makes sizeable cash transfers—around 15 percent of the per
capita expenditures of the average recipient household—to families that
agree to take preschool-aged children for regular visits to health centers,
where they are weighed and receive immunizations and food supplements,
if necessary. Families also agree to send their school-aged children to
school on a regular basis. A recent evaluation (Macours, Schady, and
Vakis 2008) found that the program had reduced developmental delays
in participating young children, especially among older preschool-aged
children, compared to nonparticipating children.

Bono de Desarrollo Humano, Ecuador

The *Bono de Desarrollo Humano* (BDH) program was introduced in
Ecuador over the three-year period, 2003–06. Its objective is to alleviate
poverty and, in the long term, contribute to social capital formation. The
program is means-tested and targets poor families,[36] covering 1,060,416
households—approximately 40 percent of the total population. As of
2006, the total budget of the program was US$194 million, of which US$8
million was allocated to administrative expenses. The average unconditional cash transfer made by the program is US$15 per month per house-
hold. This is a nontrivial amount since it represents an increase in 10
percent in family expenditure for the average family (Paxson and Schady

2007). The BDH is not conditional on health or education outcomes. Originally, the program was designed to be conditional on these, but the conditionality was never implemented.

Paxson and Schady (2007) took advantage of the built-in randomized rollout of the BDH to assess its impact on the development of children aged 3 to 7 in rural Ecuador. Using a control group (families in control parishes who were to receive the program seven years later) and treatment group, the researchers estimated the effect of the program on the average scores of children on a number of psychometric instruments that measured eight outcomes of early childhood development (including socioemotional development), comparing data from both baseline and follow-up surveys.[37]

Outcome measures were collected on physical outcomes (hemoglobin, height for age, and fine motor control), cognitive outcomes (the Spanish version of the PPVT, Woodcock-Johnson Munoz battery), and behavioral outcomes (using a mother's report scale),[38] as well as maternal outcomes, including mothers' physical and mental health. Using intent-to-treat estimates, the authors calculated the average treatment effect across all outcomes. Findings from the study indicate that income transfers per se (that is, unconditional transfers) can have a positive impact on children as long as mothers are the recipient.

The evaluation also showed substantially larger effects for the poorest families, with a positive impact on their hemoglobin levels, fine motor skills, long-term memory, and behavioral problems. The BDH also appeared to have larger effects on children in the poorest quartile whose mothers had at least completed primary school. There were no differences in impact by age when participants ages 3 and 4 were compared to participants ages 5 to 7. Of note, the program had larger effects on girls than boys across all income levels. In the absence of the program, girls appeared to be more disadvantaged, suggesting that the BDH equalizes cognitive and behavioral outcomes among girls.

With respect to fine motor skills, the evaluation found modest but statistically significant treatment effects for fine motor skills (16 percent of a standard deviation higher in the treatment than control group) and for long-term memory (19.2 percent of a standard deviation higher in the treatment than the control group).

The authors concluded that the cash transfer program improved child physical health and well-being outcomes through improved nutrition (that is, improvement in the diets of all family members, including children) and use of deworming medication. However, there was no increased usage of existing health facilities. It seems that the transfers were spent in a way that empowered mothers. The poorest mothers seemed to have experienced improvements in how they perceived themselves (in terms of wealth and physical health), but the program had no effects on mental health or maternal depression.

The authors of the 2007 evaluation suggest that it is unlikely that the BDH would have affected children's outcomes through enhanced parenting, given its limited effect on maternal health status. The data seems to indicate that cash transfers alone can have a positive impact on the development of young children, despite the absence of conditionality, if the population targeted is extremely poor or disadvantaged. It would thus appear that intensive and more responsive parenting is not necessarily the only mechanism through which child outcomes can be enhanced.

Programs That Support the Reentry of Mothers into the Workforce

Some ECD interventions are specifically designed to allow mothers to enter or remain in the workforce. As discussed in chapter 1, the average rate of female labor force participation in Latin America is around 60 percent, a rate that varies widely by country. Very low levels of female participation in the workforce among the poorest households are particularly troubling, given the strong relationship between family income and ECD outcomes. Most of the programs examined in this chapter did not specifically focus on supporting women's participation in the labor force, with the exception of HCP in Guatemala.

Programs that improve access to early childhood care and education can also have important effects on female labor force participation. For example, the evaluation by Attanasio and Vera-Hernandez (2004) of the Colombian program Hogares Comunitarios suggests that the program increased by 31 percent the average probability that mothers would work in the weeks prior to the study interview. In Argentina, Berlinski and Galiani (2005) assessed the impact of the expansion of preschool infrastructure on maternal employment, finding a positive impact on the probability of maternal employment of between 7 and 14 percentage points.

With respect to the reasons why women's labor participation rate is so low in many countries, a 2007 joint study by the World Bank, the Chilean National Service for Women (SERNAM), and the Inter-American Development Bank found several contributing factors in Chile, including: (i) lack of access to quality education and training opportunities, especially for low-income women; (ii) family structures, specifically, families with a larger number of children under the age of 15 in which mothers serve as the principal child care providers; (iii) shorter workdays for women than for men with the same employer and shorter periods of continuous employment, together with longer periods of inactivity and unemployment; and (iv) traditional cultural values and attitudes about gender roles, which constrain women's employment outside the home in the country.

Summary

Looking back at the evidence presented in this chapter, several conclusions can be reached. Early childhood development interventions in the region that offer nutrition supplements, as well as those that combine several strategies (such as parenting practices, early childhood care, and nutrition), have been shown to have positive effects on children's cognitive development, as measured by such indicators as language acquisition, reasoning, vocabulary, and educational attainment. The most rigorous evidence for these impacts comes from ECD programs in Colombia, Guatemala, and Jamaica. Preschool programs have also been found to impact children's cognitive development, improving primary school attendance and the test scores of primary students in language and mathematics. Of note, these programs appeared to benefit children from poorer backgrounds more than children from better-off households. In addition, preschool participation also positively affected children's socioemotional development, as discerned by such behavioral skills as attention, effort, class participation, and discipline. The primary evidence for these impacts comes from interventions in Argentina and Uruguay.

There is widespread use of CCT programs that require participation in ECD programs in the region, particularly to provide nutritional and educational support to young children. Such CCT programs are currently operating in Brazil, Chile, Colombia, the Dominican Republic, Ecuador, El Salvador, Honduras, Jamaica, Mexico, Nicaragua, and Peru.[39] These programs, which provide a cash transfer to low-income families along with, most commonly, a requirement that young children visit health centers for monitoring, have positive effects on the physical health and well-being outcomes of young children, but few have documented impacts on their cognitive development. The programs' impact on the utilization of health services, such as child growth monitoring and promotion, is also positive and consistent across most countries.[40,41] Such programs also appeared to have few medium-term education effects on children aged 3 to 5, although they did appear to positively affect the educational attainment of younger participants (children aged 0 to 2), possibly because this group benefited from the nutrition component of the programs. The evidence for these impacts principally comes from Mexico. Other evaluations of CCT programs in the region have found that they improve the probability of beneficiary children attending preschool (Chile) and reduce developmental delays (Nicaragua).

The evidence for the impact of ECD programs on the socioemotional development of young children is more limited. Often, ECD programs target multiple objectives and evaluations do not or cannot disentangle their effects on children's socioemotional outcomes. However, the limited evidence available from evaluations of cash transfer programs (conditional and unconditional) from Mexico and Ecuador suggests that these interventions can have positive effects on socioemotional development, as measured by a variety of widely used empirical tests.

Overall, the evaluation literature on ECD programs in Latin America and the Caribbean is much more robust concerning program effects on physical growth and well-being of young children. One strong finding is that interventions that include a nutrition component have positive effects on children's health and physical development (as measured by improvements in children's height and a reduction in the proportion of stunted children). This was the case of a subsidized milk program for children and pregnant and lactating women (Mexico), nutrition and early child care programs (Colombia and Guatemala), and certain CCT programs (Colombia and Mexico). Several programs also found that children's participation in health controls and growth monitoring also had positive effects on their health and well-being. Such was the case of programs in Mexico and Colombia that conditioned cash payments on children visiting health centers and undergoing physical monitoring. Even unconditional CCT programs appeared to have positive effects on the development of child motor skills and other developmental indicators, mainly due to better household nutrition and the use of deworming medications when they were targeted at the very poor (Ecuador).

Our review of evidence on the impacts of ECD interventions in Latin America and the Caribbean suggests that one area requires urgent attention from researchers: the need for accurate cost accounting. Not only is it difficult to track costs because funding for ECD programs is often derived from multiple sources, but also many government investments in such programs are not disaggregated from larger, sectoral categories. Although evidence from the impact evaluations helps answer the question of whether a specific program can improve ECD outcomes, it is necessary to understand the relative cost of alternative programs in order to make informed policy choices.

Notes

1. These 10 programs were chosen because they covered different countries, had evaluation results (even if such results were not rigorous), and had been in place for a few years. Mostly large-scale programs, the group examined in detail also included some small-scale, pilot programs.

2. Detailed descriptions of the programs discussed in this chapter, together with additional programs in the region, can be found in appendix 2.

3. An efficacy trial is a test of whether an intervention does more good than harm when delivered under optimal (controlled) conditions. Program implementers are usually highly trained professionals and conditions are closely monitored to ensure that targeted beneficiaries receive a maximal "dose" of the intervention. Effectiveness trials, on the other hand, test whether an intervention does more good than harm under *real world* conditions (Flay 1986, as cited in Society for

Prevention Research (SPR), 2004, "Standards of Evidence Criteria for Efficacy, Effectiveness and Dissemination," SPR, Fairfax, Virginia, USA, http://www.preventionresearch.org/commlmon.php (accessed April 2009).

4. The limitations included large attrition (only 49 percent of the original INCAP study sample were interviewed), and the inability of researchers to distinguish different effects for different exposure windows within the first 3 years of life due to data and study design restrictions.

5. In one poor, periurban community of 5,000 inhabitants, healthy children 10–30 months of age at the beginning of the study were selected from a registry of children younger than 5 years of age living in the community. Children were randomly assigned to drink 400 milliliters per day (200 milliliters in the morning and 200 milliliters in the evening) of cow's whole milk (distributed as milk powder), which was either fortified or unfortified. Infant caregivers were instructed how to reconstitute the powdered milk (which was delivered weekly to each family) and the amount of milk an infant was intended to drink daily. A fieldworker visited the household two times a day, at the usual times of milk intake by the child, to verify the correct reconstitution of milk and to register the amount of milk consumed. When mothers offered extra milk to their children or when children were not at home at the time of the visit, mothers were asked the following day to estimate the amount of milk drunk by the child (Villalpando and others 2006).

6. The evaluation compared beneficiary children and families with matched comparison groups selected from the initial sample of potential beneficiaries, but who were later excluded from the program. Data on child anthropometrics was collected six months after the benefits began to be received. Growth trajectories were reconstructed using Ministry of Health data.

7. The original survey included 127 stunted children assigned to four groups (control and three treated groups) and 32 non-stunted children. Additionally, 52 non-stunted children were included at follow-up four years later. Similarly, follow-ups on the children aged 11 to 12 years and 17 to 18 years involved 116 stunted/80 non-stunted children, and 103 stunted/64 non-stunted children, respectively (Walker and others 2000 and 2005).

8. In statistical terms, all values were $p < .05$.

9. Dropout rates in the highest grade attained or current grade if still enrolled in school (Walker and others 2005).

10. In Jamaica, "rovers" go from home to home to work with young children and parent beneficiaries, introducing them to developmentally appropriate child care practices. Each rover is assigned to about 30 families and receives training in child development. They provide colorful and interesting toys and learning material for the children, many of which are made by participants.

11. It was expected that both components would be coordinated, so that all children in CDIs would also benefit from growth monitoring and other child health services.

12. To learn more about the program go to http://www.nacer.gov.ar/index.asp.

13. The program built on the positive experiences of large-scale programs, such as the Iringa Project in Tanzania, the Indonesia Behavioral Change Program, and the Tamil Nadu Project in India, which continue to serve as best-practice examples of how nutritional issues can be addressed effectively.

14. The authors hypothesize that this result was due to the high participation of children aged 8 to 12. This age group has very high attendance rates. Older children begin to drop out of school.

15. The authors also look at other outcomes such as female labor supply.

16. A first draft of this study found higher results. It found that the program effect translated into a 2.36 centimeter gain in height among boys and a 2.39 centimeter gain among girls aged 72 months (Attanasio and Vera-Hernandez 2004a).

17. Ruel and others (2006) provided comprehensive information about program operations, identifying operational constraints and challenges. They also provided comparison information on costs incurred by beneficiary families of HCP and families using alternative care options (primarily relatives and family care).

18. Chile Solidario comprises anti-poverty programs and policies in Chile that target indigent households by providing them with intensive psychosocial support, priority access to existing transfers, connections to the public and private networks of social services, and a cash grant.

19. The results reflect only post-intervention data, as no baseline data was collected. Difficulties were also reported in the construction of the comparison group due to selection biases.

20. More information about Kallpa Wawa can be found at http://www.redin-novemos.org/content/view/458/103/lang,sp/ (last accessed August 11, 2009).

21. In statistical terms, $p < 0.07$.

22. The authors cautioned that respondents may have believed that their answers would affect their likelihood of receiving benefits. They also pointed out that interviewers were not blind to treatment and that there was only limited or partial implementation of the service-level package.

23. The average levels of expenditure of targeted households were below the level required to meet minimum calorie intake, as measured by the Nicaragua Living Measurement Standard Survey.

24. Between 1993 (the year that preschool education became compulsory) and 1999, Argentina constructed enough classrooms for approximately 176,000 children. Preschool classrooms are attached to primary schools and operate in two separate shifts of three-and-a-half hours. The program successfully impacted uptake, with all provinces experiencing increased preprimary enrollment rates by at least 10 percentage points.

25. The authors hypothesize that positive behavioral skills could be an indication that preschool participation might affect subsequent school performance and attainment, given that this provides children opportunities to socialize and facilitates their self-control, necessary skills for making the most out of classroom experience.

26. The study also used average preschool enrollment by locality and birth cohort as an instrumental variable estimate for each child's exposure; this variable served as a control for differential treatment of siblings within households.

27. A World Bank report documented that the nutritional impacts of the program were moderate to negligible (World Bank 2004a).

28. The main caveats of the study refer to its external validity, given that the sample was not representative. Further, observable and unobservable differences between children who attended the two programs (or not) were not considered. For example, it is possible that children who participated in CEI were generally better off than children who attend PRONOEI.

29. Another program in Mexico, PASL, offers subsidized milk to pregnant and lactating women to improve their and their babies' nutrition and health.

30. The Neufeld study needs to be taken with caution as its data on child outcomes came from longitudinal subsamples that were deliberately selected to complete existing surveys and thus were not randomly selected. The authors caution that the population selected for this subsample might not be representative of the total beneficiary population of the program (Neufeld and others 2006).

31. Cognitive development was measured with the Woodcock-Johnson test, the Spanish version of the Peabody Picture Vocabulary Test (PPVT) for language in 3-6 year olds, and the MacArthur Communicative Development Inventories; motor development was measured by the McCarthy scale. Socioemotional behavior was measured by the Achenbach Child Behavior Checklist. These standardized mea-

sures have been widely used in Latin America and the Caribbean, particularly the PPVT, which has been translated and adapted to Spanish-speaking populations.

32. See Verdisco and others (2007) for a detailed description of the PAININ program.

33. PAININ delivered services through nongovernmental organizations strongly rooted in their respective communities.

34. As an instrumental variable for the duration of migration, the authors used information on exogenous shocks.

35. This evidence is consistent with previous findings. An earlier program evaluation suggested that PAININ had a positive impact on preschool attendance, with a net increase in enrollment in first grade for 6-year-olds who had completed PAININ (ESA Consultores 2005). Similar positive effects were documented on children's health indicators. However, the control and treatment groups in this earlier evaluation suffered from contamination, as some control areas were exposed to the program and some treatment areas dropped out of the program. These results are therefore best interpreted in the light of the newer findings by Macours and Vakis (2007).

36. As classified by the Selben Index (levels 1 and 2). Only families in the first two quintiles of the Selben Index are eligible for the program. Selben is the beneficiary selection system for social services. It entails a proxy-means test that uses information on household demographic composition, assets, and other variables to classify households according to their welfare levels (World Bank 2004b).

37. The follow-up subsample survey included 1,479 children aged 3 to 7 whose families were interviewed both for the baseline and follow-up surveys and for whom information on all eight outcomes was available.

38. The authors reported using a subsample in order to include only those children for whom data on all child outcomes was available. This subsample was taken out of the larger sample, which included families that were in the first two quintiles of the Selben Index, had at least one child under the age of 6, no children ages 6 or older, and had not been recipients of the earlier version of the program.

39. One reason that CCT programs have spread throughout the region is that early program results were well documented and based on rigorous impact evaluations. Another reason could be that as demand-side programs, CCT interventions are more likely to attract public attention and support than traditional supply-side programs.

40. *Bolsa Alimentação* in Brazil; see Morris, Olinto, and others (2004a).

41. It is important to emphasize that CCTs can be conditional on a variety of things. Some conditionalities (like improving cognitive test scores) might (or might not) lead to desired outcomes. We thank an anonymous reviewer for noting this point.

5

Increasing Early Childhood Development Program Coverage in the Region: The Need for Comprehensive Approaches

Comprehensive approaches to early childhood development are developed to make the well-being of children from birth through ages 6 or 8 a national, government priority. Countries with high-quality ECD programs that reach significant numbers of potential beneficiaries generally tend to have national policies. If the countries of Latin America and the Caribbean are to successfully expand coverage of existing programs, they will need corresponding national policies.

This chapter begins with a current snapshot of ECD policies in the region, after which it outlines the basic steps involved in building a comprehensive ECD policy. Throughout the chapter, illustrations are drawn from countries in the region, as well as from member states of the OECD. Options for expanding ECD services in the region are offered at the end of the chapter.

There are several reasons why comprehensive approaches are invaluable for helping build and sustain ECD programs. First, key stakeholders—specifically, children and working mothers—often do not have sufficient voice in the public arena to effectively participate in or influence the political debate. Second, ECD policies typically cut across sectoral boundaries—involving health, education, and social planning ministries—which can result in the isolation, fragmentation, and, in some cases, lack of cohesion of ECD programs. In the absence of a comprehensive approach that lays out an institutional anchor for these programs, it can be difficult to name a "champion" for ECD among government institutions. Third, the long time horizon required to achieve tangible results from ECD investments, coupled with the short-to-medium-term planning horizon of many political actors, makes it difficult for such investments to become a high priority.

A national policy is a useful way to articulate and coordinate various ECD policies under a common vision. It makes explicit a country's vision and long-term goals for early childhood development and provides a framework for designing and implementing ECD programs. Although some countries in the region with longstanding successful ECD programs do not have a national policy, such a policy signals that early childhood development is a governmental priority.

The degree to which a national ECD policy is needed depends on the particular context of an individual country. A study on South Africa (Aidoo 2006) notes that countries with robust and adequate social policies, integrated sectoral policies and strategies, and well-defined children's policies may not need a national ECD policy. What is necessary in those contexts is an integrated framework, or plan of action, to ensure coordination and prioritize sector responsibility, thus facilitating effective implementation. In contrast, countries with a weak understanding of ECD, and that place a low priority on vulnerable children or have low levels of intersectoral coordination, would benefit from a national policy.

Status of Comprehensive ECD Policies in the Region

Countries in Latin America and the Caribbean are slowly moving toward a comprehensive approach to early childhood development (UNESCO 2006). For example, Colombia and Jamaica first financed comprehensive ECD programs, then acknowledged the need for a policy framework that could provide the necessary leverage to ensure their sustainability. Both countries are now in the process of developing national policies, which will no doubt be built on strong existing sectoral policies. Peru has adopted a policy framework for the development of ECD programs—the National Plan of Action for Infancy and Adolescence (2002–2010), which supports the work of the country's Non-Formal Program for Initial Education (PRONOEI).

In Colombia, Chile, and Mexico, new approaches to ministerial leadership and coordination are seeking to overcome sectoral boundaries, aligning ECD strategies with overall poverty reduction and development goals, and making the most effective use of scarce resources. One impetus for better coordination in these countries was the launch of large-scale conditional cash transfer programs, which have forced a realignment of social protection expenses. The coordination role of a strong ministry, whether of finance, planning, or social development, is crucial because these organizations have the convening power to promote dialogue between sectors and forge a national consensus. Critical issues that must be decided by these countries include who will take the lead for ECD policy design and implementation, which ministry will coordinate interventions for children from birth to age 3 (and their parents), and how programs will coordinate their activities to maximize coverage and quality.

Chile has already designed and introduced a national ECD policy. In 2006, President Michelle Bachelet charged the Ministry of Planning with implementing her national ECD policy *Chile Crece Contigo* (CCC, or Chile Grows with You), which promotes child development and protection interventions in multiple sectors. The Ministry of Planning in Chile is the central coordinating agency for the policy, working with the ministries of health and education, as well as the two main agencies that provide ECD services in the country: *Junta Nacional de Jardines Infantiles* (JUNJI) and *Fundación Educacional para el Desarrollo Integral del Menor* (Fundación INTEGRA). As of this writing, CCC was reported to be in a transition stage. The Chilean Ministry of Planning and other organizations are in the process of creating a legal basis for the new system and its expanded ECD services, with the goal of enabling it to continue functioning beyond the term of the current administration.

Building a Comprehensive ECD Policy: The Basic Steps

A comprehensive ECD policy helps define institutional leadership and creates an umbrella framework for intersectoral coordination. It may also provide a general framework for articulating the sources of program funding and defining a limited number of high-stakes national priorities, based on past program successes. To be effective, a comprehensive policy needs to be consistent with social practices and other, related national policies, such as labor market policy. Because the policy formulation process goes beyond the scope of this book, this section concentrates on the principal building blocks of such a policy, all of which must be considered at the outset of the process.

The review of ECD policies, both in the region and the OECD, suggest that a set of initial steps is required to develop a comprehensive policy. These steps include:

(i)   defining an institutional anchor and achieving intersectoral coordination
(ii) ensuring adequate funding
(iii) defining core national priorities
(iv) building on the successes of existing and past programs, while remaining aware of the limitations of impact evaluations
(v)   ensuring the coherence of ECD policy with other related policies

Defining an institutional anchor

A comprehensive ECD policy is by definition multidisciplinary and multisectoral. Ideally, such policies create links among different policy areas that affect young children, such as health, nutrition, education, water, hygiene, sanitation, and legal protection. In essence, national policies help create coordination systems to implement integrated ECD programs.

The experiences of certain OECD countries are particularly illustrative of the institutional anchoring of ECD plans and the need to facilitate coordination among multiple ministries. For instance, England and Scotland (both in 1998) and Sweden (in 1996) have all transferred national responsibility for early childhood education and care (that is, services for young children), as well as child care for school-age children (that is, services for school-age children), from national welfare to national education departments.

The spectrum of centralization-decentralization arrangements adopted in OECD countries is also instructive for the countries in Latin America and the Caribbean. In Norway, the Ministry of Social Affairs is responsible for national policy making and administration, but the delivery and implementation of ECD programs is handled locally. After a long period of strict regulation and centralized control, Sweden delegated responsibility for implementation of early childhood services to the municipal level. In Germany, nearly all ECD legislation, as well as the regulation and administration of ECD programs, takes place at the state level. Countries also vary as to whether private, early child education centers are regulated. In Germany, the private sector is unregulated, while in Denmark and Sweden, private centers are subject to public regulation (OECD 2006).

One continuing challenge of countries in the OECD is that programs supporting the entire 0-to-6-year-old age period lack coherence and coordination (Vegas and others 2006). This failing has several important, negative consequences for early childhood development. First, children end up switching teachers, programs, and services frequently. Second, services are fragmented, particularly links between early and later services, but also between part-time formal programs and out-of-school care. Third, the pedagogical techniques and curricula used in programs can be inappropriate for the specific age group concerned. Fourth, there are often wide disparities in the training and status of care providers and early education staff. As a result, even if the provision of child services is becoming universal, the level and quality of these services is heterogeneous.

Ensuring adequate funding

The development of a comprehensive ECD policy and the process leading to its adoption typically have a significant impact on the overall sustainability of national ECD interventions because the process also develops innovative funding mechanisms. One funding option is to create a national fund for ECD programming or to use existing social investment funds, sometimes through the use of earmarked taxes. Another option is to directly fund services through grants and transfers from national, provincial, and municipal budgets, sometimes combined with a fee-sharing system. In other cases, fee sharing can be complemented with demand-side funding mechanisms.

Some countries, such as Colombia, have recently established national funds to support early childhood development. The Colombian Ministry of Education, together with municipalities, jointly finance the *Fondo de Fomento a la Atención Integral de la Primera Infancia* (Fund to Promote Integrated Services for Early Childhood). Brazil recently made local public preschools eligible for funding by the federal education fund (FUNDEB). Examples of national funds in OECD countries include the New Opportunities Fund in Scotland and England (funded through the National Lottery), and the U.S. Child Care and Development Fund, which provides block grants to states.

A number of countries use existing social funds to finance ECD-related investments. For example, Jamaica's Social Investment Fund supports community-based early childhood development services and early education. The Dominican Republic uses resources from its Competitive Fund for Educational Innovations to fund early childhood and basic education programs. And France uses part of the payroll-funded *Caisse Nationale des Allocations Familiales* to support the provision of child care services, whether directly by the state or through private providers. General budget sources for social funds include annual ministerial contributions from each ministry that participates in an ECD program (typically, the health, education, social protection, or social development ministries); a presidential or prime minister's fund managed by either the relevant officeholder's administration or a ministry of finance or planning (whichever has the highest convening power and coordination authority); and a dedicated national budget for young children.

Although earmarked taxes for ECD programs have been considered by countries worldwide, their advantages need to be carefully assessed in light of the negative effects that they may generate in the labor market. Earmarked taxes have, for example, been found to create disincentives for formalizing contracts and hiring workers; decrease the disposable income of all employees; and suffer from the cyclical nature of tax revenues. Examples of earmarked taxes for ECD programming are outlined below.

- The French *Caisse Nationale des Allocations Familiales*, which is funded through payroll taxes, supports comprehensive ECD services for most young French children and their families (Belfield 2006).
- In Colombia, a 3 percent payroll tax on all public, private, and international enterprises of all sizes funds *Instituto Colombiano de*

Bienestar Familiar programs throughout the nation (Vargas-Barón 2006). These programs cumulatively serve over 50 percent of the nation's vulnerable children. Revenue from ECD payroll taxes for 2004 amounted to US$541 million—close to 0.6 percent of GDP.

- Dedicated income tax revenue is used to fund child development programs in several industrialized and certain middle-income nations. Income taxes for ECD are imposed at various levels: municipal income and property taxes in some U.S. states and Sweden, and state income taxes in Brazil. Often taxes at all three levels of government (national, state or provincial, and municipal) contribute to ECD programs, as is the case in the United States and Sweden.

- England levies taxes on products or activities that are potentially damaging to health and family welfare (such as tobacco, alcohol, and gambling) to fund ECD programs. On the other hand, many countries exempt certain items from taxes in order to help parents (such as paper and cloth diapers in Canada). In Kentucky, taxes on tobacco contribute to Kids Now, an early childhood program. Tobacco taxes in California created the California Children and Families First Trust Fund, which is expected to yield millions of dollars to support ECD programs in the state. In Missouri, the Children's Trust Fund for the Prevention of Child Abuse and Neglect was created through the sale of a special car license plate, dedicated fees on marriage licenses and other vital records, voluntary contributions designated on the Missouri state income tax return, other donations, and interest income from the fund itself. The Missouri fund provides parent education and support services throughout the state.

- In Jamaica, the CHASE Fund established by the Ministry of Finance and Planning is funded by taxes from gaming. The fund is used to support early childhood education. In 2004–05, approximately US$2.5 million of these monies funded 203 early childhood projects in the country (Young 2007).

- Tax concessions for certain businesses are permitted in some areas of the United States in exchange for grants for children's services.

- Natural resource taxes for ECD programming are an option for countries with extractive industries (such as mining or logging) to ensure that the revenues from these activities benefit young children.

- England, Jamaica, Scotland, and the states of Georgia, North Carolina, and Tennessee, in the United States use public lottery earnings to help support children's services. Because revenue from these funds usually fluctuates greatly, it should be considered only "add-on" support for program innovations and other nonredundant costs. Critics of lotteries as a funding source fear that the negative impacts of gambling on poor families outweigh the funding generated.

In the absence of specific designated funds, the funding of ECD services varies within and across countries, with different levels of government involved to varying degrees. Grants and transfers from national, provincial, and municipal budgets may provide direct funding for services or support decision-making groups at the local level to allocate and administer funds according to local priorities (box 5.1).

In some countries, grants are given to specific preapproved programs within a given province or state. For example, in the United States, the statewide "Smart Start" North Carolina Partnership for Children funds specific approved programs through local partnerships, providing technical assistance and training grants to both municipalities and ECD programs.[1] These program grants substitute for or supplement vouchers or tax credits given to parents.

Another form of funding is the creation of a sliding fee scale for ECD services, usually based on per capita family income (either gross or taxable). In the United States, each state has a different approach to using available child care funding to maximize coverage and equity. In the case of early childhood development interventions, issues of equity need to be carefully weighed. In France, transfer payments to individual families vary according to the "family coefficient," which is derived from information on the national income tax form (that is, family composition, income, and assets).

Box 5.1 Multilevel Funding of ECD in OECD Countries

Governments often fund ECD services directly or through transfers from one governmental level to another. For example, in French preschools (children aged 3 to 6), the national government finances teacher salaries, while local governments provide the facilities, administration, and other services. For child care centers in France, the national government covers 36 percent of expenses; departments, 47 percent; and local governments, 17 percent. In Sweden, public funding for Early Child Care and Education (ECCE) is primarily the responsibility of municipalities (60 percent) and is funded through local income taxes. Local authorities receive block and equalization grants from the national government to cover the remainder. In the United States, the federal government provides around 60 percent of public funding for ECCE programs, with state and local governments contributing the rest.

Source: France (Neuman and Peer 2002), Sweden (Gunnarsson and others 1999), United States (Belfield 2006).

Some countries provide parents with subsidies to use on children's health care, nutritional supplements, or educational services. Examples include the U.S. Women's Infants and Children's Program (WIC), which provides food vouchers and related services for income-eligible mothers (and, in some states, child care vouchers that eligible parents may use at various centers). France and other European countries also provide tax abatements. The United States gives parents of young children tax credits as a form of indirect support of child care costs, with the amount of the credit dependent on family income.

To stimulate the provision of services, the national government and several states (Iowa, Minnesota, and Vermont) in the United States (as well as the Canadian government and certain Canadian provinces) provide low-cost loans for child care centers and preschools in low-income areas. For example, the U.S. Small Business Administration provides loans for child care centers in minority ethnic communities (Vargas-Barón 2007a).

Defining a set of core national priorities

Defining a set of core national priorities is another initial step in building a national ECD policy. Decisions about the cut-off age for mandatory provision of preschool and the level of public contributions to the funding of child care are core strategic priorities that need to be made explicit up front. These decisions will likely vary from country to country. A national policy should also define the main problems it seeks to address, that is, it should respond to the challenges facing children in the country. For example, in Central America and several Andean countries, the focus of several programs is on ensuring proper nutrition and the early stimulation of young children. In Brazil, the focus is on expanding access to child care centers (at the municipal level) and preschools (at the federal level) so as to promote school preparedness and on-time enrollment in primary school.

The public share of investment in ECD programs varies widely across OECD countries. While in the United States, the federal government covers only 25 to 30 percent of the cost of child care (Committee for Economic Development 2002), in many western European countries for which data are available—including Denmark, Finland, France, Norway, and Sweden—the national government funds between 68 and 100 percent of the costs of early child care (box 5.2). The OECD (2006) recommends that public investment provide direct rather than indirect public support to ECD programs, as the latter entails extensive administrative burdens and does not easily allow for the qualitative improvement of ECD services.

Countries in the OECD have a longstanding tradition of investing in ECD, but differ in how they conceive of and provide early childhood services. However, certain common policy trends are emerging. One such trend is providing affordable universal preschool services, starting one or two years before a child reaches the age of primary school. Many OECD countries provide these services as a right or, alternatively, use them to

Box 5.2 The Emergence of the Swedish Preschool System

The Swedish Preschool System was conceived with the dual purpose of "edu-care." The expansion of the preschool system took place over slightly more than 30 years and was influenced by changes at the macro level, that is, by the economic, social, and political context in the country.

Sustained economic growth and a need for a larger labor force. Sweden experienced periods of economic growth that directly impacted female participation in the labor force. During World War II, it became necessary to offer child care for children, as well as to reform family policy to attract women to the workplace. Later, during the economic boom of the 1960s, municipalities had to offer child care services to attract competent workers. Economic growth also contributed to sustained, stable financing of child care. Even in periods of slow economic growth, the central government provided incentives to local governments to encourage the expansion of preschool. Today, approximately 2 percent of national GDP is spent on preschool services.

A strong women's movement. The history of the Swedish preschool system parallels that of the Swedish women's movement. Sweden is characterized by a strong female presence in labor unions and public administration, which contributed to the passage of important child care reforms. In the 1930s, female politicians focused on removing the stigma of poverty associated with child crèches. In the 1960s, women strongly advocated for their own professionalization and liberation and thus became strong advocates of child care. In that era, Sweden implemented a series of important reforms, including universal, affordable child care. As a result, it took the lead among countries worldwide in the design and implementation of family policy. By the 1990s, Swedish parents viewed child care as a right and the expansion of the preschool system was grounded in an articulated child care agenda. This achievement provided additional leverage for others to benefit from ECD interventions, since the ECD interventions concerned all Swedes who wanted to work or study.

A firm interest across political parties in child care and preschool policy. Over decades, political parties in Sweden have been concerned about child care and early education issues. Contentious debates on child care and preschool are a regular part Sweden politics, with differences relating to aspects of the provision, costs, and coverage of ECD programs. However, the role that political leaders have played in championing preschool and child care issues cannot be downplayed. One of these champions was Prime Minister Olof Palme, who served in the office twice, first in the late 1960s and then later in the early 1980s. Palme took the debate on child care and preschool to the highest level and seized the initiative to scale up child care as a foundation of the educational system, arguing for a pedagogical orientation of ECD services. Different political parties have also had a chance to influence the public policy debate to suit their vision and agendas when they have been in office.

Source: Martin Korpi (2007).

reach out to more vulnerable children, such as those from poor families. In some countries, these services are used to promote the role of fathers as well as mothers in the upbringing of children.

Countries thus have to decide between establishing the universal legal right to preschool or socially targeting ECD interventions to the most vulnerable groups who attend preschool. Many OECD countries have laws guaranteeing children access to preschool as of the age of 3 or 4 (see table 5.1). Even countries in which this level of schooling is not a legal right (such as Australia, the Czech Republic, Norway, and the United States) they still ensure broad access to this level of education, despite the lack of legislation. In two of these countries—the United States (with respect to kindergarten) and Australia—the programs are free. With or without legal status, many OECD countries offer one or two years of free early education to all children immediately before they reach enrollment age for primary school. In general, early childhood education (ECE) is publicly provided.

Only three countries—Denmark and Sweden (as of age 1), and Finland (from birth)—have made ECE for younger children a legal right, although several countries offer subsidized or free services to broad or selected groups of children. For countries that do not make lower-level ECE widely available, access can be a major problem. In the United States, for example, very low-income families qualify for free early child care and education. But low-income families above the cut-off line, together with middle-income families, are independently responsible for caring for their young children, which makes access to and the affordability of child care serious problems. Care for younger children, as opposed to older children, is more often privately provided, often on a full-day basis.

Build on successful programs

A national ECD policy should build on past experiences and programmatic achievements, not only to gain legitimacy, but also to increase its chances of being successfully scaled up. In general, carefully designed impact evaluations have helped programs weather regime transitions and gain the credibility needed to expand their resources and coverage.[2] In Latin America and Caribbean, this is especially true of CCT programs, such as *Oportunidades* in Mexico and *Familias en Acción* in Colombia. However, evidence of positive results does not necessarily imply guaranteed program survival. For instance, the Peruvian program PAIN, the Bolivian *Kallpa Wawa* program, and the Nicaraguan *Red de Protección Social* program all struggled to survive even in the presence of positive evaluation results.

In particular, impact evaluations of pilot programs face the specific challenge of external validity. The success of a pilot in a particular province or institutional arrangement may, for example, not be replicable in

Table 5.1 Early Childhood Education Services, Select OECD Countries

Country	Name of provision	Setting	Ages served	Full/part time	Government administration	Locus of policy making	Compulsory school age (years)
Australia	Extended day care	Center	0–5	FT	Social Welfare	Commonwealth	6
	Family day care (FDC)	FDC home	0–5	FT	Social Welfare	Commonwealth	
	Preschool	School/center	4–5	PT	Education	State/territories	
Belgium (Fl)	Kinderdagverbliff	Center	0–3	FT	Social Welfare	Community	6
	Diensten voor opvanggezinnen (DOGs)	FDC home	0–3	FT	Social Welfare		
	Kleuterschool	School	2.5–6	PT	Education		
Belgium (Fr)	Crèche	Center	0–3	FT	Social Welfare	Community	6
	Gardienne encadrée	FDC home	0–3	FT	Social Welfare		
	École maternelle	School	2.5–6	PT	Education		
Czech Republic	Crèche	Center	0–3	FT	Health/Welfare	Local	6
	Materska skola	School	3–6	FT	Education	National and local	
Denmark	Vuggestuer	Center	0.5–3	FT	Social Welfare	National and local (primarily)	7
	Aldersintegrerede	Center	0.5–6+	FT	Social Welfare		
	Bornhaver	Center	3–6	FT	Social Welfare		
	Dagplejer	FDC home	0.5–3	FT	Social Welfare		
	Bornhaveklasser	School	5/6–7	PT	Education		

(Table continues on next page)

Table 5.1 (continued)

Country	Name of provision	Setting	Ages served	Full/part time	Government administration	Locus of policy making	Compulsory school age (years)
Finland	Paivakoti	Center	0–7	FT	Social Welfare	National and local	7
	Perhepaivahoio	FDC home	0–7	FT	Social Welfare		
	6-vuotiadiden esiopetus	Center/school	6–7	PT	Education		
Italy	Asilo nido	Center	0–3	FT	Health/Welfare	Local	6
	Scuola materna	School	3–6	Varies	Education	National	
The Netherlands	Kinderopvang	Center	0–4	FT	Social Welfare	National and local (primarily)	5
	Gastouderopvang	FDC home	0–4	PT	Social Welfare		
	Peuterspeelzaal	Center	2–4	PT	Social Welfare		
	Bassischool	School	4+	PT	Education		
Norway	Barnehage	Center	0–6	FT & PT	Children and Family Affairs	National and local	6
	Familliebarnehage	FDC home	0–6	FT & PT			
Portugal	Crèche	Center	0–3	FT	Social Welfare	Regional and local	6
	Crèche familiare	FDC home	0–3	FT	Social Welfare		
	Jardin de infancia	Center/school	3–6	FT (varies)	Education/Social Welfare	National	

Country	Program	Setting	Age	FT/PT	Sector	Governance	Compulsory school age
Sweden	Forskola	Center	0–6	FT	Education	National and local (primarily)	7
	Familiedaghem	FDC home	0–6	FT			
	Forskoleklass	School	6–7	PT			
United Kingdom	Day nursery	Center	0–5	PT	Education	National and local	Great Britain: 5 Northern Ireland: 4
	Nursery class/school	School	3–5	PT			
	Preschool playgroup	Center	2–5	PT (varies)			
	Child minder	FDC home	0–5	FT			
	Reception class (not in Scotland)	School	4–5	FT			
United States	Child care center	Center	0–5	FT	Social Welfare	State	5–7 (varies by state)
	Family child care	FDC home	0–5	FT		State	
	Head Start	Center	4–5	PT (varies)		National and local	
	Prekindergarten	School/center	4–5	PT (varies)	Education	State	
	Kindergarten	School	5–6	PT (varies)		State	

Source: Vegas and others (2006).

other provinces or under different arrangements. One study (Attanasio and others 2003) simulated the results of the *Oportunidades* program in different Mexican states, using a model constructed for the first states that participated in the program. The simulated impacts were notably different from the real impacts. This outcome is especially relevant to programs when they expand from rural to urban areas and need to change their rules of operation, or when they attempt to reach different target groups. A further examination of the operations and processes of a pilot program is often important to understand how impacts were obtained, as well as to identify good practices and bottlenecks. Research evaluations that focus on processes and operations help planners and managers understand the systemic aspects of program design and operations.

Experimental evaluations of ECD programs also face several challenges. One common argument against implementing experimental programs in order to facilitate their evaluation is that they deprive vulnerable children of services that have proven short- and long-term benefits. When a pilot program is scaled up, however, logistics and supply constraints—such as those in Rio de Janeiro (see box 5.3)—offer such programs an opportunity to adopt more transparent allocation rules, either by randomizing access or adopting transparent rules for determining who will qualify for the program.

Another challenge relates to the design and implementation of an intervention itself, which in turn affects the identification of its effects. Early child care development programs generally provide a bundle of services, which depend on the specific characteristics of a child and the care provider, as well as the child's needs and the providers' capacity. While care practices or education curricula can be standardized, the form in which they are applied varies widely.

A third issue is the ethical consideration related to the measurement of ECD outcomes. For instance, testing for micronutrient deficiencies may require blood tests and other biological samples. Preparation for this kind of testing needs to be implemented carefully, so that the informed consent of all participating children's parents or caregivers is ensured. When severe malnutrition or cognitive development delays are found, evaluation or program staff should provide parents with information about and referrals to complementary services, if possible.

A fourth issue of evaluating ECD programs is that their most important impacts accrue much later in life, making it necessary to plan for longitudinal data collection. This task entails considerable information gathering and funding. In the course of this long process, potential beneficiary children may lose the opportunity to access program services. Nevertheless, obtaining evidence on the long-term impacts of ECD programs is the key to making a case for such programs before decision makers.

In Latin America and the Caribbean, Jamaica is currently conducting a follow-up study of a supplementation and early stimulation program

---

Box 5.3 Impact Evaluation and ECD Expansion in Rio de Janeiro

The municipality of Rio de Janeiro, Brazil, has a severe shortage of ECD services: it currently provides approximately 11,000 spots in municipal crèches, when the demand for those spots is estimated to be tenfold that number. World Bank and Brazilian researchers paired up with the municipal government to randomize access to the 242 municipal day care centers in the city. A team of 430 enumerators registered applications from 25,000 families who applied for the approximately 11,000 municipal day care spots in October–November 2007. After entering the data and checking the veracity of information, 20 randomization workshop sessions were held for approximately 900 combinations of day care centers and grades (almost all day care centers have approximately four grades).

The majority of participants agreed that the randomization process was the fairest way to deal with excess demand for day care center spots. In the past, this problem had been handled on a first-come, first-serve basis, which obviously penalized certain mothers who needed day care services the most. Most important to the randomization experiment was the buy-in of participants, who agreed that randomization actually provides equality of opportunity and should be applied to other government programs for which there is excess demand and no obvious prioritization criteria. A baseline survey was planned for the launch of services in early 2008, which aimed to include all households listed on the application forms (although locating houses in poor informal settlements might turn out to be quite difficult). Other municipalities in Brazil, such as Belo Horizonte and Niteroí, are also considering this approach to allocating scare day care services.

Source: Paes de Barros and others (2007).

---

from the 1980s (see Walker and others 2005). Researchers in Guatemala have continued to follow adults who received food supplements as infants and toddlers (see Murphy and others 2005; Maluccio and others 2006). In Argentina, researchers are tracking the performance of children who attended preschool during the country's preschool expansion of 1995–2002 (Berlinski and others 2007) and in Mexico, a study is tracking the school attainment of children whose families were beneficiaries of the *Oportunidades* program.

A fifth issue relates to the long-term welfare impacts of CCTs. Most impact evaluations for this type of intervention contemplate follow-up studies, so that at least the medium-term welfare impact of a program can be determined. Long-term evaluations are needed, however, because without them, the initial successful experience of a handful of programs in the early stages of operation cannot be generalized into lessons that are applicable under a variety of circumstances. Such generalized information is particularly important to policy makers.

Certain situations raise questions about the external validity of evaluation results. For instance, can programs be successfully exported to countries where the administrative infrastructure for successful program implementation (for example, for monitoring compliance, ensuring timely payments, and so forth) is limited? Would such programs be appropriate for populations with particular characteristics, such as indigenous peoples? These questions have become more pertinent as CCT programs have been scaled up within countries, such as the recent expansion of *Oportunidades* into urban areas of Mexico, and adopted internationally, as is being contemplated with *Oportunidades* in parts of Africa and Asia (Rawlings 2004).

Finally, there is often a temptation to draw conclusions about the positive effects of a program based on partial or incomplete information. In the search for solutions to pressing development challenges, there is always a risk of jumping to conclusions by extrapolating from the appearance of success. This is a temptation to be resisted, in the words of Fiszbein and Gevers (2005), by keeping an "inquisitive eye on the evaluation ball."

Ensuring the coherence of ECD policy with related policies

As previously discussed, a national policy can help formalize the links between ECD interventions and relevant social sector and labor market policies, including the use of maternity policies and child care as a means of fostering the labor force participation of women. This integration can lead to different models for providing ECD services, which are strongly dependent on the values, attitudes, and preferences of a given society.

For example, paid maternity leave complements the provision of ECD services. According to a recent report (UNESCO 2006), 80 percent of the 126 nations surveyed had some form of maternal leave policy. However, these countries offer a wide range of maternal and paternal leaves, ranging from one week to over a year, with a median of 12 weeks. The rationale behind maternity leave is to enable parents to provide essential infant care themselves and thus bond well with their new child. However, as chapter 2 pointed out, this type of leave mainly benefits working mothers from middle- and upper-income brackets, who are formally employed.[3] Yet in many countries in Latin America, a considerable share of working mothers are employed in the informal sector and would not have access to these benefits.

As already noted, female labor force participation is intimately linked to the availability of affordable, acceptable, and reliable child care services. Access to child care is one of most frequent barriers to finding and keeping employment cited by mothers. Conversely, when affordable, acceptable, and reliable child care services are available, poor women are more likely to work outside the home and hold full-time, formal jobs, such as in the Guatemala slums, where the *Programa de Hogares Comunitarios* operates (Hallman and others 2005). Ideally, increasing child care coverage should go hand in hand with the provision of flexible work schedules, which improve parental choices and minimize the trade-offs between the needs of children (child care) and their parents (labor force participation and income).

In general, the timing and intensity of a child's transition from parent care to provider care or preschool depends on labor market regulations. For example, maternity and paternity leave gives parents an option for infant care. Some labor laws also typically protect mothers against discrimination, for instance, by granting them time to breastfeed at work or including a provision for the use of sick leave when a child is sick. As more and more women enter and stay in the labor force, they increasingly seek family-friendly work environments. Yet only middle-income women in the formal or public sectors are likely to find such environments. In general, their poorer counterparts, whose jobs tend to be more unstable, less formal, and provide fewer benefits, face greater challenges.

Service provision also follows very different models, reflecting in part a country's attitudes toward gender equity and female labor force participation, children's rights, the quality of child care, and the role of the state in providing equal opportunities. Finland's child care model creates incentives for mothers to stay at home and raise young children, as well as incentives for families to hire private child care, via financial allowances for stay-at-home mothers and tax credits and other monetary incentives for private child care providers. These incentives were put in place in 1986 and as a result, about 60 percent of 2-year-olds in Finland are now cared for at home and female labor participation has dropped markedly. Mahon (2002), however, suggests that this model can undermine gender equity and female labor participation, decrease child care quality, and create greater social inequity by building a market for low-skilled, low-wage private child care providers.

The model adopted by the Netherlands and the United Kingdom focuses on demand-side incentives, such as tax credits, to encourage parents to enroll their children in early childhood education. But these incentives focus on education for older children (aged 3–6) and are generally part-time. Both features result in female labor participation that is frequently part-time or temporary in nature. There are also large disparities between the number of regular work hours for women and men in both countries. Private costs for child care remain high, averaging 44 percent of total costs in the Netherlands and 30 to 60 percent in the United Kingdom. Both countries have targeting policies that further subsidize child care for children from poor families. Yet Mahon (2002) suggests that the focus on demand-side provisions, limited access, and such targeting mechanisms are likely to exacerbate gender inequity in the labor market and insufficiently address the quality of child care.

In Denmark and Sweden, the model for ECD and provision of services seeks to support gender equity (at home and in the workplace), promote high rates of labor market participation among both genders, provide universal ECE for children 1 year old and older, and ensure high-quality care with a strong educational base. In these two countries, which are members of the OECD, parental leave policies are designed to be attractive to both men and women, regardless of income. Parents are subsidized to stay home based on their salaries, and fathers have significant leave rights. At the same time, cash transfers for parental leave are relatively short in duration, encouraging parents to return to work. In both countries, children age 1 and older have the legal right to ECD services, with parents paying either a very low percentage of costs (Sweden) or on a sliding-fee scale (Denmark). Most children, including those in disadvantaged groups, are entitled to at least 525 hours of ECE from the age of 4 or younger, and both countries have strong policies in place to ensure the quality of this education.

In Sweden, ECE services, including those for children under 3 years old, are administered by the Ministry of Education and Science, which has established a national curriculum with clear standards. In Denmark, public ECE centers are organized into networks, have parent boards, and collaborate closely with primary school systems. In both countries, a great deal of ECD programming is publicly provided, but private provision has been growing. Private providers frequently receive public subsidies and are subject to the same rules as public centers, a requirement that provides some quality assurance (Mahon 2002). Table 5.2 summarizes the ECD policies of selected OECD countries.

Expanding ECD Services in the Region

Expanding coverage to larger population groups is an overarching priority of most national ECD policies in Latin America and the Caribbean. This goal is particularly relevant in Latin America, where coverage of early childhood services remains low and significant population segments remain without access.

National policies across the region are expected to become useful frameworks to support ongoing ECD programs and their expansion. However, as explained in chapter 2, most countries in the region have only recently started to consider national policies and only one among them—Chile—actually has such a policy in place. These policies take time to develop and, in many instances, special, sectorwide funding mechanisms may not be immediately available. Therefore, a bottom-up approach in which sup-

Table 5.2 ECD Policies in Selected OECD Countries

Country	Policy focus	Coverage	Financing
Australia	Statutory entitlement to extended, but unpaid, parental leave, with some state financial support Subsidized day care	7% of children 0–1 26% of children 1–2 40% of children 2–3 61.5% of children 3–4 81% of children 4–5	• Preprimary education: 0.1% of GDP • All services for children under 3: 0.45% • Parents cover 31% of child care and 22% of preschool costs
Denmark	Gender equity and high labor force participation with quality child care	12% of children 0–1 83% of children 1–2 94% of children 3–5	• Day care service: 2.1% of GDP; parents contribute 22% of costs, on average • Average cost per child in center-based daycare: US$19,550 for young child, US$10,200 for older child
Finland	Incentives for staying home and private day care provision; preschool begins at age 6	27.5% of children 1–2 43.9% of children 2–3 62.3% of children 3–4 68.5% of children 4–5 73% of children 5–6 100% of children 6–7	• Daycare service: 1.1% of GDP; parents contribute 15% of costs, on average. • Average cost per child: €8,000 per year
France	Public provision and incentives for part-time work Incentives for private provision for child care	61% of children 0–3	• Daycare service: 0.7% of GDP; parents pay up to 27% of average costs for children 0–3 • Average cost per child: US$4,512 • Distribution of public cost on ECE: national 36%, department 47%, local government 17%

(Table continues on next page)

Table 5.2 (continued)

Country	Policy focus	Coverage	Financing
Norway	Incentives for staying home to care for children, high female labor force participation, generous parental leave policies	48% of children 1–3 88% of children 3–6	• Daycare service: 1.7% of GDP; parents pay up to 20% of average costs • Average annual cost per child: €9,773 (children 0–3), €5,355 (children 3–6)
Sweden	Gender equity and high female labor force participation with quality care	45% of children 1–2 86% of children 2–3 91% of children 3–4 96% of children 4–6	• Daycare service: 1.9% of GDP; parents pay up to 9% of average costs • Average cost per child per year: US$12,097 • Local government: 60% of public ECE expenditure
United Kingdom	Demand-side incentives	20% of children 0–3 96% of children 3–4 100% of children 4–5	• Day care service: 0.47% of GDP; parents pay close to 45% of average costs • Average annual cost per child: US$8,452
United States	Unpaid parental leave (some states pay disability benefits), high female labor force participation, but no incentives to stay home	38% of children 0–3 56.4% of children 3–5 90% of children 5–6	• Daycare service: Public funding is 0.4% of GDP, but private contributions cover two-thirds of cost • Average annual cost per child (aged 3–6): US$7,881 • Federal: 60% of ECE public expenditure

Source: Coverage and financial data: OECD (2006). The executive summary and country profiles from the report are available on the OECD Website, http://www.oecd.org/document/63/0,3343,en_2649_39263231_37416703_1_1_1,00.html#C (accessed April 2009).

110

port is maintained at the programmatic level will be needed to ensure the continuity of existing interventions.

As explored earlier in this chapter, developing a national ECD policy in intended to stimulate a national dialogue on issues of early childhood development, help identify a high-level champion for these issues, strengthen government commitment to ECD investments, and foster intersectoral coordination. As a consequence, these policies lay the foundation for the long-term sustainability of early childhood interventions. Some countries that are moving toward the adoption of national policies are anchoring them on some of the oldest programs in the region, such *as Hogares Comunitarios de Bienestar Familiar* in Colombia or JUNJI in Chile, which already benefit from strong policy, political, legal, and financial support. The ability of these programs to obtain and secure these four types of support is thus providing important data for the design of national policies.

On the funding side, diversification of funding sources (with a high share of public funding) may be advisable in the region. Some programs have incorporated loans from international financial institutions as part of their strategy to promote program continuity across administrations. For example, *Oportunidades* in Mexico was supported by a loan from the Inter-American Development Bank. On the other end of the spectrum, Colombia's *Hogares Comunitarios de Bienestar Familiar* has succeeded in maintaining a single funding source: the tax system.

International groups and operating foundations that are committed to long-term program funding in low-income communities, such as the Christian Children's Fund, Save the Children, Plan International, and World Vision, can on occasion provide bridge funding to a national program. These international NGOs usually depend on private donors and benefactors who are willing to provide long-term, sustainable funding for selected children or communities. However, the level of this support is rarely large enough to enable ECD programs to grow to scale without significant additional bilateral government funding or that of other donors. Increasingly, these organizations are seeking to find ways to become involved in national policy planning processes, offering their programs as models for national implementation. *Madres Guías* in Honduras is a good example of this approach; the program seems to be having a positive impact on national policy and specific public sector education and health programs.

Political support and a solid legal anchoring are two additional ingredients of eventual program sustainability. Political support may come from different sources, but a high-level champion in the government is crucial. Sustained presidential involvement in Chile and Colombia, the support of *Programa de Hogares Comunitarios* on the part of the First Lady in Guatemala, and the support of the Minister of Finance of Mexico for *Oportunidades* have all played an important role in advancing these programs in their respective countries. In addition, programs may be based on national laws, be backed by legal decrees, or use national codes or regulations governing children's services. Pilot programs perhaps can afford to use temporary measures or decrees, but if these programs scale up, they will need to buttress their legal foundations.

On the operational side, human resource, information management, and procurement systems are critical. Well-functioning and competent personnel structures help programs withstand political change. For instance, capacity-building programs for care providers can improve the quality of care and decrease staff turnover. At the local level, high staff turnover can be a crucial bottleneck for the sustainability of programs that place a great deal of responsibility on volunteers. This has been particularly true for the AIN-C program in Honduras and CCT programs. In addition, an efficient management and information system should be nested in the government accounting system in order to provide accountability for both financial and operational inputs. At present, JUNJI in Chile uses the National Information System for Financial Management (SIGFE) to track this type of data; *Hogares Comunitarios* in Colombia uses the information system of the National Comptroller's Office. Procurement and financial systems, moreover, need to be flexible enough to accommodate the realities of service provision in poor environments, yet sufficiently robust to provide a reasonable structure of controls that strengthen program management.

The quality of ECD services is also important for program survival. At the local level, service providers rely mostly on word of mouth, with their reputation becoming an important element of program success and survival. Given the multitude of providers involved in providing services, setting standards and assuring quality remains a major challenge worldwide. Setting standards refers both to ensuring minimum levels of quality care for all children and that ECD services address the diverse needs of vulnerable children. Effective use of technology can be critical to ensuring the quality of delivery. Two examples of such technology are (i) user-friendly, Internet-based applications that ensure confidentiality of information, and (ii) document management systems that can scan and digitize paper-based forms in a central office, as has been done by the *Red de Protección Social* program in Nicaragua. Finally, solid monitoring systems that are accessible by local program managers can provide useful feedback to central program offices and thus support quality assurance. This type of feedback is particularly important, as many programs lose valuable information about local operations because of the lack of a systematic mechanism for this purpose.

Summary

Countries in Latin America and the Caribbean have rich experience in developing child care programs. However, the region as a whole faces many challenges in scaling up promising programs and assuring access to quality services for all children, especially the most vulnerable among them. This chapter has argued that a coherent, well-defined, long-term national policy can facilitate the sustainability of existing programs, especially if it is developed through a consensus-oriented process. The main advantages of a national policy are that it fosters the sustainability of ECD programs (in other words, their funding) and promotes intersectoral coordination between different levels of government—both the result of increasing the visibility of early childhood development issues. To gain legitimacy, however, a national policy has to leverage lessons learned from existing successful local programs, not only in terms of impact, but also in terms of operational processes.

Selectively and strategically scaling up ECD interventions (or parts thereof) should become a main priority for policy makers seeking to increase coverage of early childhood development services. The recent experience of large-scale CCT programs provides some indications on how to expand such programs, but holistic ECD interventions face specific and complex institutional coordination challenges. In parallel with the development of a national policy, countries also need to ensure that existing successful programs continue to receive support through traditional mechanisms. They also need to ensure that adequate information about program costs, processes, and impacts is made available to policy makers. Existing programs, then, can provide important building blocks for national policy, in terms of the strategies needed to secure their financial, political, and legal sustainability, as well as to promote coordination among a nation's health, education, and social protection ministries.

One crucial element of any program expansion is the availability of properly trained providers, whose role and status are recognized by the given society. These workers are crucial for ensuring the quality of both the care and education services provided to children. Quality services, moreover, maximize the returns to ECD investments. Building an ECD policy on the basis of existing successful programs means that comprehensive policies will follow different routes in different countries, as they seek to resolve country-specific challenges. Most importantly, countries need to develop information systems that collect data about the costs, impacts, and processes of ECD interventions. Only this kind of data can identify which programs are replicable and which are worth replicating. The overall process requires a long-term commitment, which must be kept in mind when building the financial sustainability of ECD programs. Finally, a comprehensive policy should strive to promote tailored interventions that can provide equal opportunities for all children. Such interventions are thus likely to vary according to children's ages, local conditions (for example, rural/urban implementation, the needs of ethnic minorities, and local government capacity), and the specific vulnerabilities of targeted groups.

Notes

1. For details on the program, see the Smart Start Website at http://www.ncsmartstart.org (accessed April 2009).

2. For an excellent resource on methodologies for evaluating the impact of ECD programs, see World Bank (2007).

3. For a useful discussion on the relative benefits of alternative leave policies, see Kamerman (2000).

6

Conclusion

The adverse effects of poor early childhood development outcomes are often long lasting—affecting a child's future income-earning capacity, productivity, longevity, and health. This is particularly the case of children living in poverty. Recent research on ECD programs suggests that these interventions are powerful policy levers in the fight against poverty and inequality. Most such programs are multisectoral, involving interventions in health, hygiene and nutrition, education, and poverty alleviation. They provide services not simply to children, but to their parents and caregivers as well. Because these interventions help equalize opportunities, they hold particular promise for children in Latin America and the Caribbean, where poverty rates hover near 20 percent and the proportion of poor children in some countries exceeds 40 percent.

Indicators for the region suggest that early childhood development is inadequate in many countries. For example, the average infant mortality rate in the region overall is 22 percent, but exceeds 50 percent in Bolivia. Close to 50 percent of children in the region suffer from iron-deficiency anemia, high proportions suffer from other vitamin deficiencies, and 12 percent have stunted growth (in Guatemala, this rate is over 40 percent). With a few exceptions, access to health services and health care coverage is also limited and inequitable in the region. All of these conditions are exacerbated by poverty and inequality. Regional diversity is, moreover, extensive. In some countries very few children suffer from one or more of these conditions, while in other countries, a majority of children do. All countries in the region, however, continue to face challenges in providing equal opportunities to all young children for their development.

Based on the ample evidence of the many benefits of ECD interventions in both developed and developing countries, early childhood development should be a national priority in Latin America and the Caribbean. ECD interventions offer a particularly important tool for reducing income and social gaps between poor and nonpoor populations—gaps that are becoming exceedingly difficult to bridge. Such interventions also appear to be more cost-effective than many interventions that attempt to improve conditions for poor people later in their lives. Perhaps most importantly, ECD programs are an important tool for removing the most glaring obstacles to children's development in the region (malnutrition, illness, stunting, and illiteracy) and are ideal for targeting support to poorer, disadvantaged groups.

Current Efforts and Their Track Record

At present, investments in ECD range from less than 1 percent to roughly 12 percent of the total educational expenditures of countries in the region. On the whole, existing ECD programs show exceptional promise for improving the cognitive and socioemotional development of young children, as well as their physical well-being and growth. The evidence on ECD programs in Bolivia, Colombia, Guatemala, Jamaica, and Nicaragua suggests that interventions offering nutritional supplements, as well as those that combine several strategies (such as parenting practices, early childhood care, and nutrition) have positive effects on language acquisition, reasoning, vocabulary, and schooling.

Nutrition and supplementation programs appear especially important in the region for improving physical well-being and growth, as well as certain cognitive outcomes. This was the case of subsidized milk programs for children and pregnant and lactating women (Mexico), nutrition and early child care programs (Colombia and Guatemala), and CCT programs (Mexico and Colombia). This evidence suggests that the nutrition component of ECD interventions targeted to low-income children seems to be particularly beneficial.

Several programs also found positive effects of children's compliance with health controls and growth monitoring. Such was the case of CCT programs in Colombia, Honduras, and Mexico, which tied cash payments to children's attendance at health centers and continued participation in physical monitoring. Even unconditional cash transfer programs appear to have positive effects on the development of child motor skills and other developmental indicators when programs are targeted at very poor families, mainly due to better household nutrition and use of deworming medications (Ecuador).

Of note, despite their large positive effects on physical ECD outcomes, CCT programs in the Mexico did not appear to improve cognitive outcomes for beneficiary children and had few medium-term education effects for older children (aged 3 to 5). The programs did appear to improve schooling for the youngest participants (from birth through age 2) in Mexico, possibly because this group was the intended target of the program's nutrition component. However, evaluations of other CCT programs in the region have found that they improved the probability of attending preschool (Chile) and reduced developmental delays (Nicaragua).

Early education and care programs also show important positive benefits. Parenting programs in Bolivia, Honduras, Jamaica, Nicaragua, and elsewhere suggest that parents do improve their childrearing and stimulation techniques, resulting in children with better cognitive and language development and better motor, social, and other skills. In Jamaica, certain parenting programs that have been rigorously evaluated also show benefits for the mothers, such as reduced maternal depression rates. Early education and preschool programs in Argentina and Uruguay, moreover, show that children's language and math test scores, behavioral skills, as well as their long-term educational attainments, benefit from attending preschool.

The Road Ahead: Expanding ECD Services in the Region

ECD services offer governments a proven mechanism to help poor and otherwise disadvantaged children. By equalizing opportunities at a crucial period in the lives of young children and their parents, these interventions enable children from low-income families to achieve equal footing with nonpoor children at the start of their learning years, a period that affects their development for the rest of their lives. Three recommendations are offered here to help countries in the region scale up ECD services in the most efficient manner possible.

Build the data to analyze cost-effectiveness

From a social policy perspective, ECD programs are cost effective because they avoid many of the moral hazard problems inherent in programs that seek to equalize outcomes in adulthood, such as tax and income transfers, which are often seen as inequitable. In order to examine the crucial policy question of cost-effectiveness, however, individual countries and programs need to begin collecting disaggregated administrative and cost data that make cost-benefit analysis of various ECD interventions possible. One possibility would be to design impact evaluations that use similar (or comparable) outcome measures, thus facilitating the comparison of alternative policies to inform decision making on investments.

Estimates on the cost per measure of effectiveness of different interventions would provide policy makers guidance on how to allocate resources based on the benefits and costs of each alternative. Options could then be compared by ranking their costs and effects to estimate the additional cost per unit of effectiveness required to move from a less costly, less effective intervention, to the next more costly, but more effective, alternative. Final allocations will, of course, reflect resource availability and a society's willingness to invest in improving specific outcomes. Analysis of the cost-effectiveness of programs can also provide useful information on the cost and benefits of scaling up ECD interventions.

A common criticism of this type of analysis is that it focuses on a single measure of effectiveness out of many outcomes that could be used to evaluate an intervention. Often these outcomes are hard to observe, which makes their measurement approximate at best. Such is the case of educational outcomes, where scores on cognitive assessments or tests are frequently used to measure a broader concept of learning. Additionally, cost-effectiveness measures are likely to change over time, necessitating information on the long-term impacts of ECD programs. At present, this information is scant or nonexistent in most developing countries. In addition, there is a general lack of solid cost information about ECD interventions. Some programs, such as AIN-C in Honduras and CCT programs in Honduras, Mexico, and Nicaragua provide cost information. Information on other programs in the region, however, mostly focuses on results.

Countries in Latin America and the Caribbean are accordingly urged to begin collecting disaggregated administrative and cost data, especially for multidimensional interventions such as CCTs. On the operational side, information management systems are crucial for tracking program inputs and outputs. As noted above, it is recommended that program managers in a country use similar impact evaluation methods whenever feasible in order to allow for more meaningful comparisons, as well as to promote the accountability and transparency of program operations. Solid monitoring systems that are accessible by local managers can also provide useful feedback to central program offices and thus support the quality assurance of individual programs. This type of feedback is particularly important, as many programs lose valuable information about local operations due to the lack of a systematic mechanism for this purpose.

On the government side, an efficient management and information system nested in the government accounting system is needed in order to provide accountability for both financial and operational inputs of ECD programs. Procurement and financial systems, moreover, need to be flexible enough to accommodate the realities of service provision in poor environments, yet sufficiently robust to provide a reasonable structure of controls that strengthen program management.

Plan upfront for long-term impact studies

Because many of the benefits of ECD interventions accrue later in life, long-term data collection is needed to measure the outcomes of the programs. It is crucial that interventions plan for longitudinal data collection that includes several follow-up surveys (or rounds of information gathering from beneficiaries). This type of data collection requires considerable information and funding, but is indispensable for demonstrating both the benefits and cost-effectiveness of ECD programs to policy makers.

Long-term evaluations are needed, moreover, because without them, the initial successful experience of a handful of programs in the early stages of operation cannot be generalized into lessons that are applicable under a variety of circumstances. Such generalized information is particularly important to policy makers. With respect to multidimensional ECD interventions, future impact studies would benefit from a design that allows data on individual components to be disaggregated, so that policy makers can understand which components work best, and which work best together.

Develop and implement national ECD policies

Although the region has made important improvements in early childhood development, many countries in Latin America and the Caribbean have only recently begun to implement national ECD policies. Similar to other social programs, ECD programs face considerable barriers to their survival. Funding is always a challenge. Moreover, their integrated nature, and the fact that the most effective interventions include components that are usually the domain of different government sectors (such as education, health, welfare, and labor), makes it complicated to implement and sustain them. Furthermore, the main beneficiaries of ECD policies are young children, with little voice in politics or civil society. The populations that stand to gain the most from ECD also do not have a strong voice in the public domain: low-income, disadvantaged, and often indigenous families.

All of these factors reduce the chances of ECD becoming a priority without a national policy. Developing a national policy builds consensus for investing in early childhood, creates funding mechanisms to sustain ECD interventions, and musters the interdepartmental and interministerial cooperation needed to deliver integrated services well. Such a policy also helps formalize links between ECD interventions and relevant social sector and labor market policies, including the use of maternity policies and child care as a means of fostering the labor force participation of women. This integration will lead to different models for providing ECD services, depending on the values, attitudes, and preferences of a given society.

Some countries that are moving toward the adoption of national policies are anchoring them on some of the oldest programs in the region, such as *Hogares Comunitarios de Bienestar Familiar* in Colombia or JUNJI in Chile, which already benefit from strong policy, political, legal, and financial support. The ability of these programs to obtain and secure these types of support provides important data for the design of national policies. Building an ECD policy on the basis of existing successful programs means that national policies will follow different routes in different countries, as they seek to resolve their own specific challenges.

Access to child care, for example, is one of the most frequent barriers to finding and keeping employment cited by mothers. Conversely, when affordable, acceptable, and reliable child care services are available, poor women are more likely to work outside the home and hold full-time, formal jobs, such as in the Guatemala slums, where the *Programa de Hogares Comunitarios* operates (Hallman and others 2005). Ideally, increasing child care coverage goes hand in hand with flexible work schedules that allow minimal trade-offs between the needs of children and the need for family income.

Stepping into the Future

Comprehensive policies across the region are expected to become useful frameworks to support ongoing ECD programs and their expansion. The main advantages of a national policy are that it fosters the sustainability of ECD programs (in other words, their funding) and promotes intersectoral coordination between different levels of government—both the result of increasing the visibility of early childhood development issues. To gain legitimacy, however, a national policy has to leverage lessons learned from existing successful local programs, not only in terms of impact, but also in terms of operational processes.

However, these policies take time to develop. Selectively and strategically scaling up ECD interventions (or parts thereof) should become a main priority for policy makers seeking to increase coverage of early childhood development services in the region, while they build national policies and create information systems to track the impact and cost of individual programs. The recent experience of large-scale CCT interventions provides some indications on how to expand such programs, but holistic ECD interventions face specific and complex challenges of institutional coordination. In parallel with the development of a national policy, countries also need to ensure that existing successful programs continue to receive support through traditional mechanisms and that adequate information about program costs, processes, and impacts is made available to policy makers. Existing programs, then, can provide important building blocks for national policy, in terms of the strategies needed to secure their financial, political, and legal sustainability, as well as to promote coordination among a nation's health, education, and social protection agencies.

Appendixes

Appendix 1. Data on Early Child Development Indicators in Latin America

Table A1.1 Poverty around the World (Percent of Population)

Region	Extreme poverty rates (US$ 1.08 per day)		Poverty rates (US$2.15 per day)	
	1981	*2004*	*1981*	*2004*
Latin America and the Caribbean	10.77	8.64	28.45	22.17
East Asia and the Pacific	57.73	9.05	84.80	36.58
Eastern Europe and Central Asia	0.70	0.94	4.60	9.79
Middle East and North Africa	5.08	1.47	29.16	19.70
South Asia	51.75	34.33	88.53	77.12
Sub-Saharan Africa	42.26	41.10	74.52	71.97

Source: Chen and Ravallion (2007).

Figure A1.1 Children Aged 18 Years or Younger Living below the Relative Poverty Line (Percent)

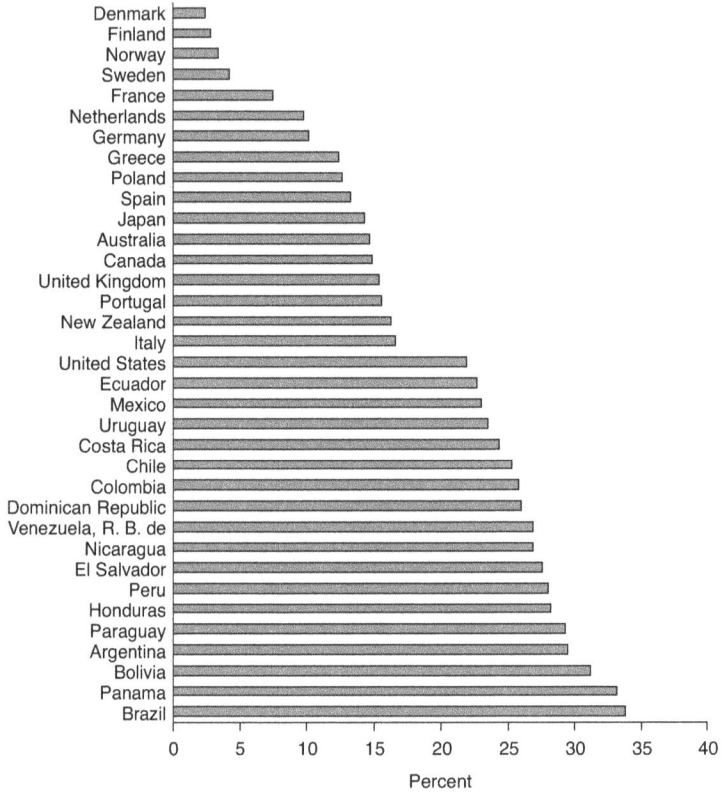

Source: UNICEF ECLAC 2005.

Figure A1.2 Poverty Rates by Country (Percent)

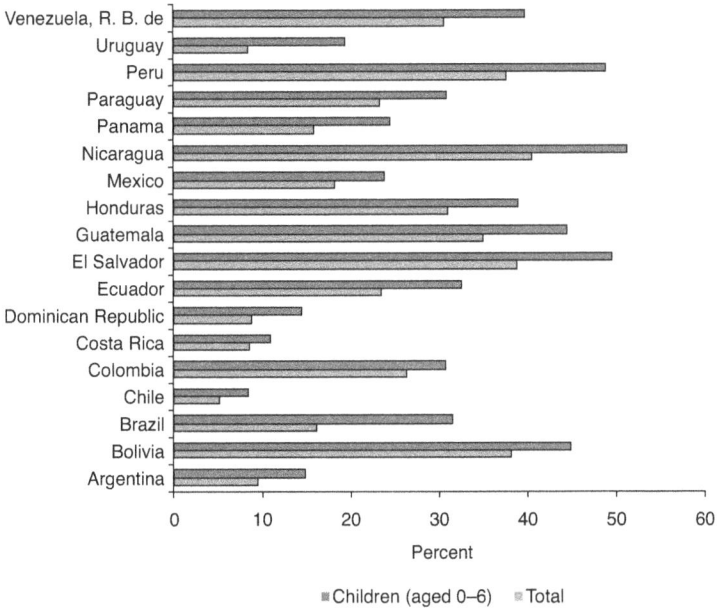

Source: World Bank calculations using SEDLAC household survey data (CEDLAS and World Bank, 2007)

Note: For socioeconomic, demographic, and ECD access indicators, data come from household surveys. In Argentina, El Salvador, Honduras, Peru, and República Bolivariana de Venezuela, these rates are for children aged 3–6. In Bolivia, Colombia, Costa Rica, Mexico, Panama, and Paraguay, rates are for children aged 5–6. In the Dominican Republic and Nicaragua, they are for children aged 4–6. In all other countries, the rates are for children aged 0–6. Preprimary education includes preschool and early education services.

Figure A1.3 Households and Children Living in Poor Housing Conditions, by Country (Percent)

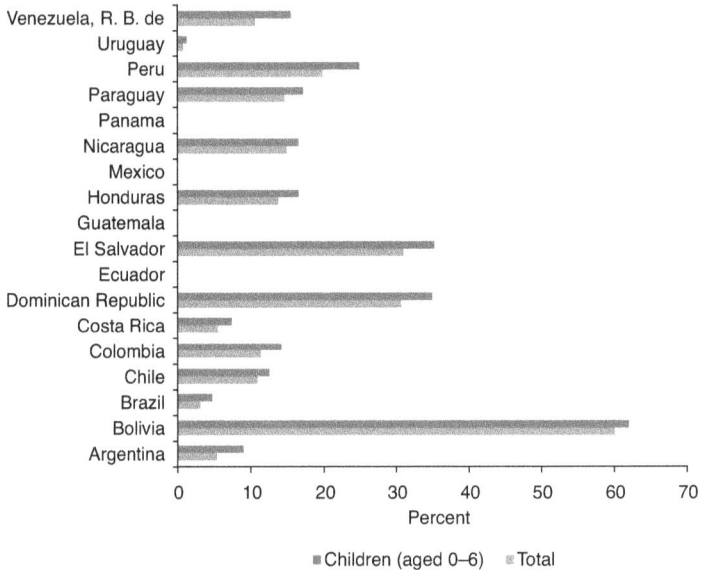

Source: World Bank calculations using SEDLAC household survey data (CEDLAS and World Bank, 2007)

Note: Ages are 0–6 except for the following cases. In El Salvador, Honduras, Peru and República Bolivariana de Venezuela, enrollment rates are for children aged 3–6. In Bolivia, Colombia, Costa Rica, Mexico, Panama, and Paraguay, rates are for children aged 5–6. In the Dominican Republic and Nicaragua, enrollment rates are for children aged 4–6.

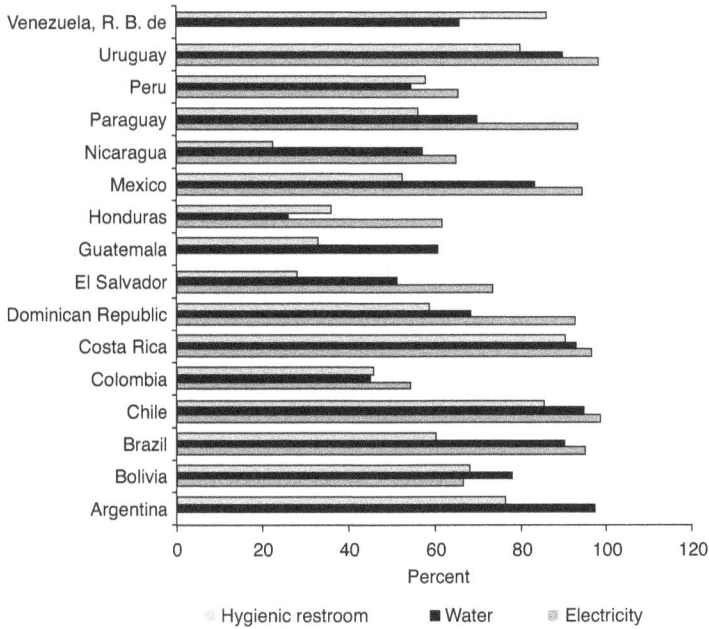

Figure A1.4 Children with Access to Electricity, Water, and Hygienic Restrooms at Home (Percent)

Source: World Bank calculations using SEDLAC household survey data (CEDLAS and World Bank, 2007)

Note: This information was not available for Ecuador and Panama.

Figure A1.5 Children Aged 0–6 Years by Income Decile
(Percent)

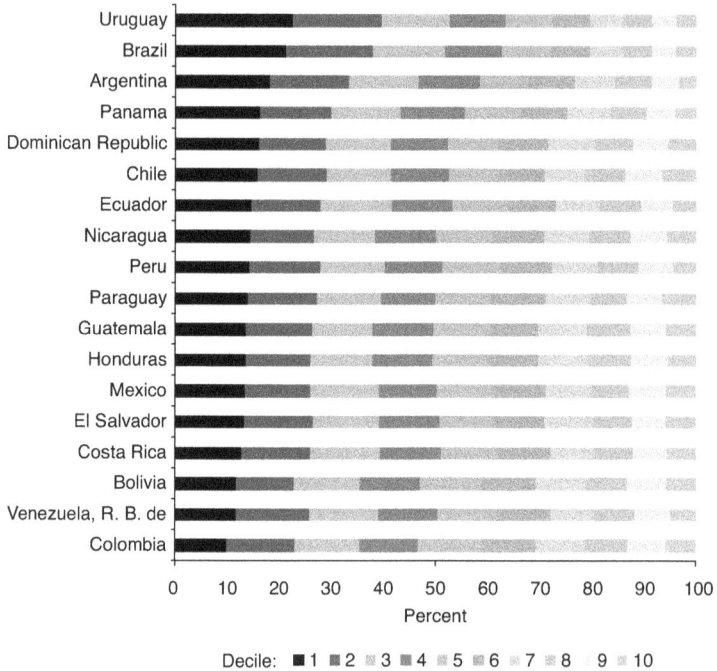

Source: World Bank calculations using SEDLAC household survey data
(CEDLAS and World Bank, 2007).

Table A1.2 Poverty and Education Indicators, by Country

	25 years						25–59 years					
	Average years of schooling			At least completed secondary school (%)			Average years of schooling			At least completed secondary school (%)		
Country	Poor	Non-poor	All	Poor	Non-poor	All	Poor	Non-poor	All	Poor	Non-poor	All
Argentina	9.0	11.7	11.4	26	63	59	7.6	10.8	10.5	15	52	49
Bolivia	5.9	10.7	9.1	17	57	44	4.7	9.2	7.5	9	41	29
Brazil	5.3	8.9	8.4	14	51	45	4.0	7.5	7.1	9	37	33
Chile	9.0	12.4	12.3	22	73	71	8.2	10.9	10.8	22	54	53
Colombia	7.7	9.7	9.4	41	59	56	5.8	8.4	7.8	23	44	39
Costa Rica	6.1	9.3	9.2	18	40	39	5.5	8.4	8.2	9	34	32
Dominican Republic	8.8	9.9	9.8	32	48	46	5.4	8.4	8.1	11	32	30
Ecuador	7.2	10.3	9.5	19	50	42	6.2	9.6	8.6	15	44	36
El Salvador	5.9	9.8	8.6	18	50	40	4.2	8.2	6.9	10	36	28
Guatemala	3.3	6.6	5.8	6	29	24	2.2	5.4	4.5	2	22	16
Honduras	4.3	7.6	6.5	3	19	14	3.4	7.4	6.0	3	24	17
Mexico	6.1	10.2	9.8	12	37	35	4.9	8.8	8.3	6	31	27
Nicaragua	4.9	7.5	6.5	9	29	22	3.6	6.7	5.5	6	24	17
Panama	6.0	11.0	10.2	12	57	50	5.6	10.2	9.7	11	48	44
Paraguay	6.3	10.0	9.2	15	43	38	4.9	8.1	7.5	5	29	24
Peru	6.2	10.7	9.7	22	72	62	4.5	9.5	8.3	14	60	49
Uruguay	7.2	11.0	10.8	4	45	43	6.8	10.1	9.9	3	40	38
Venezuela, R. B. de	8.0	10.5	9.7	12	32	25	6.7	9.5	8.6	7	25	20
Average	6.1	9.7	9.1	16	49	44	4.8	8.4	7.9	10	37	33

Source: World Bank calculations using SEDLAC household survey data (CEDLAS and World Bank, 2007).

Figure A1.6 Indigenous Children and Population, by Country (Percent)

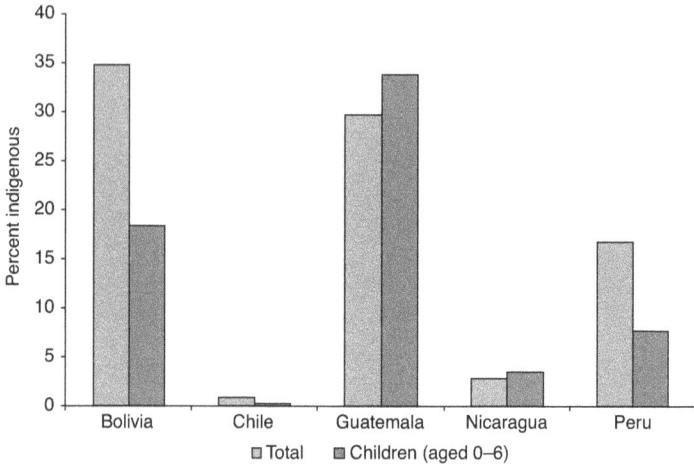

Source: World Bank calculations using SEDLAC household survey data (CEDLAS and World Bank, 2007).

Note: Argentina, Brazil, Colombia, Costa Rica, the Dominican Republic, Ecuador, El Salvador, Honduras, Mexico, Panama, Paraguay, República Bolivariana de Venezuela, and Uruguay did not report this information on the household survey.

Children's ages are 0–6 except in Bolivia (5–6), Nicaragua (4–6), and Peru (3–6).

Table A1.3 Prevalence of Selected Nutritional Deficiencies in
Children Aged 0–4, by Region

Region	Vitamin A deficiency	Iron deficiency anemia	Zinc deficiency
Latin America and the Caribbean	15	46	33
East Asia and the Pacific	11	40	7
Eastern Europe and Central Asia	1	22	10
Middle East and North Africa	18	63	46
South Asia	40	76	79
Sub-Saharan Africa	32	60	50
High-income Countries	0	7	5

Source: Caulfield et al. (2006).

Figure A1.7 Socioeconomic Differences on Child
Development in St. Lucia

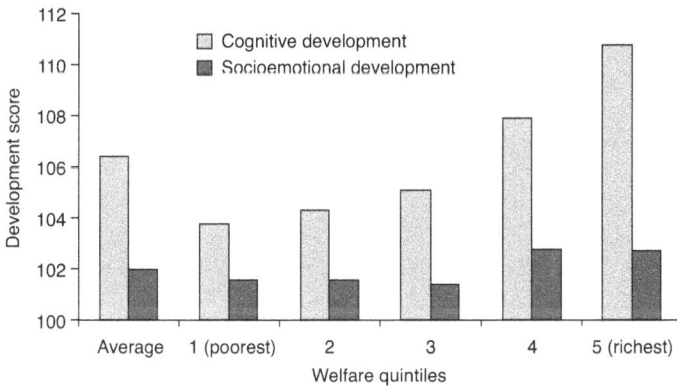

Source: Janssens (2006).

Table A1.4 Employment Indicators for Women, by Country

Country	Total participation (all women)	Women who are HH or spouses aged 20–55	HH or spouses aged 20–55 with children
Argentina	0.650	0.640	0.539
Bolivia	0.710	0.719	0.687
Brazil	0.696	0.682	0.638
Chile	0.540	0.510	0.436
Colombia	0.657	0.624	0.580
Costa Rica	0.510	0.469	—
Dominican Republic	0.497	0.498	0.442
Ecuador	0.656	0.644	0.596
El Salvador	0.549	0.531	0.463
Guatemala	0.490	0.466	0.422
Honduras	0.470	0.455	0.387
Mexico	0.527	0.494	0.411
Nicaragua	0.549	0.533	0.458
Panama	0.556	0.534	0.462
Paraguay	0.657	0.641	0.630
Peru	0.704	0.714	0.688
Uruguay	0.731	0.731	0.663
Venezuela, R. B. de	0.637	0.632	0.570

Source: World Bank calculations using SEDLAC household survey data (CEDLAS and World Bank, 2007).

Note: HH = head of household.

Figure A1.8 Women Employed in the Informal Sector, by Country (Percent)

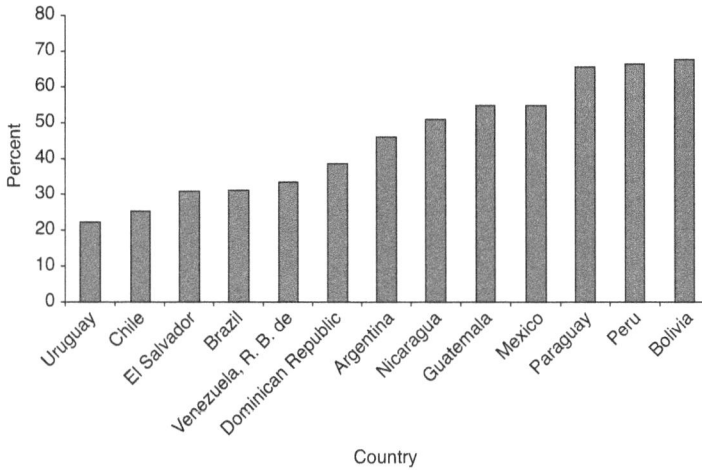

Source: World Bank calculations using SEDLAC household survey data (CEDLAS and World Bank, 2007).

Note: Informal sector includes jobs that offer no social security benefits.

Figure A1.9 Preprimary Gross Enrollment Rates, by Country, 2004 (Percent)

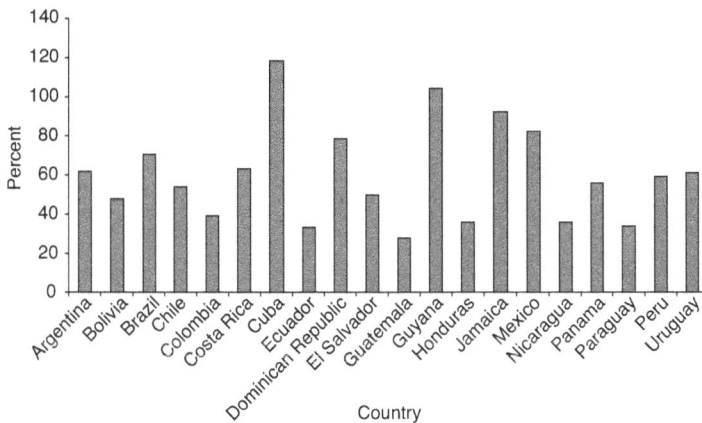

Source: UNESCO 2006.

Figure A1.10 Children Who Enter Grade 1 and Reach Grade 5, by Region (Percent)

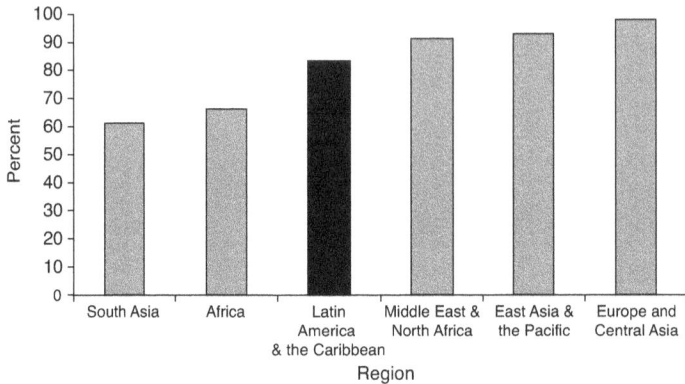

Source: UNESCO 2006.

Figure A1.11 Enrollment Rates by Income Quintile (1st and 5th), Children under Six Years Old

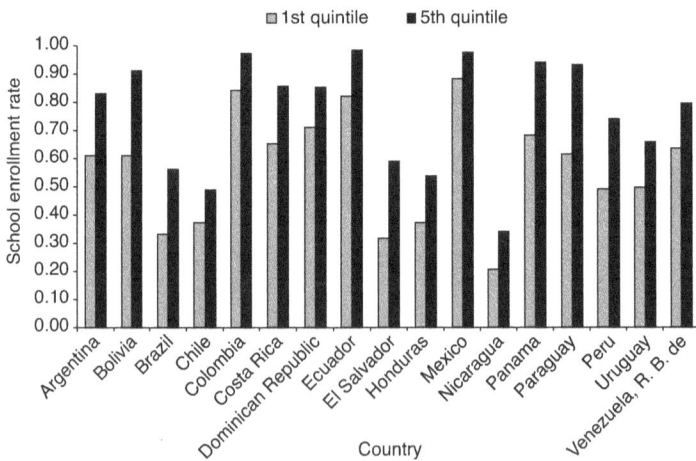

Source: World Bank calculations using SEDLAC household survey data (CEDLAS and World Bank, 2007).

Note: In Argentina, El Salvador, Honduras, Peru, and República Bolivariana de Venezuela, these rates are for children aged 3–6. In Bolivia, Colombia, Costa Rica, Mexico, Panama, and Paraguay rates are for children aged 5–6. In the Dominican Republic and Nicaragua, they are for children aged 4–6. In all other countries, the rates are for children aged 0–6.

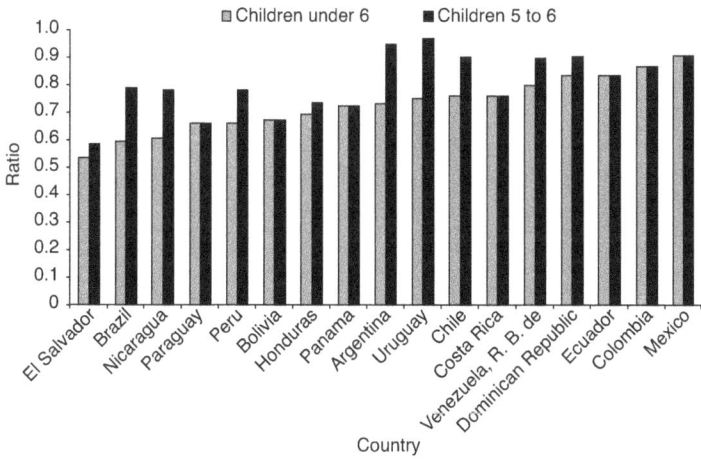

Figure A1.12 Ratio of School Enrollment Rates, First to Fifth Quintile

Source: World Bank calculations using SEDLAC household survey data (CEDLAS and World Bank, 2007).

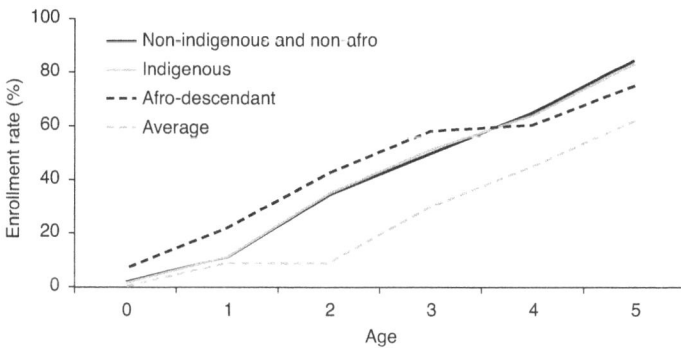

Figure A1.13 ECD Enrollment Rates by Age and Ethnic Group, Ecuador

Source: Reveco and Cruz 2006.

Figure A1.14 Children Younger than Six Years with Access to Health Insurance, by Country (Percent)

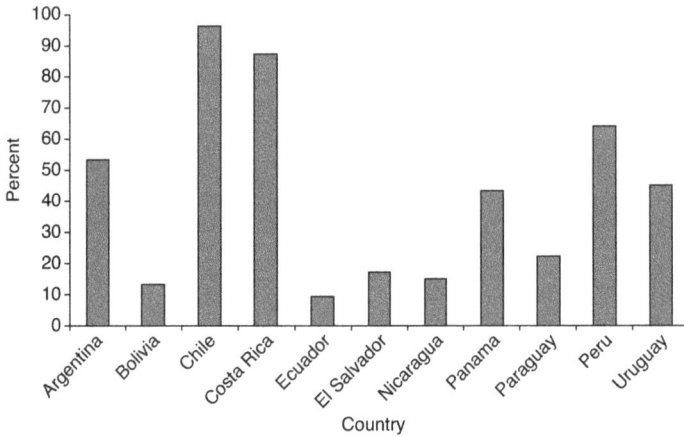

Source: World Bank calculations using SEDLAC household survey data (CEDLAS and World Bank, 2007).

Figure A1.15 Ratio of Health Insurance Coverage Rates of the First to the Fifth Quintile, by Country

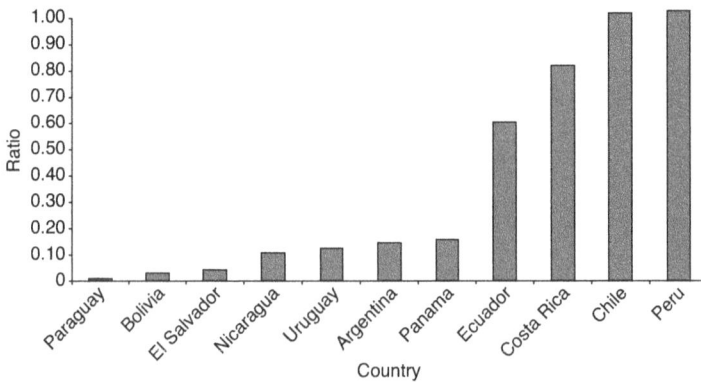

Source: World Bank calculations using SEDLAC household survey data (CEDLAS and World Bank, 2007).

Figure A1.16 Prenatal Care and Breastfeeding Indicators, by Country (Percent)

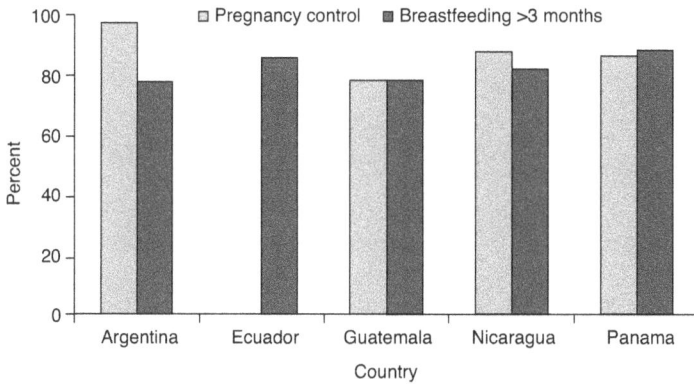

Source: World Bank calculations using SEDLAC household survey data (CEDLAS and World Bank, 2007).

Figure A1.17 Children Younger than Six Years Receiving Vaccinations, by Country (Percent)

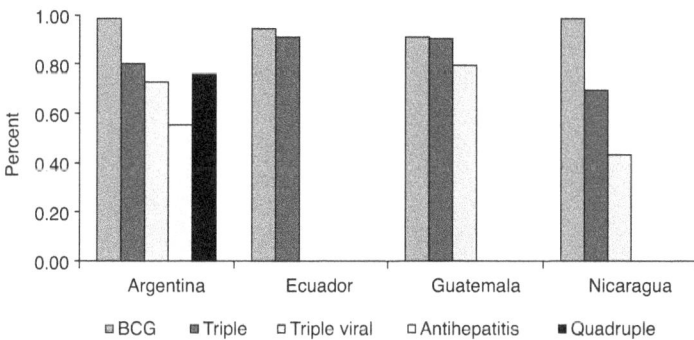

Source: World Bank calculations using SEDLAC household survey data (CEDLAS and World Bank, 2007).

Figure A1.18 Households That Benefit from Poverty Alleviation Programs, by Income Quintile and Country (Percent)

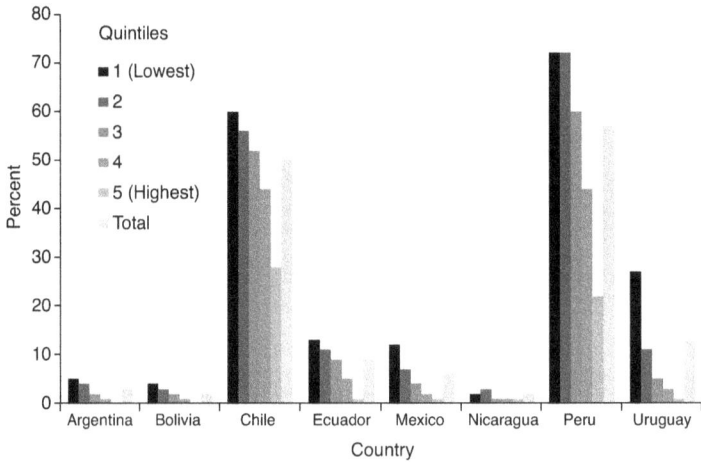

Source: World Bank calculations using SEDLAC household survey data (CEDLAS and World Bank, 2007).

Appendix 2. Detailed Descriptions of Early Childhood Development Programs

This appendix provides detailed descriptions of the ECD programs discussed in Chapter 4, as well as for programs without rigorous impact evaluations (or with evaluations underway) that deserve attention for their scope, preliminary results, or innovative program features. The discussion is organized by program focus: those primarily addressing health, hygiene, and nutrition; those primarily addressing educational interventions (parenting practices, preschool and early childhood education, and early childhood care); and poverty alleviation programs (including conditional and unconditional cash transfers). We also discuss briefly programs that promote female labor force participation or programs that have indirectly affected this outcome.

Of the interventions discussed in this appendix and Chapter 4, eleven are analyzed in depth regarding program participation, organization, institutional support, results, and evaluation features. Table A2.1 lists the selected programs and table A2.2 describes some of their key features.

Table A2.1 Selected Programs

Program name	Type of program	Country	First implemented
Junta Nacional de Jardines Infantiles (JUNJI)	Early education and care	Chile	1970
Fundación Educacional para el Desarrollo Integral del Menor (Fundación INTEGRA)	Early education and care	Chile	1990
Conozca a su Hijo (CASH)	Combined health, nutrition, and education	Chile	1980
Hogares Comunitarios	Combined health, nutrition, and education	Colombia	1987
Familias en Acción	Conditional cash transfer	Colombia	1999
Proyecto Integral de Atención a Niños y Niñas Menores de 6 Años de la Sierra Rural (PAIN)	Early education and care	Peru	2001
Atención Integral a la Niñez Comunitaria (AIN-C)	Combined health, nutrition, and education	Honduras	1991
Proyecto Nutrición y Protección Social (AIN-C Nutrition)	Combined health, nutrition, and education	Honduras	2006
Madres Guías	Combined health, nutrition, and education	Honduras	1992
Oportunidades	Conditional cash transfer	Mexico	1997
Educación Inicial no Escolarizada (CONAFE)	Early education and care	Mexico	1993

Table A2.2 Key Features of Selected Programs

Program name	Types of services	Target	Services delivered mostly to	Services delivered mostly by	Services delivered at
JUNJI	Parent education and support, early stimulation and nutrition for children	Periurban, rural, and indigenous families living in poverty	Children aged 0–6 and parents	Preschool teachers	Preschools and daycare centers
Fundación INTEGRA	Early education and stimulation, nutrition, parent education, child assessments	Families living in poverty	Children aged 0–6 and parents	Preschool teachers	Homes, preschools, and daycare centers
CASH	Early education and stimulation, nutrition services, parent education	Rural and indigenous mothers	Mothers and their children aged 0–5	*Monitora* (community educational agent)	Schools, community space, health care facilities
Hogares Comunitarios	Child care, nutrition (including supplements), parent education, early stimulation, preventive health services, health assessments	Families living in poverty; preference given to displaced and indigenous families	Pregnant women, mothers and their children	*Madre comunitaria* (community mother) and professional supervisors	Preschools, community space, health care facilities
Familias en Acción	Cash payments, nutrition services (including supplements), health services for children, child health and growth monitoring, child care, parent education	Families living in poverty (particularly displaced and indigenous families)	Pregnant women and mothers with children aged 0–7	Community mother leaders	Community space
PAIN	Preschool, health referrals, health education, nutrition services (including supplements)	Rural indigenous children living in severe poverty in highland areas	Children aged 3–6	Preschool teachers and *animadoras* (community mother leaders)	Preschools and daycare centers

(Table continues on next page.)

Table *A2.2* (continued)

Program name	Types of services	Target	Services delivered mostly to	Services delivered mostly by	Services delivered at
AIN-C	Nutritional and health assessments and education, treatment for illnesses, assistance with health care services	Municipalities with severe poverty levels	Children aged 0–2	Volunteers	Homes and community space
AIN-C Nutrition	Prenatal education, newborn screening, nutrition services, preventive health, parent education	Pregnant women and families living in severe poverty	Pregnant women, children aged 0–2, and parents	Health care personnel and volunteers	Health centers
Madres Guías	Prenatal education, newborn screening, nutrition, preventive health, parent education, community sanitation, child care, early and preschool education	Families living in poverty in municipalities with high child mortality and malnutrition rates	Children aged 0–6, parents, and community	*Madre guías* (mother guides), community educators, preschool teachers	Homes, community space, preschools
Oportunidades	Cash payments, prenatal education and health care, newborn screening, nutrition services (including supplements), parent education, preventive and primary health services, child assessments	Families living in poverty	Pregnant and lactating women, children aged 0–15, emphasis on young children aged 0–2	Teachers, health care personnel	Schools, community space, public health care facilities
CONAFE	Early education and stimulation, parent services, prenatal education, child assessments	Urban, periurban, and rural and indigenous families living in poverty	Children aged 0–4 and their parents, pregnant women	Community instructors	Homes and community space

Source: Authors.

Health, Hygiene, and Nutrition Interventions

In Central America, the *Atención Integral a la Niñez Comunitaria* (AIN-C) program[1] is a community-based, preventive health, and nutrition model that targets young children and their families. Honduras, El Salvador, Guatemala, and Nicaragua currently implement AIN-C. AIN-C aims to improve child feeding and child care practices; diagnose, treat and/or refer common illnesses; and improve the utilization of existing health-related services.

The Honduran AIN-C program is the only one that has been evaluated so far (evaluations are ongoing for other AIN-C model programs in the other countries). The program was piloted by the Ministry of Health in 1991 to address malnutrition in children less than 5 years of age, and scaled up to a national program in 1999. It is a community-based health and education program that focuses on serving municipalities with the highest levels of poverty. Services include nutritional assessments and measurements of children; nutrition and health education for mothers; identification, diagnosis, and treatments for usual childhood illnesses; referrals for more serious illnesses, diseases, or accidents; health care promotion; and assistance with accessing health care services. Children identified as malnourished are referred to health services for treatment and nutrition supplementation. In addition to evaluating children's health and conducting health education sessions for parents, the program seeks to assess and address the causes of health and nutritional problems in home and community settings.

The program focuses mainly on children aged 0 to 2 years in order to reduce infant mortality and identify early those children with poor weight gain or height. Teams composed of three volunteers provide monthly monitoring visits for approximately 25 children 0 to 2 years and their older siblings and mothers. The AIN-C program is characterized by frequent contact with the center (once a month). In 2000, coverage was estimated at 92 percent of Honduran children 0 to 2 years of age (Fiedler 2003). Evaluation results suggest program participation was associated with a 0.39 z-score increment in weight for age over nonparticipants (Griffiths and McGuire 2005).

In 2006, a new *Proyecto Nutrición y Protección Social* (Nutrition and Social Protection Project) was developed to complement the AIN-C program. The program targets children from prenatal to 2 years of age from families living under the poverty line, or in severe poverty in rural areas where high rates of malnutrition and child mortality are found.

Project services are provided by health centers and NGOs and include prenatal education, support for the newborn child, newborn screening, nutrition services, preventive health education and services, parent education and support groups, and community participation. The program has not developed standards as yet. Families participate by taking their children to assessment sessions, attending support groups and parent education sessions, and participating in community gatherings. Communities receive general sensitization to nutritional needs, select and support program volunteers, and promote parental and community participation in project activities.

The project was initially piloted in four health centers in two departments. Its coverage targets are 10,000 boys, 10,000 girls, and 15,000 mothers in 1,000 exclusively rural communities. The most recent information on the program includes a new target for the coverage of children from 3 to 6 years of age, which is reported to be 50,000 children.

Founded in 1992 by the Christian Children's Fund of Honduras (CCF-H), *Madres Guías* (Mother Guides) provides continuous services for pregnant women and children from 0 to 4 or 6 years of age. The program is based on the U.N. Convention on the Rights of the Child that guarantees access to integrated services for children. The program serves rural, urban, and periurban families living under the poverty line in departments and municipalities with the highest rates of child mortality, malnutrition, at-risk children, and chronically ill and developmentally delayed children.

Madres Guías uses a combined strategy of parent education, health, and nutrition services to improve child development. Services include prenatal education, newborn screening, child development assessments, individualized child and family development plans, early stimulation, parent education and support, nutrition services and school feeding, primary health services, community sanitation services, social protection services, daycare centers, child care and preschool education, transition to primary school, community participation, and basic education. Some 60 percent of participant families live in poverty, 26 percent live in severe poverty, and 70 percent live in rural areas. Some 5 percent of the families are from indigenous communities, and 10 percent of the children are reported to have disabilities.

Services are provided by community mothers, or *madres guías*. Most madres guías have some basic education (grades 1 to 6). They are aided by paid community educators who have completed secondary education. The program provides pre-service and in-service training for all actors involved (madres, community educators, preschool teachers).[2] Madres Guías' services include both home visits and group sessions. Home visits are provided once a week for approximately one hour. Parent meetings last 1.5 hours and are held once a month, and preschool classes are held daily for 3.5 hours. Program standards have been developed for home visits and the program's assessments of child development.[3]

Families are very much involved in Parents' Committees. They administer and implement the program, and manage follow-up activities at the community level. They conduct activities for early stimulation, health, nutrition, and environmental sanitation, and they become "multipliers" of program activities through their extended families and others in the community. They participate actively and continuously in training sessions that are held to strengthen services for children, motivate direct service providers, and keep personnel apprised of developments in ECD. Communities as a whole are involved in projects to develop sources of potable water, build latrines, and improve sanitation. They participate in health fairs and immunization campaigns, improve the physical condition of the community, and provide school feeding services in various educational settings.

External and internal evaluations have found that program objectives have been achieved especially in three areas: reducing infant and maternal mortality, expanding literacy, and improving the nutritional status of children. The program has developed and is applying a scale for measuring child development as well as several other evaluation and monitoring instruments. In addition, the program reports that women's self-esteem has greatly increased; men recognize and accept the importance of program activities with women and that they benefit children and the community; communities have become more committed to actions for the improvement of educational quality; and youth participate in the application of early stimulation programs. Importantly, the early stimulation program is transmitted in an intergenerational manner to the extended families of beneficiaries.

A number of similar programs are currently being implemented but have not yet been evaluated. In Nicaragua, the *Programa Comunitario de Salud y Nutricion* (PROCOSAN, or Community-based Health and Nutrition Program) has been the official community-based nutrition strategy in the country since 2003. The program supports three interventions: growth monitoring, early stimulation, and attention to illnesses or morbidity.[4] In 2006 the program reached 72,400 children under 2 years of age and their mothers in the poorest communities of Nicaragua. To date, the program has not been formally evaluated. A draft process evaluation was based on data collected from a sample of 90 communities using self-report questionnaires. The results are mixed but promising. They indicate that the program has been functioning well in about 70 percent of the communities. The majority of mothers (85 percent) understand the program's growth promotion aspect in terms of weighing children. However, fewer mothers (40 percent) know that the program also provides information on child development and even fewer know about aspects of the program such as obtaining referrals for treatment of illness. Nonetheless, mothers and health providers report that mothers' knowledge on child development has been enhanced. The evaluation did not collect data on child health and nutrition outcomes (Flores and others 2007).

In Peru, UNICEF has supported since 2000 a health education program in four departments (Apurimac, Cajamarca, Cusco, and Loreto) called *Buen Inicio,* which offers an integrated package of preventive and promotional activities on health and nutrition and early stimulation. The program aims to improve practices and utilization of services. It provides health education to pregnant women and mothers of children up to 3 years old and reaches approximately 75,000 children and 35,000 pregnant women in 200 rural communities. The program has been evaluated using two approaches: an evaluation of process, outputs, and outcome indicators at selected communities in two points in time, and an evaluation based on program progress indicators collected by the Ministry of Health in a sample of health centers. Results show a decrease in the prevalence of chronic malnutrition ranging between 24 to 41 percentage points. In communities were the program was implemented, a reduction in the prevalence of anemia and vitamin A deficiencies was also reported. The results of the evaluation need to be taken with care as there were reported problems with the baseline data and processing.[5] These findings suggest that if a proper impact evaluation (with baseline data and a control group) were carried out, it would demonstrate positive effects of the program (UNICEF 2005).

Educational Interventions

As discussed in Chapter 2, education programs designed to improve ECD outcomes can take on a variety of forms. These include programs that educate parents on how to better care for their children (parenting practices), programs to ensure that children 0 to 2 years old have adequate early childhood care in centers, and preschool education programs for children 3 to 6 years old.

Education programs to improve parenting practices

There are a number of parenting programs in Latin America and the Caribbean, but only a few have been rigorously evaluated. We describe below some of the most important parenting programs and their effects.

Conozca a Su Hijo (CASH, or Know Your Child Program) was developed in the 1980s to help develop poverty-stricken rural areas of Chile. It began as a pilot program and was not based on a prior model. A situation analysis was conducted in two rural communities, and subsequently the program and its educational materials were developed and field-tested during a three-year pilot period. Although its scale has improved, it remains a small-scale program.

CASH targets rural mothers, preferably belonging to *Sistema de Protección Social de Chile Solidario,* and/or indigenous mothers under the poverty line who have children aged 0 to 5 years and who live in dispersed rural sectors that lack preschool education centers. Services include early stimulation, parent education and support, nutrition services, social protection, preschool education, early childhood intervention services for children with developmental delays or disabilities, and participatory activities with communities. Initially the program tried to work with both parents but decided to focus instead on mothers and train them to provide key messages to the rest of the family. Initially they tried to work solely with mothers, but soon found that it was necessary to provide play spaces for children to ensure mothers would be able to attend parenting group sessions.

A combined strategy of mother education and child services is used, with mothers meeting once a week (for approximately 80 hours per year) in community gatherings led by an educational agent called a *monitora* who is elected by the mothers' group. The monitora must be literate and she is paid an honorarium. There are approximately 13 mothers per monitora and no volunteers are used. Mothers remain in the program for approximately 20 months. Monitoras are trained by CASH and JUNJI professionals using a variety of educational materials including a manual for monitoras, workbooks for mothers, and activities for children. Educational materials have been developed in the Mapudungun language for Mapuche families. No program standards have been developed as yet but they are planned.

Program coverage is not wide, and it has experienced slow growth since the 1990s. In 1993–94 the program served 3,810 children and 2,738 mothers. In 2006, the program served 3,983 children and 3,917 mothers living in 312 communities. Some 27 percent of the mothers belong to the Sistema de Protección Social de Chile Solidario that serves the poorest populations in Chile.[6] CASH works closely with municipalities and community nonprofit organizations to deliver its services. Rural schools, health services, and community organizations give spaces for the mothers to meet.

Early childhood care

In Colombia, the *Hogares Comunitarios de Bienestar Familiar* (HCBF) program was developed in 1987 to serve pregnant women, mothers, and children living in poverty. HCBF is a large-scale child care and nursery program with a nutrition component. At the HCBF center, children receive a lunch and two snacks that include a nutritional beverage called *bien-estarina*. The program targets urban, semiurban, and rural populations living in level 1 (severe poverty) and level 2 (under the poverty level) as measured by the *Sistema de Selección de Beneficiarios* (SISBEN, or System for the Selection of Beneficiaries), with priority given to female-headed households, internally displaced families,[7] and indigenous families.[8]

Hogares Comunitarios uses a combined approach of parent education and child services. Services include parent education and support; early stimulation, nutrition and feeding services; health education and preventive health care; height/weight measurements; daycare centers; child care

services; and preschool education. Feeding and child care services are provided by one of the mothers in the community, called a *madre comunitaria*
or mother educator. Madres comunitarias are unpaid paraprofessionals
with at least a few years of secondary school[9] who reside in the communities and report to the community's Parents' Associations. HCBF serves 12
to 14 children per madre comunitaria.[10]

Early childhood education

The *Educación Inicial* program was started in 1993, and is one of the
compensatory programs of *Consejo Nacional de Fomento Educativo*
(CONAFE).[11] Educación Inicial is an early childhood education center and
community-based program that seeks to expand preschool and primary
school education in impoverished communities of Mexico. Educación
Inicial targets children, pregnant women, and the parents of children aged
0 to 4 years living in rural, periurban, and urban areas with high levels of
marginalization, as well as indigenous populations.

Early childhood education, parenting, and other educational programs
are offered by *instructores comunitarios* (community instructors). These
individuals usually have completed only primary education, but also have
experience with community-based education and often are familiar with
the community, its context, and culture. Instructores comunitarios work
directly with parents and children, serving an average of 10 children at
a time. Nineteen percent of the program participants were very highly
marginalized and 47 percent were highly marginalized. Some 70 percent were rural, 21 percent were indigenous, and the remainder urban or
periurban.[12]

Educación Inicial uses a combined strategy of parent education and
child services. Its services include prenatal education, education for moth-
ers-to-be, child assessments, early stimulation, parent education, and support. Over an eight-month period, home visits of one hour each are conducted twice a week, individual consultations of one hour are held once a
week, and two-hour parent meetings are held once a week. At the age of
4, children are expected to enroll in public preschool.

Educación Inicial has strong family and community participation components, including parent (or family) and child sessions, providing learning spaces as needed, conducting learning activities at home, and promoting the program throughout the community. Community participation
includes selecting community instructors, providing spaces for educational
sessions, convening community meetings for monitoring and evaluation
activities (for example, to learn about program progress and conduct self-
evaluations), requesting the support of the authorities, and interacting
with them as needed.

The *Junta Nacional de Jardines Infantiles* (JUNJI, or National Board
of Early Childhood Care,) is a public network of daycare and preschools

developed and implemented in Chile in 1970. With a combined strategy of parent education, child-centered early education, and support for working women, its services include parent education and support, early stimulation, nutrition services, child assessments, early intervention for children with delays and disabilities, and support for the transition to primary school. The program is delivered in daycare centers and preschools.

JUNJI targets urban, periurban, rural, and indigenous families living in severe poverty or under the poverty level. It focuses on serving at-risk children and those with developmental delays. When it began in 1970, JUNJI served 2,738 children from birth to age 6.[13] According to the program director, 80 percent of the children served by JUNJI live in poverty and 20 percent in severe poverty. Some 85 percent of the children live in urban settings and 15 percent in rural areas, with 3 percent from indigenous groups.[14]

Services are delivered by professional teachers (with university or technical degrees) or technical personnel. The program does not rely on volunteers, although in a few clinics volunteers help with daycare centers and other activities. Community participation is strongly sought. Communities help develop educational activities in each preschool center, participate in communication and training activities, conduct outreach to identify participants, and help to rehabilitate buildings for local services. Teacher/child ratios for daycare centers (serving children from 3 months to 2 years of age) are one educator for 40 children plus one technical educator for 10 children.[15] In the middle and transition levels there is one educator for every 64 children, and between one and two technical educators for each group of 32 children.

Another Chilean program, *Fundación INTEGRA,* was established in 1990 as a nonprofit agency to provide daycare and preschool education for children aged 0 to 4 years living in poverty. It evolved from a private foundation to a government program. INTEGRA is a public sector, early-education program based in daycare centers and preschools. The program pursues a combined strategy of parent education and child services. Its services include early childhood care and preschool, child assessment including cognitive and socioemotional assessments, early stimulation, nutrition services, parent education and support, transition to primary school, sanitation services, social protection, and community participation. INTEGRA has developed program standards and applies them at all levels.

The program targets urban, periurban, and rural populations, with special emphasis on severely impoverished families. Indigent families make up 26.4 percent of the program's beneficiaries. Families living under the poverty line represent 64.7 percent of the program's beneficiaries.[16] The program targets adolescent mothers, working mothers or those looking for work, female heads of household, and families who are classified as socially vulnerable by the Ministry of Planning.[17]

The program respects and values cultural, geographical, linguistic, and ethnic diversity and promotes close linkages with the families of the children they serve. Families participate actively in the preschools through parent centers and parent education sessions. They are usually involved in improving school facilities. Home-based activities are conducted to promote family learning. Communities conduct consultations for planning, hold gatherings of neighbors, collaborate with the police and preschools for child protection, and build support networks for child rights and development. Family and community linkages are expected to increase knowledge and understanding of the context in which children and their families live. INTEGRA's daycare centers and preschools conduct activities with children that are appropriate to their physical and sociocultural realities.

Program services are delivered mostly by preschool teachers with a technical degree. Educators receive continuous training; INTEGRA does not rely on volunteers or paid paraprofessionals. In daycare centers for infants between 3 and 23 months, teacher/child ratios are one caregiver for six children. For children aged two to four years, one teacher is provided for 15 children. The cost per day of children in crèches (from 3 months to 2 years of age) is US$10 or approximately US$2,400 per child per year. The cost per child in preschool (2 to 5 years of age) is US$5 or approximately US$1,200 per child per year. Administrative costs are reported to be 10 percent.

The program is externally evaluated to analyze its implementation process, contents, materials, methods, and results. Evaluations are conducted annually, and they have found that the approved curriculum is being used, the well-being of children is ensured, and children have developed a good attachment with adults, which promotes learning and positive interaction in groups. After one year in the educational program, children have achieved statistically significant gains in cognitive, language, and socioemotional development. With respect to targeting and achieving the mission of INTEGRA, the program currently contributes to reaching 10 percent of the population of children in income levels 1 and 2, and 91.1 percent of the families are from those income levels.

In 2001, the National Directorate for Initial and Primary Education (DINEIP) of the Ministry of Education of Peru developed the Project for Integrated Services to Children Less than Six Years in the Rural Mountainous Region (PAIN) as a pilot ECD program (Ministerio de Educación del Perú 2004; Espejo, Arakaki, and Ulloa 2005). After initial donors withdrew their funding, DINEIP funded the program in its first two years. In 2003–04, the program was supported by the Inter-American Development Bank. Although external evaluations showed positive results of PAIN, the program lost its funding and was shut down in 2004. Nonetheless, the program was the subject of a detailed external evaluation that found it to be successful in achieving its ECD outcome goals (Espejo, Arakaki, and Ulloa 2005).

PAIN was a community-based, child-oriented preschool program run by the Ministry of Education. It sought to develop culturally competent preschool education of high quality for rural highland indigenous families and children living in severe poverty. PAIN targeted children from 3 to 6 years of age. Services were provided in 310 rural indigenous communities and included culturally and linguistically appropriate preschool education. Preschool classes were held five days per week for three hours per day during nine months each year, for a total of 450 to 520 contact hours per year. Other program services included referrals to preventive and primary health care services, nutritional supplementation through a preschool feeding program, education in personal hygiene, and participatory community support and decision making. No home visits or individual parent education services were provided, although parents attended occasional group sessions led by *animadoras* (community mother leaders).

PAIN encouraged parents to diagnose their children's educational and socioemotional development and identify problems and needs. These evaluations were the basis for program design at the local level. Indigenous languages and local cultural items were used as educational resources in order to help ensure continuity for children and parents. Services were provided by trained early education teachers and community mother leaders called animadoras. Animadoras had a secondary education, but were given additional training and small stipends. Their responsibilities included direct work and interaction with parents and children in culturally appropriate ways. Animadoras served from 15 to 25 children at a time, depending upon population density in each community. When it began in 2001, PAIN served 3,076 children each year. The program increased its coverage substantially to 7,554 children in 2004, but was discontinued thereafter.

Poverty Alleviation Interventions

Several multisectoral policies help alleviate the detrimental effects of poverty on young children, including income support, maternal and family leave policies, improvements in household infrastructure, and policies designed to increase female labor force participation. Most empirical research has focused on income support programs, especially conditional cash transfers. There is also some recent research focusing on the relationship between female labor force participation and ECD outcomes in Latin America and the Caribbean.

Income support programs

Conditional cash transfer programs are being implemented widely in Latin America and the Caribbean, including Brazil, Chile, Colombia, the

Dominican Republic, Ecuador, El Salvador, Honduras, Jamaica, Mexico, Nicaragua, and Peru.[18] Several programs have been externally evaluated to capture their impact on a broad range of outcomes, including child development outcomes. Most of the evaluations have focused on the nutritional and health outcomes. The evaluation of the Mexican CCT program also looked at cognitive and socioemotional development outcomes in the short term as well as medium-term educational outcomes of very young children who were program beneficiaries before starting school.

The Mexican *Oportunidades* program is the most studied of all CCT programs. It began in 1997 and today targets five million extremely poor families (25 percent of the Mexican population) in 86,091 localities in 32 Mexican states.[19] Of these close to one-third are families living in urban areas, and close to two-thirds live in rural areas. The program serves an impressive total of 3.8 million indigenous families (close to two-thirds of all indigenous families in Mexico). The program was originally designed to overcome severe poverty and "jump-start the economy" after the Mexican financial crisis of 1995. The program was called PROGRESA from 1997 until 2002, when a new federal administration renamed it Oportunidades. The program was also designed to replace several previous national nutrition programs that had not been evaluated, were assessed to be flawed, or had been found to have low impact levels

Originally designed as a cash transfer program to families living in poverty who could demonstrate compliance with the program's education and health conditions, Oportunidades is increasingly becoming a combined parent and child strategy through cooperative agreements with health, nutrition, and educational services. In addition to providing cash payments to families, program services include prenatal education and health care, childbirth support, services for newborns, nutritional supplements for pregnant women and children from birth to 24 months, child screening and assessments, parent education and support, primary health care services, and protective services. Malnourished children aged 2 to 5 years receive nutritional supplements. Target ages for enrollment in Oportunidades include pregnant and lactating women and their children from birth until secondary school (approximately 15 years old), with a major emphasis on children from birth to 24 months of age. The target populations are urban, periurban, and rural families who are marginalized and living in conditions of severe poverty.

Cash payments are deposited to the family's bank account. This has the indirect program effect of linking very poor families to banking and credit institutions for the first time.[20] Payments are conditional on health and nutrition behaviors, and educational responsibilities for families with older children. Community and family participation in various aspects of the program is strongly encouraged. Families' roles in the program are to guarantee that their school-age children attend school and comply with controls regarding health and nutrition; attend health self-care workshops; become members of the Committees for Community Promotion; attend sessions on information, training, and guidance, and especially those regarding nutrition; and participate actively in the system of social accountability (oversight).

Community responsibilities include to establish Committees for Community Promotion that receive training and create linkages between program beneficiaries and health, education, and Oportunidades services; ensure requests and suggestions are channeled to the appropriate groups; enable program transparency, supervision, and follow-up in accordance with program guidelines; develop youth groups for students with educational scholarships for upper-secondary school that will support the Committees; participate in the System of Services for the Population, which are mechanisms that enable beneficiaries and Committees to present their complaints, petitions, and appreciation for services; and encourage the participation of beneficiaries in the exercise of their social rights and in the promotion of community development. State health and education services, teachers, and health personnel provide the program's direct services. These paid community workers have health and education certificates that are required by state service providers, and the number of professionals per child varies according to the type of center, school, teacher, or specialist.

Founded in 1999 in Colombia, *Programa Familias en Acción* (FA, or Families in Action Program) is a CCT program based on Oportunidades. Program leaders studied the Mexican program, made adjustments, and added new processes such as the use of the SISBEN as a targeting system. A pilot project was first conducted in 22 municipalities to field test the program design before it was scaled up.

Programa Familias en Acción is a parent-oriented CCT program providing direct services to mothers. Cash transfers and nutritional supplements are conditioned on use of health services for children, such as immunizations and controls regarding physical growth and development. Older children are required to be enrolled in school. The program targets pregnant women and mothers with children less than 7 years of age. Families served live in SISBEN Level 1 communities located in urban, periurban, or rural or indigenous areas of selected municipalities with high levels of poverty or officially registered internally displaced families. Although currently focused on parents, the program is increasingly becoming a combined parent and child strategy.

"Mother leaders" guide assemblies of participating mothers. Child care and family workshops are provided to mothers covering health, nutrition, hygiene, contraception, child development, and play, as well as literacy topics. Educational materials, learning toys, and other items have been included in the program. To make the program more culturally competent, program leaders have chosen to include ritual elements of regions and communities, promote learning play, and include traditional folklore. They reported that they place a value on questions and conversations about culture, emphasize the symbolic role of food as a gift, and encourage professionals who lead training workshops to converse with rather than dictate to participants.

Program standards have been developed and they are routinely used to monitor the program. Participating families are responsible for meeting their commitments. They are expected to participate in municipal assemblies and child care, as well as development groups that are aimed at benefiting both mothers and their children. They are also asked to play a role in citizen oversight activities (*veeduría*), and some are asked to serve on the municipal certification committee for the program, along with other community members.

Female labor force participation

In Latin America, the average rate of female labor force participation is almost 60 percent, and as seen in Chapter 2, this rate varies widely by country. Very low levels of female participation in the work force among the poorest households are particularly troubling given the strong relationship between family income and ECD outcomes. A 2007 joint study by the World Bank, the Chilean National Service for Women, and the Inter-American Development Bank found that several factors contribute to Chilean women's low labor force participation, including (i) a lack of access to quality education and limited training opportunities, especially for low-income women; (ii) family structures, specifically families with a larger number of children under the age of 15, in which mothers serve as the principal child care providers; (iii) shorter workdays for women than men with the same employer, and longer periods of inactivity and unemployment than men; and (iv) traditional cultural values and attitudes about gender roles in Chile that constrain women's employment outside the home.

Some program evaluations have documented the effects of female labor force participation. For example, evaluation of the Colombian program *Hogares Comunitarios* by Attanasio and Vera-Hernandez (2004) suggested that, in the weeks prior to the interview, the program increased by 0.31 percentage points the average probability that mothers would be working.

Notes

1. The AIN-C strategy centers upon frequent contact with the families; tailored counseling to meet their needs; prioritization of children under 2 years, the period when most nutritional damage can occur; and a community action tool for analysis of factors influencing children's growth beyond a family's control.

2. Madres guías serve five to seven mothers at a time with children aged 0 to 4 years. The program's teachers for nonformal preschools serve children aged 4 to 6 years, with an average of 15 to 20 children per class.

3. In 2006, home visits and sessions were provided in 233 communities for parents and children aged 0 to 3 years, including 3,802 boys and 3,719 girls for a total of 7,521 children and 11,325 families. Preschool services were offered for children aged 3 to 6 years, including 645 boys and 621 girls for a total of 1,266 children. Services for prenatal and postnatal education and care were provided for 890 mothers, 641 pregnant women, and 890 newborns.

4. Program activities include promoting and monitoring growth through regular weighing; early stimulation provided at the community health centers during the growth monitoring visit; individual counseling of mothers on improving health and nutritional practices based on a child's nutritional status and developmentally appropriate guidelines; and referrals when needed. Home visits are also encouraged, as well as community meetings every four months. The program is carried out by volunteers or *brigadistas*. Three brigadistas work with an average of 20 to 25 children per community

5. The firm hired to do the baseline data faced problems with the sample size and the application of the survey questionnaire. Additional baseline data on nutritional status was collected by the program implementers in selected communities, but here again there were problems with data collection and processing of the enumerators.

6. Indigenous families make up some of the program's beneficiaries, but no statistics were provided by program officials.

7. These are families who have had to leave their place of residence due to the violent conflict (guerrilla warfare) in Colombia.

8. The program began in Cali with 102 hogares serving 530 children. By 2006, 799,979 children were served. Children served by Familia, Mujer e Infancia (FAMI, or Family, Women and Infancy)—a subprogram of Hogares Comunitarios that targets pregnant women and children aged 0 to 3 years—included 389,820 children, for a total of 1,189,799 children served by Hogares Comunitarios and related programs in 2006. Program standards have been developed, and they are linked to program supervision and results-based planning.

9. Efforts are currently underway to provide these mothers with training that would lead to a professional or technical preschool teaching degree.

10. Many professional advisors (including social workers and nutrition specialists) and supervisors work in the program. They form interdisciplinary teams to provide integrated support and improve service quality.

11. These programs are designed to "compensate" children living in extreme poverty by providing them with school materials, books, and other educational resources.

12. In May 2007, the program reached 2,085 municipalities and 22,855 communities serving 367,986 parents, or 97.1 percent of their target parent population, and 409,871 children, or 98.6 percent of their target child population.

13. As of 2007, JUNJI served 90,650 children from three months to three years of age (74 percent) and 31,315 children from ages three to six (26 percent), totaling 121,965 children.

14. JUNJI's service target for 2008 for children living in severe poverty was 45 percent, with a total of 80 percent under the poverty line.

15. As of January 1, 2008, there will be one educator for every 20 children and one technical educator for every 6 children.

16. Impoverished and severely impoverished families (poverty levels 1 and 2, respectively) make up 10 percent of Chile's population.

17. Since its early years, INTEGRA's coverage has increased substantially. In 1994, INTEGRA served 44,142 children from birth to 6 years of age, or 3 percent of the children in that age group. In 2007, INTEGRA served 78,000 children from birth to 6 years or 6.3 percent of children in the same age group according to the

2002 census. Ninety-six percent of the beneficiaries come from the most impoverished families in Chile.

18. Part of their success is based on rigorous evaluations that have documented
their impact. Part is based on the nature of CCT programs, which, as demand side
programs, are more likely to attract public attention and support than traditional
supply side programs.

19. The program's total budget in 2007 is US$3.2 billion (of which less than
5 percent is for operative costs). The size of the "food" cash transfers is US$6 per
month (more than that for the total transfer), which is offered to the mother to
improve income and food intake in the household. The transfer size represents
as much as 20 percent of household income (Schady 2006). Nutritional complements are provided to children under 5 years and pregnant and lactating women.
Compliance with basic preventive health care visits and attendance at workshops
on health and nutrition are required. During these visits children are immunized,
their growth is monitored, and they receive micronutrient supplements if they are
malnourished. Other components include increasing cash transfers for students
in grades 3 to 12 (US$11 to US$60 per scholarship holder), savings accounts of
US$300 upon graduation from high school, and cash transfers for the elderly
(Hermosillo 2006).

20. It is reported that as a result, many families are beginning to amass savings
and make small investments in businesses and other vehicles, thus encouraging
upward socioeconomic mobility (Székely 2007).

References

Abramo, L., and M. Valenzuela. 2005. "Women's Labour Force Participation Rates in Latin America." *International Labour Review* 144(4). Special issue on "Women's Labour Force Participation." International Labour Office, Geneva.

Acción Social. 2008. "Familias en Acción. Informe de Estado y Avance. Segundo Semestre de 2008." Bogotá, Colombia. Available at: http://www.accionsocial.gov.co/documentos/3742_Informe_a_la_Banca_Multilateral_(2do_semestre_2008).pdf

Aidoo, A. A. 2006. "Facing the Challenge of Defining Early Childhood Development Models that can be Scaled Up. Ensuring a Supportive Policy Environment." Paper for the Association for the Development of Education in Africa, Biennale on Education in Africa. Libreville, Gabon, March 27–31, 2006. Available at: http://www.adeanet.org/adeaPortal/adea/biennial-2006/doc/document/PL4_1_aidoo_en.pdf.

ANEP (Administración Nacional de Educación Pública). 2001. "Estudio de evaluación de impacto de la educación inicial en Uruguay." Montevideo, 2001. República Oriental del Uruguay. Available at: http://www.mecaep.edu.uy/docs/EEIEIU.pdf.

———. 2005. "Panorama de la educación en el Uruguay, Una década de transformaciones. 1992–2004." Montevideo, 2005. República Oriental del Uruguay. Available at: http://www.anep.edu.uy/gerenciagrl/ger_inv_eva/publicaciones/Panorama_de_la_educuc_Uruguay.htm.

Akimushkina, I. 2008. "Contemporary Women: Between Productive and Childcare Activities." Review of the World Bank Projects and Research Papers on Child Care and Women's Participation in the Labor Market. Background Paper for the Virtual Workshop on Childcare Policies and Gender: Experiences from Latin America and the Caribbean and Europe and Central Asia. January 16. Processed. World Bank, Washington, DC.

Alderman, H. 2007. "Improving Nutrition through Community Growth Promotion: Longitudinal Study of the Nutrition and Early Child Development Program in Uganda." *World Development* 35(8): 1376–1389.

Arango, M. M, G. P. Nimnicht, and F. Peñaranda. 2004. *Twenty Years On: A Report on the PROMESA Program in Colombia.* Bernard van Leer Foundation, The Hague, Netherlands.

Armecin, G., J. Behrman, P. Duazo, S. Ghuman, S. Gultiano, and E. King. 2006. "Early Childhood Development through an Integrated Program: Evidence from the Philippines." Policy Research Working Paper No. 3922. World Bank, Washington, DC.

Attanasio, O., C. Meghir, and M. Szekely. 2003. "Using Randomized Experiments and Structural Models for 'Scaling Up': Evidence from the PROGRESA Evaluation." IFS Working Paper EWP04/03. Institute for Fiscal Studies, London.

Attanasio, O., and M. Vera-Hernandez. 2004 (revised 2007). "Nutrition and Child Care Choices: Evaluation of a Community Nursery Program in Rural Colombia." Centre for the Evaluation of Development Policies. The Institute for Fiscal Studies, EWP04/06. November 2004, revised March 2007. Institute for Fiscal Studies, London.

———. 2004a. "Medium and Long Run Effects of Nutrition and Child Care: Evaluation of a Community Nursery Program in Rural Colombia." Working paper. November. Institute for Fiscal Studies, London.

Attanasio, O., and others. 2005. "The Short-Term Impact of a Conditional Cash Subsidy on Child Health and Nutrition in Colombia." The Institute for Fiscal Studies, Report Summary: Familias 03. December. Institute for Fiscal Studies, London. Available at: http://www. ifs.org.uk/publications/3503.

Aughinbaugh, A., and M. Gittleman. 2003. "Does Money Matter? A Comparison of the Effect of Income on Child Development in the United States and Great Britain." *The Journal of Human Resources* 38(2): 416–440.

Barnett, S. 2002. "Early Childhood Education." In *School Reform Proposals: The Research Evidence,* ed. Alex Molnar, pp. 1–27. CT: Information Age Publishing.

Baker, M., J. Gruber, and K. Milligan. 2005. "Universal Childcare, Maternal Labor Supply and Family Well-Being." Unpublished paper. National Bureau of Economic Research, Cambridge, MA.

Baker-Henningham, H., C. Powell, S. Walker, and S. Grantham-McGregor. 2005. "The Effect of Early Stimulation on Maternal Depression: A Cluster Randomised Controlled Trial." *Archives of Disease in Childhood* 90: 1230–1234.

Bardon, Agnes. 2006. "Ireland: Mothers Talking to Mothers." *UNESCO Courier,* October. Online at http://portal.unesco.org/en/ev.php-URL_ID=34823&URL_DO=DO_TOPIC&URL_SECTION=201.html.

Becker, G. 1964. *Human Capital: A Theoretical and Empirical Analysis.* New York: Columbia University Press.

———. 1981. *A Treatise on the Family.* Cambridge, MA: Harvard University Press.

Behrman, J., and J. Hoddinott. 2001. "Program Evaluation with Unobserved Heterogeneity and Selective Implementation: The Mexican *Progresa* Impact on Child Nutrition." PIER Working Paper No. 02-006. Penn Institute for Economic Research, Philadelphia, PA.

———. 2004 "An Evaluation of the Impact of PROGRESA on Pre-School Child Height". FCND Discussion Paper No 104. International Food Policy Research Institute, Washington, DC.

Behrman, J., P. Sengupta, and P. Todd. 2005. "Progressing through *Progresa*: An Impact Assessment of a School Subsidy Experiment in Mexico." *Economic Development and Cultural Change* 54(1): 237–76.

Berhman, J., S. Parker, and P. Todd. 2000. "The Impact of Progresa on Achievement Test Scores in the First year". International Food Policy Research Institute, Washington DC.

———. 2004. "Medium-Term Effects of the *Oportunidades* Program Package, Including Nutrition, on Education of Rural Children Age 0–8 in 1997." Technical document number 9 on the Evaluation of *Oportunidades*. Philadelphia, PA: University of Pennsylvania.

———. 2008. "Medium-Term Impacts of the *Oportunidades* Conditional Cash Transfer Program on Rural Youth in Mexico." In *Poverty, Inequality, and Policy in Latin America*, ed. S. Klasen and F. Nowak-Lehmann. Cambridge, MA: MIT Press.

Behrman, J., Y. Cheng, and P. Todd. 2004. "Evaluating Pre-school Programs when Length of Exposure to the Program Varies: A Nonparametric Approach." *Review of Economics and Statistics* 86(1): 108–32.

Belfield, C. R. 2006. "Financing Early Childhood Care and Education: An International Review." Background Paper for the 2007 Global Monitoring Report on Education for All. UNESCO, Paris.

Benasich, A., and J. Brooks-Gunn. 1996. "Maternal Attitudes and Knowledge of Child-Rearing: Associations with Family and Child Outcomes." *Child Development* 67: 1186–1205.

Berger, L., C. Paxson, and J. Waldfogel. 2005. "Income and Child Development." Unpublished manuscript. World Bank, Washington, DC.

Berlinski, S., and S. Galiani. 2005. "The Effect of a Large Expansion of Pre-Primary School Facilities on Preschool Attendance and Maternal Employment." WP04/30. August. Institute for Fiscal Studies, London.

Berlinski, S., S. Galiani, and G. Gertler. 2006. "The Effect of Pre-Primary Education on Primary School Performance." WP06/04. London, Buenos Aires, Washington DC: University College London, Institute for Fiscal Studies, Universidad de San Andres, and World Bank.

Berlinski, S., S. Galiani, and M. Manacorda. 2007. "Giving Children a Better Start: Preschool Attendance and School-Age Profiles." Processed. University College, London.

Bingswanger, H., and A. Swaminathan. 2003. "Scaling-up Community-Driven Development: Theoretical Underpinnings and Program Design Implications." World Bank, Washington, DC.

Bitler, M., and J. Currie. 2005. "Does WIC Work? The Effects of WIC on Pregnancy and Birth Outcomes." *Journal of Policy Analysis and Management* 24: 73–91.

Blau, D. 1999 "The Effect of Income on Child Development." *Review of Economics and Statistics* 81(2): 261–27.

Black, M., S. Walker, T. Wachs, N. Ulkuer, J. Gardner, S. Grantham-McGregor, B. Lozoff, P. Engle, and M. de Mello. 2008. "Policies to Reduce Undernutrition Include Child Development." *Lancet* 371(9611): 454–5.

Brooks-Gunn, W-J Han, and J. Waldfogel. 2002. "Maternal Employment and Child Cognitive Outcomes in the First Three Years of Life: The NICHD Study of Early Child Care." *Child Development* 73(4): 1052–1072.

Campbell, F., E. Pungello, S. Miller-Johnson, M. Burchinal, and C. Ramey. 2001. "The Development of Cognitive and Academic Abilities: Growth Curves From an Early Childhood Educational Experiment." *Developmental Psychology* 37(2): 231–242.

Campbell, F., C. Ramey, E. Pungello, J. Sparling, and S. Miller-Johnson. 2002. "Early Childhood Education: Outcomes as a Function of Different Treatments." *Applied Developmental Science* 6: 42–57.

Carneiro, P., and J. Heckman. 2003. "Human Capital Policy." In *Inequality in America: What Role for Human Capital Policy?* ed. J. Heckman and A. Krueger. Cambridge, MA: MIT Press.

Center on the Developing Child. 2007. *A Science-Based Framework for Early Childhood Policy.* National Forum on Early Childhood Program Evaluation, National Forum on the Developing Child (http://www.developingchild.harvard.edu/). Cambridge, MA: Harvard University.

Chen, S. and Ravallion, M. 2007. "Absolute Poverty Measures for the Developing World, 1981–2004." *Proceedings of the National Academy of Science of the United States of America* 104(43): 16757–16762. Available at: http://www.pnas.org/content/104/43/16757.full.pdf+html.

Cohen, M., and M. Rubio Pardo. 2007. "Violence and Crime in Latin America." Paper prepared for the Consulta de San Jose. Available at: http://www.copenhagenconsensus.com.

Colchero, A., O. Galárraga, J. Leroy, J.P. Guttierez, and S. Bertozzi. 2007. "Comparative Cost Effectiveness Analysis of Early Childhood Development Interventions in Latin America: An Economic Evaluation of Three Interventions in Mexico." Processed. Mexican National Institute of Public Health, Cuernavaca, Mexico.

Committee for Economic Development. 2002. "Preschool for All: Investing in a Productive and Just Society." Committee for Economic Development, Washington, DC. Available at: http://www.ced.org/images/library/reports/education/early_education/report_preschool.pdf.

Cueto, S., and J. Diaz. 1999. "Impacto de la educacion inicial en el rendimiento en primer grado de primaria en escuelas publicas urbanas de Lima". *Revista de Psicología* 1: 74–91.

Cunha, F., J. Heckman, L. Lochner, and D. Masterov. 2005. "Interpreting the Evidence on Life Cycle Skill Formation." NBER Working Paper 11331. National Bureau of Economic Research, Cambridge, MA.

Cunha, F., and J. Heckman. 2007. "The Technology of Skill Formation." *American Economic Review* 97(2): 31–47.

Curi, A., and N. Menezes Filho. 2006. "Os Efeitos da Pré-Escola sobre Salários, Escolaridade e Proficiência." Ibmec Working Paper WPE-02-2006. Ibmec, São Paulo. Available at: http://www.ibmecsp.edu.br/pesquisa/download.php?recid=3059.

Currie, J. 2000. "Early Childhood Intervention Programs: What Do We Know?" Processed. The Brooking Institution, Washington, DC. Available at: http://www.brookings.edu/es/research/projects/cr/doc/currie20000401.pdf.

———. 2001. "Early Childhood Education Programs." *Journal of Economic Perspectives* 15(2): 213–238.

Currie, J., and D. Thomas. 1995. "Does Head Start Make a Difference?" *American Economic Review* 85(3): 341–364.

———. 2000. "School Quality and the Longer-Term Effects of Head Start." *Journal of Human Resources* 35(4): 755–774.

Davis, D. 2004. "Scaling-Up Action Research Project, Phase One, Lessons from Six Case Studies." Unpublished. World Bank, Washington, DC. Available at: http://siteresources.worldbank.org/INTCDD/550121-1138894027792/20806147/CDDAFRSynthCAseStudies.pdf.

De Ferranti, D., G. Perry, F. Ferreira, and M. Walton. 2003. *Inequality in Latin America and the Caribbean. Breaking with History?* Washington, DC: World Bank.

Desai, S., P. Chase-Lansdale, and R. Michael. 1989. "Mother or Market? Effects of Maternal Employment on the Intellectual Ability of 4-Year-Old Children." *Demography* 26(4).

Devaney, B., L. Bilherman, and J. Schre. 1990. "The Savings in Medicaid Costs for Newborns and Their Mothers from Perinatal Participation in the WIC Program." Mathematical Policy Research, Washington, DC.

Duncan, G., and J. Brooks-Gunn, eds. 1997. *Consequences of Growing Up Poor*. New York: Russell Sage Foundation.

Duncan, G. and S. Raudenbush. 1999. "Assessing the Effects of Context in Studies of Child and Youth Development." *Educational Psychologist* 34(1): 29–41.

Duncan, G., P. Morris, and C. Rodrigues. 2004. "Does Money Really Matter? Estimating Impacts of Family Income on Children's Achievement with Data from Random-Assignment Experiments." Processed. Next Generation Projects, New York, NY.

Engle, P., and M. Pedersen. 1989. "Maternal Work for Earnings and Children's Nutritional Status in Urban Guatemala." *Ecology of Food and Nutrition* 22(3): 211–223.

ESA Consultores. 2005. "Diseño e implementación del sistema de evaluación del Programa de Atención Integral a la Niñez Nicaragüense. Evaluación Final. Informe Final." Tegucigalpa, Honduras.

Eickmann, S., A. Lima, and M. Guerra. 2003. "Improved Cognitive and Motor Development in a Community-Based Intervention of Psychosocial Stimulation in Northeast Brazil." *Developmental Medicine & Child Neurology* 45: 536–41.

Espejo, Ronald, Milagros Arakaki, and Luis Ulloa. 2005. *Evaluación de la experiencia de atención integral a niños y niñas menores de 6 años en la sierra rural: lecciones aprendidas y mejores practices*. Lima, Peru: Panez y Silva Consultores.

Fernald, L., A. Raikes, and R. Dean. 2006. "Summary of Child Development Assessments and Application to Evaluations in the Developing World." Report prepared for the World Bank Development Group. World Bank, Washington, DC.

Ferreira, F., and J. Gignoux. 2007a. "Inequality of Economic Opportunity in Latin America." Processed. World Bank, Washington, DC.

———. 2007b. "Towards an Understanding of Socially Inherited Inequalities in Educational Achievement: Evidence from Latin America and the OECD." Processed. World Bank, Washington, DC.

Fiedler, J.. 2003. "A Cost Analysis of the Honduras Community-Based Integrated Child Care Program (Atención Integral a la Niñez Comunitaria, AIN-C)." Health, Nutrition and Population Discussion Paper. World Bank, Washington, DC.

Fiszbein, A., and C. Gevers. 2005. "Learning and Scaling Up through Evaluation". In *Reducing Poverty on a Global Scale: Learning and Innovating for Development,* ed. B. Moreno-Dodson. Washington, DC: World Bank.

Flay, B. 1986. "Efficacy and Effectiveness Trials (and Other Phases of Research) in the Development of Health Promotion Programs." *Preventive Medicine* 15: 451–474.

Flores, R., M. Ruiz, and others. 2007. "Evaluación de proceso del Programa Comunitario de Salud y Nutrición (PROCOSAN) de Nicaragua." PROCOSAN. Available at: http://nicaragua.nutrinet.org/publicaciones/publicaciones/Evaluaci%C3%B3n-de-proceso-del-Programa-Comunitario-de-Salud-y-Nutrici%C3%B3n-%28PROCOSAN%29-de-Nicaragua/.

Galasso, E. 2006. "Assessing the Impact of the SEECALINE: Improving Malnutrition through Behavioral Change." Processed. Development Research Group. World Bank, Washington, DC.

———. 2006a. "With Their Effort and One Opportunity: Alleviating Extreme Poverty in Chile." Processed. Development Research Group. World Bank, Washington, DC.

Galiani, S. 2007. "Reducing Poverty in Latin America and the Caribbean." Processed. Report for the Copenhagen Consensus Center and the Inter-American Development Bank. Washington University in St. Louis.

Garces, E., D. Thomas, and J. Currie. 2002. "Longer-Term Effects of Head Start." *American Economic Review* 92(4): 999–1012.

Gertler, P. 2004. "Do Conditional Cash Transfers Improve Child Health? Evidence from *Progresa's* Control Randomized Experiment." *AEA Papers and Proceedings* 92(2).

———. 2000. "Final Report: The Impact of PROGRESA-Oportunidades on Health." International Food Policy Research Institute, Washington, DC.

Gertler, P., and L. Fernald. 2004. "The Medium Term Impact of *Oportunidades* on Child Development in Rural Areas." Available at: http://www.sarpn.org.za/documents/d0001264/P1498-Child_dev_terminado_1dic04.pdf.

Glewwe, P., and E. King. 2001. "The Impact of Early Childhood Nutritional Status on Cognitive Development: Does the Timing of Malnutrition Matter?" *The World Bank Economic Review* 15(1): 81–113.

Glick, P. 2002. "Women's Employment and its Relation to Children's Health and Schooling in Developing Countries: Conceptual Links, Empirical Evidence, and Policies." Cornell Food and Nutrition Policy Program Working Paper No. 131. Cornell University, Ithaca, New York. Available at: http://papers.ssrn.com/sol3/papers.cfm?abstract_id=424101.

Goodman, A., and B. Sianesi. 2005 "Early Education and Children's Outcomes: How Long Do the Impacts Last?" *Fiscal Studies* 26(4): 513–548.

Government of the Philippines. Republic Act No. 8980: Early Childhood Care and Development (ECCD) Act. Signed December 05, 2000. Manila.

Gragnolati, M. 1999. "Children's Growth and Poverty in Rural Guatemala." Policy Research Working Paper No. 2193. World Bank, Washington, DC.

Grantham-McGregor, S. 1995. "A Review of Studies of the Effect of Severe Malnutrition on Mental Development," *Journal of Nutrition* 125(8): 2233.

Grantham-McGregor, S., and C. Ani. 2001. "A Review of Studies on the Effect of Iron Deficiency on Cognitive Development in Children." *Journal of Nutrition* 131(2S-2): 649S–666S.

Grantham-McGregor, S., et al. 2006. "Preventing the Loss of Children's Developmental Potential." PowerPoint presentation given at Colloquia on Measuring Early Child Development, Centre for Excellence on Child Development April 26–28. Château Vaudreuil, Vaudreuil, Québec, Canada. Available at: http://www.excellence-earlychildhood. ca/documents/Grantham-McGregorANG.pdf

Grantham-McGregor, S., C. Powell, S. Walker, S. Chang, and P. Fletcher. 1994. "The Long Term Follow-up of Severely Malnourished Children Who Participated in an Intervention Program." *Child Development* 65: 428–293.

Grantham-McGregor, S., C. Powell, S. Walker, and J. Himes. 1991. "Nutritional Supplementation, Psychosocial Stimulation, and Mental Development of Stunted Children: The Jamaican Study." *Lancet* 338: 1–5.

Grantham-McGregor, S., Y. Cheung, S. Cueto, and the International Child Development Steering Group. 2007. "Developmental Potential in the First 5 Years for Children in Developing Countries." *Lancet* 369: 60–70.

Gregg, P., and J. Waldfogel. 2005. "Symposium on Parental Leave, Early Maternal Employment and Child Outcomes: Introduction." *The Economic Journal* 115 (February). Royal Economic Society.

Griffiths, M., and J. McGuire. 2005. "A New Dimension for Health Reform—The Integrated Community Child Health Program in Honduras." In *Health System Innovations in Central America. Lessons and Impact of New Approaches*, ed. Gerard La Forgia. World Bank, Washington, DC.

Grunewald, R., and A. Rolnick, 2005. "A Proposal for Achieving High Returns on Early Childhood Development." Draft paper prepared for Building the Economic Case for Investments in Preschool. Forum convened by the Partnership for America's Economic Success, with support from the Committee for Economic Development and PNC Financial Services, Inc. New York, NY.

Gunnarsson, L., B. Martin Korpi, and U. Nordenstam. 1999. *Early Childhood Education and Care Policy in Sweden.* Ministry of Education and Science, Stockholm, Sweden.

Haggerty, P. 1981. "Women's Work and Child Nutrition in Haiti." Master of Science Thesis, Massachusetts Institute of Technology.

Hallman, K., A. Quisumbing, M. Ruel, and B. de la Brière. 2005. "Mothers' Work and Child Care: Findings from the Urban Slums of Guatemala City." *Economic Development and Cultural Change* 53: 855–885.

Hamadani, J., S. Huda, F. Khatun, and S. Grantham-McGregor. 2006. "Psychosocial Stimulation Improves the Development of Undernourished Children in Rural Bangladesh." *Journal of Nutrition* 136(10): 2645–2652.

Halpern, R., F. Barros, B. Horta, and C. Victora. 1996. "Desenvolvimento neuropsicomotor aos 12 meses de idade em uma coorte de base populacional no Sul do Brasil: diferenciais conforme peso ao nascer e renda familiar." Cad. Saúde Púb. 12(Supl. 1): 73–78.

Hart, B., and T. Risley. 1995. *Meaningful Differences in the Everyday Experience of Young American Children.* Baltimore, MD: Paul H. Brookes Publishing Co.

Haskins, R. 2008. Testimony to the U.S. House Committee on Education and Labor January 23, 2008. Available at: http://www.brookings.edu/testimony/2008/0123_education_haskins.aspx?emc=lm&m=212252&l=40&v=173795.

Hermosillo, R. 2006. "*Oportunidades,* the Mexican Human Development Program." Paper presented at the Third International Conditional Cash Transfer Program in Istanbul, June 26 to 30.

Heaton, T., and R. Forste. 2008. "Domestic Violence, Couple Interaction and Children's Health in Latin America." *Journal of Family Violence* 23(3): 183–193.

Heckman, J. 2006. "Skill Formation and the Economics of Investing in Disadvantaged Children." *Science* 312(5782): 1900–1902.

Hoddinott, J., and A. Quisumbing. 2003. "Investing in Children and Youth for Poverty Reduction." April 24. International Food Policy Research Institute, Washington, DC.

Hoddinott, J., and L. Bassett. 2008. "Conditional Cash Transfer Programs and Nutrition in Latin America: Assessment of Impacts and Strategies for Improvement." International Food Policy Research Institute, Washington, DC.

Holzer, H., D. Whitmore-Schanzenbach, G. Duncan, and J. Ludwig. 2007. "The Economic Costs of Poverty in the United States: Subsequent Effects of Children Growing Up Poor." Center for American Progress, Washington, DC.

Institute of Medicine. 1996. *WIC Nutrition Risk Criteria: A Scientific Assessment.* Washington, DC: National Academy Press.

Janssens, W. 2006. "St. Lucia Child Development Study—Baseline Report 2006: An Impact Evaluation of the Roving Caregivers Programme in St Lucia." Amsterdam Institute for International Development.

Johnson, Z., and others. 2000. "Community Mothers Programme—Seven Year Follow Up of a Randomized Controlled Trial of Non-Professional Intervention in Parenting." *Journal of Public Health Medicine* 22(3): 337–342.

Kagitcibasi, C. 1992. "A Model of Multipurpose Nonformal Education: The Case of the Turkish Early Enrichment Project." Proceedings of the First International Council on Education for Women.

Kagitcibasi, C., D. Sunar, and S. Berkman. 1988. *Comprehensive Preschool Education Project.* Ottawa: IDRC.

———. 2001. "Long-Term Effects of Early Intervention: Turkish Low-Income Mothers and Children. *Journal of Applied Development Psychology* 22: 333–61.

Kamerman, S. 2000. "Parental Leave Policies: An Essential Ingredient in Early Childhood Education and Care Policies." Social Policy Report XIV (2). Society for Research on Child Development, Ann Arbor, MI.

Keating, D., and C. Hertzman. 1999. *Developmental Health as the Wealth of Nations: Social, Biological, and Educational Dynamics.* New York: Guilford Press.

Khandke, V., E. Pollitt, and K. Gorman. 1997. "Maternal Education and Its Influences on Child Growth and Cognitive Development in Rural Guatemala." Paper presented at the Biennial Meeting of the Society for Research in Child Development, April 3–6, Washington, DC.

Levy, D., and J. Ohls. 2007. "Evaluation of Jamaica's PATH Program: Final Report." March. Mathematica Policy Research Inc.

Lewin, H., and H. Schwartz. 2006. "Costs of Early Childhood Care and Education Programs." Paper prepared for UNESCO 2006 Global Monitoring Report.

Lewin, H., and P. McEwan. 2001. *Cost Effectiveness Analysis. Methods and Applications.* Second Edition. London: Sage Publications.

Loeb, S., M. Bridges, D. Bassok, B. Fuller, and R. Rumberger. 2005. "How Much Is Too Much? The Influence of Preschool Centers on Children's Social and Cognitive Development." NBER Working Paper 11812. National Bureau of Economic Research, Cambridge, MA.

Londoño, B., and T. Romero Rey. 2005. "Colombia: Challenges in Country-level Monitoring." Paper prepared for the World Bank Symposium, September 28 29, Washington, DC.

Love, J., et al. 2005. "The Effectiveness of Early Head Start for 3 Year Old Children and their Parents: Lessons for Policy and Programs." *Developmental Psychology* 41(6): 885–901.

Ludwig, J., and D. Phillips. 2007. "The Benefits and Costs of Head Start." NBER Working Paper No. 12973. National Bureau of Economic Research, Cambridge, MA.

Lynch, R. 2004. *Exceptional Returns: Economic, Fiscal, and Social Benefits of Investment in Early Childhood Development.* Washington, DC: Economic Policy Institute.

Macours, K., and R. Vakis. 2007. "Seasonal Migration and Early Childhood Development." Social Protection Discussion Paper No. 0702. World Bank, Washington, DC.

Macours, K., N. Schady, and R. Vakis. 2008. "Can Conditional Cash Transfer Programs Compensate for Delays in Early Childhood Development?" Processed. World Bank, Washington, DC.

Magnuson, K., C. Ruhm, and J. Waldfogel. 2004. "Does Prekindergarten Improve School Preparation and Performance?" NBER Working Paper 10452. National Bureau of Economic Research, Cambridge, MA.

Mahon, R. 2002. "What Kind of 'Social Europe?' The Example of Child Care." *Social Politics* 9(4).

Maluccio, J., and R. Flores. 2005. "Impact Evaluation of a Conditional Cash Transfer Program: The Nicaraguan Red de Proteccion Social." International Food Policy Research Institute, Washington, DC.

Maluccio, J., J. Hoddinott, J. Behrman, R. Martorell, A. Quisumbing, and A. Stein. 2006. "The Impact of an Experimental Nutritional Intervention in Childhood on Education Among Guatemalan Adults." FCND Discussion Paper 207. International Food Policy Research Institute, Washington DC.

Martin Korpi, B. 2007. "The Politics of Preschool—Intentions and Decisions Underlying the Emergence and Growth of the Swedish Preschool." The Ministry of Education and Research, Sweden.

Martorell, R. 1995 "Promoting Healthy Growth: Rationale and Benefits." In P. Pinstrup-Andersen, D. Pelletier, and H. Alderman, eds., *Child Growth and Nutrition in Developing Countries: Priorities for Action.* New York: Cornell University Press.

———. 1999. "The Nature of Child Malnutrition and Its Long-Term Implications." *Food and Nutrition Bulletin* 20(3): 288–292. The United Nations University.

Mincer, J. 1958. "Investment in Human Capital and the Personal Distribution of Income." *Journal of Political Economy* 66(4): 281–302.

Ministerio de Educación de Chile. 1998. *Evaluación de Programas de Educación Parvularia en Chile: Resultados y Desafíos.* Santiago de Chile, Chile.

Ministerio de Educación del Perú. 2004. *Proyecto de Atención Integral a niñas y niños menores de 6 años de la Sierra Rural.* Lima, Peru: Dirección Nacional de Educación Inicial y Primaria, Ministerio de Educación.

Morenza L, O. Arrazola, I. Seleme, and F. Martinez. 2005. "Evaluación Proyecto Kallpa Wawa." UNICEF, Santa Cruz, Bolivia.

Morris, S., P. Olinto, and others. 2004a. "Conditional Cash Transfers Are Associated with a Small Reduction in the Rate of Weight Gain of Preschool Children in Northeast Brazil." *Journal of Nutrition* 134: 2336–2341.

Morris, S., P. Olinto, R. Flores, and J. Medina. 2004b. "Monetary Incentives in Primary Health Care and Effects on Use and Coverage of Preventive Health Care Interventions in Rural Honduras: Cluster Randomised Trial." *Lancet* 364: 2030–37.

Murphy, A., R. Grajeda, J. Maluccio, P. Melgar, L. Asturias de Barrios, and S. Saenz de Tejada. 2005. "Social and Economic Development and Change in Four Guatemalan Villages: Infrastructure, Services and Livelihoods." Publication INCAP MI/007. INCAP, Guatemala City, Guatemala.

Myers, R. 2004. "In Search of Quality in Programmes of Early Childhood Care and Education." Paper prepared for the 2005 EFA Global Monitoring Report. April.

———. 2007. Presentation at World Bank, Washington, DC.

Neufeld, L., A. García-Guerra, M. Flores-López, A. Fernández-Gaxiola, and J. Rivera-Dommarco. 2006. "Impacto del Programa Oportunidades en nutrición y alimentación en zonas urbanas de México." In *Evaluación externa de impacto del Programa Oportunidades 2006,* ed. B. Hernández-Prado and M. Hernández-Ávila. Cuernavaca, México: Instituto Nacional de Salud Pública.

Neuman, M., and S. Peer. 2002. "Equal from the Start: Promoting Educational Opportunity for All Pre-School Children. Learning from the French Experience." Franco-American Foundation, New York, NY.

Oberlin, E., and others. 2007. "Family Allowances: Policy, Practice and the Fight against Poverty in Europe and Latin America?" Technical report 2. International Social Security Association (ISSA), Geneva, Switzerland.

Oden, S., L. Schweinhart, and D. Weikart. 2000. *Into Adulthood: A Study of the Effects of Head Start.* MI: High/Scope Press.

OECD (Organisation for Economic Co-operation and Development). 2007. *Understanding the Brain: The Birth of a Learning Science.* Paris: OECD. Available at: http://www.oecd.org/document/60/0,334 3,en_2649_35845581_38811388_1_1_1_1,00.html.

OECD. 2007. Family Database. Available at: www.oecd.org/els/social/ family/database.

OECD. 2006. *Starting Strong II.* Paris: OECD.

Paes de Barros, R., M. De Carvalho, R. Mendonça, P.Olinto, J. Rocha, and A. Rosalém. 2007. "Uma Proposta para a Construção de uma Linha de Base para a Avaliação do Impacto dos Programas de Atenção à Primeira Infância no Município do Rio de Janeiro." Processed. Instituto de Estudios de Trabalho e Sociedade, Rio de Janeiro, Brazil.

Patel, V., and others. 2004. "Effect of Maternal Mental Health on Infant Growth in Low Income Countries: New Evidence from South Asia." *British Journal of Medicine* 328: 820–823.

Patrinos, H. 2007. "Living Conditions of Children." In *Solutions for the World's Biggest Problems: Costs and Benefits*, ed. Bjørn Lomborg. Cambridge, UK: Cambridge University Press.

Paxson, C., and N. Schady. 2005. "Cognitive Development among Young Children in Ecuador: The Roles of Wealth, Health and Parenting." Policy Research Working Paper No. 3605. World Bank, Washington, DC.

———. 2007. "Does Money Matter? The Effects of Cash Transfers on Child Health and Development in Rural Ecuador." Policy Research Working Paper No 4226. World Bank, Washington DC. Available at: http://papers.ssrn.com/sol3/papers.cfm?abstract_id=984618.

Plowman B, J. Picado, M. Griffiths, K. Van Roekel, and V. Vivas de Alvarado. 2004. "BASICS II: Evaluation of the AIN Program in Honduras, 2002." Arlington, VA: Basic Support for Institutionalizing Child Survival Project (BASICS II) for the United States Agency for International Development.

Powell, C. 2004. "An Evaluation of the Roving Caregivers Programme of the Rural Family Support Organization, *May Pen*." UNICEF, Clarendon, Jamaica.

Powell, C., H. Baker-Henningham, S. Walker, J. Gernay, and S. Grantham-McGregor. 2004. "Feasibility of Integrating Early Stimulation into Primary Care for Undernourished Jamaican Children: Cluster Randomized Controlled Trial." *British Journal of Medicine* 329: 89.

Quisumbing, A., K. Hallman, and M. Ruel. 2007. "Maquiladoras and Market Mamas: Women's Work and Childcare in Guatemala City and Accra." *Journal of Development Studies* 43(3): 420–455.

Radke-Yarrow, M., M. Pedro, and others. 1998. *Children of Depressed Mothers from Early Childhood to Maturity.* New Cork: Cambridge University Press.

Rawlings, L. 2004. "A New Approach to Social Assistance: Latin America's Experience with Conditional Cash Transfer Programs." Social Protection Discussion Paper 0416. World Bank Institute, Washington, DC.

Reveco, O., and Cruz. 2006. "Acceso y Calidad de la Educación Infantil Dirigida a Poblaciones Indígenas y Afro descendientes. Evaluación a Partir de Tres Casos: Colombia, Ecuador y Perú." Presentation at the Inter-American Development Bank, Washington, DC.

Reynolds, A., J. Temple, D. Robertson, and E. Mann. 2001. "Long-term Effects of an Early Childhood Intervention on Educational Achievement and Juvenile Arrest: A 15-Year Follow-up of Low-Income Children in Public Schools." *Journal of the American Medical Association* 285: 2339–2346.

———. 2002. "Age 21 Cost-Benefit Analysis of the Title I Chicago Child-Parent Centers." *Educational Evaluation and Policy Analysis* 24(4): 267–303.

Rosenzweig, M., and E. Bennett. 1996. "Psychobiology of Plasticity: Effects of Training and Experience on Brain and Behavior." *Behavioural Brain Research* 78(1): 57–65.

Ruel, M.T.B. de la Briere, K. Hallamn, A. Quisumbing, and N. Coj. 2002. "Does Subsidized Childcare Help Poor Working Women in Urban Areas? Evaluation of a Government Sponsored Program in Guatemala City." FCND Discussion Paper No 131. International Food Policy Research Institute, Washington, DC.

———. 2006. "The Guatemala Community Day Care Program. An Example of Effective Urban Programming." Research Report 144. International Food Policy Research Institute, Washington, DC.

Samons, P., K. Sylva, E. Melhuish, I. Siraj-Blatchord, B. Taggart, Y. Grabbe, and S. Bareau. 2007. "Effective Preschool and Primary Education Project 3-11 (EPPE 3-11). Summary Report. Influences on Children's Attainment and Progress in Key Stage 2 Cognitive Outcomes in Year 5." Institute of Education, University of London. Available at: http://k1.ioe.ac.uk/schools/ecpe/eppe/eppe3-11/eppe3-11%20pdfs/eppepapers/Tier%202%20short%20report%20-%20Final.pdf.

Save the Children. 2003. "What's the Difference? The Impact of Early Chlidhood Development Programs. A Study from Nepal of the Effects for Children, Their Families, and Communities." Kathmandu, Nepal.

Schady, N. 2005. "Early Childhood Development in Latin America and the Caribbean." Unpublished manuscript. The World Bank, Washington, DC.

———. 2006. "Early Childhood Development in Latin America and the Caribbean." Policy Research Working Paper 3869. World Bank, Washington, DC.

Schaetzel, T., and others. 2008. *Evaluation of the AIN-C Program in Honduras*. Arlington, VA: Basic Support for Institutionalizing Child Survival (BASICS) for the United States Agency for International Development (USAID).

Schweinhart, L. 2005. "The High/Scope Perry Preschool Study Through Age 40: Summary, Conclusions, and Frequently Asked Questions." MI: High/Scope Press.

Schultz, T. 1961. "Investment in Human Capital." *American Economic Review* 51(1): 1–17.

———. 1971. *Investment in Human Capital: The Role of Education and Research*. New York: The Free Press.

Shamah, T., S. Villalpando, V. Mundo, L. Cuevas, and J. Rivera. 2007. "Lecciones aprendidas en la evaluacion de Liconsa." In *XII Congreso de Investigación en Salud Pública Edición Especial* 49: 250–54.

Shonkoff, J., and D. Phillips. 2000. *From Neurons to Neighborhoods: The Science of Early Childhood Development*. Washington, DC: National Academy Press.

Sidiqi, A., L. Irwin, and C. Hertzman. 2007. "Total Environment Assessment Model for Early Childhood Development: Evidence Report for the World Health Organization's Commission on the Social Determinants of Health." WHO, Geneva.

Simmons, R., J. Brown, and M. Diaz. 2002. "Facilitating Large-Scale Transitions to Quality of Care: An Idea Whose Time Has Come." *Studies in Family Planning* 33(1): 61–75.

Stewart, K., and C. Huerta. 2006. "Reinvesting in Children? Policies for the Very Young in South Eastern Europe and the CIS." Innocenti Working Paper No. 2006-01. Florence, UNICEF Innocenti Research Centre.

Sylva, K., E. Melhuish, P. Sammons, I. Siraj-Blatchford, and B. Taggart. 2004. "The Effective Provision of Pre-School Education (EPPE) Project: Findings from Preschool to the End of Key Stage 1." London: DfES/Institute of Education, University of London. Available at: http://k1.ioe.ac.uk/schools/ecpe/eppe/eppe/eppefindings.htm.

Székely, M. 2007. "Mexico's Oportunidades." An interview with Miguel Székely, Undersecretary for Social Development, IDB Website, July 4.

Tan-Torres Edejer, T., M. Aikins, R. Black, L. Wolfson, R. Hutubessy, and D. Evans. 2005. "Cost Effectiveness Analysis of Strategies for Child Health in Developing Countries." *British Medical Journal* 331: 1177. Available at: http://www.bmj.com/cgi/content/full/331/7526/1177?ehom.

Tanaka, S. 2005. "Parental Leave and Child Health Across OECD Countries." *Economic Journal* 115 (February).

Taylor, B., E. Dearing, and K. McCartney. 2004. "Incomes and Outcomes in Early Childhood." *Journal of Human Resources* 39(4): 980–1007.

UNICEF (United Nations Children's Fund). 2000. "Domestic Violence against Women and Girls." *Innocenti Digest* 6 (June). Available at: http://www.unicef-icdc.org/publications/pdf/digest6e.pdf.

———. 2005. "Proyecto Supervivencia Crecimiento y Desarrollo Temprano Cooperación UNICEF-USAID Iniciativa Buen Inicio. Reporte de Resultados finales e intermedios 2000–2004." UNICEF Peru, Noviembre 2005.

———. 2009. *The State of The World's Children 2009*. New York: UNICEF. Available at: http://www.childinfo.org/files/The_State_of_the_Worlds_Children_2009.pdf.

United Nations. 1924. *Geneva Declaration of the Rights of the Child*. New York: United Nations. Available at: http://www.un-documents.net/gdrc1924.htm.

———. 1948. *The Universal Declaration of Human Rights*. New York: United Nations. Available at: http://www.un.org/en/documents/udhr/.

———. 1959. *Declaration of the Rights of the Child*. New York: United Nations. Available at: http://www.unhchr.ch/html/menu3/b/25.htm.

———. 1966. *International Covenant on Economic, Social and Cultural Rights*. New York: United Nations. Available at: http://www.unhchr.ch/html/menu3/b/a_cescr.htm.

———. 1989. *Convention on the Rights of the Child*. New York: United Nations. Available at: http://www.unhchr.ch/html/menu3/b/k2crc.htm.

———. 2005. *5th Report on the World Nutrition Situation*. New York: United Nations.

United Nations Development Programme (UNDP). 2004. *Human Development Report 2004. Cultural Liberty in Today's Diverse World*. New York: UNDP. Available at: http://hdr.undp.org/en/media/hdr04_complete.pdf.

UNESCO (United Nations Educational, Scientific and Cultural Organization). 2006. *Global Monitoring Report for Education for All 2007. Strong Foundations: Early Childhood Care and Education*. Paris: UNESCO.

———. 2007. "Situación Educativa de América Latina y el Caribe: Garantizando La Educación de Calidad para todos." Informe Regional de Revisión y Evaluación del Progreso de América Latina y el Caribe hacia la Educación para Todos en el marco del Proyecto Regional de Educación (EPT/PRELAC). Oficina Regional de Educación para América Latina y el Caribe (REALC/UNESCO Santiago) con colaboración del Instituto de Estadística de la UNESCO (UIS).

UNICEF ECLAC (United Nations Children's Fund and UN Economic Commission for Latin America and the Caribbean). 2005. "Child Poverty in Latin America." *Newsletter on Progress Towards the Millennium Development Goals from a Child's Rights Perspective*, Number 1 (September).

Van Roekel, K., B. Plowman, M. Griffiths, V. Vivas de Alvarado, J. Matute, and M. Calderon. 2002. "Evaluación de Medio Término del Programa AIN en Honduras, BASICS II, 2000)." Published by the Basic Support for Institutionalizing Child Survival Project (BASICS II) (*Proyecto de Apoyo Básico para la Institucionalización de la Sobreviviencia Infantil*) of the U.S. Agency for International Development, Arlington, VA.

Vargas-Barón, E. 2006. "Payroll Taxes for Child Development: Lessons from Colombia." Policy Brief on Early Childhood. UNESCO, Paris.

———. 2007a. "Early Childhood Finance: An Exploration of Investment Opportunities and Challenges." Paper prepared for the Consultative Group on Early Childhood Care and Development and for the Bernard van Leer Foundation. Processed. Rice Institute, Washington, DC.

———. 2007b. "Going to Scale and Achieving Sustainability: Early Childhood Development in Latin America." Processed. World Bank, Washington, DC.

Vegas, E., P. Cerdán-Infantes, E. Dunkelberg, and E. Molina. 2006. "Evidencia Internacional sobre Políticas de la Primera Infancia que Estimulen el Desarrollo Infantil y Faciliten la Inserción Laboral Femenina." Working Paper 01/06 of the World Bank Office for Argentina, Chile, Paraguay, and Uruguay. World Bank, Buenos Aires.

Verdisco, A., E. Naslund-Hadley, F. Regalia, and A. Zamora. 2007. "Integrated Childhood Development Services in Nicaragua." *Child Health and Education* 1(2): 104–111.

Villalpando, S., T. Shamah, C. Ramirez, F. Mejia, and J. Rivera. 2003. "Prevalence of Anemia in Children 6 Months to 12 Years of Age. Results of a Nationwide Probabilistic Survey in Mexico." *Salud Publica Mex* 45: 490–8.

Villalpando, S., T. Shamah, J. Rivera, Y. Lara, and E. Monterrubio. 2006. "Fortifying Milk with Ferrous Gluconate and Zinc Oxide in a Public Nutrition Program Reduced the Prevalence of Anemia in Toddlers." *Journal of Nutrition* 136: 2633–2637.

Waber, D., L. Vuori-Christiansen, N. Ortiz, and others. 1981. "Nutritional Supplementation, Maternal Education, and Cognitive Development of Infants at Risk of Malnutrition." *American Journal of Clinical Nutrition* 34: 807–13.

Waiser, M. 1998. "Early Childhood Care and Development Programs in Latin America: How Much Do They Cost?" Human Development Department, LCSHD Paper Series No 19. World Bank, Washington, DC.

Walker, S., S. Grantham-McGregror, C. Powell, and S. Chang. 2000. "The Effects of Growth Restrictions in Early Childhood on Growth, IQ, Cognition at Age 11 to 12 Years and the Benefits of Nutritional Supplementation and Psychosocial Stimulation." *Journal of Pediatrics* 137(1): 36–41.

———. 2005. "The Effects of Early Childhood Psychosocial Stimulation and Nutritional Supplementation on Cognition and Education in Growth-Stunted Jamaican Children: Prospective Cohort Study." *Lancet* 366: 1804–07.

Walker, S., T. Wachs, J. Meeks Gardner, B. Lozoff, G. Wasserman, E. Pollitt, J. Carter, and the International Child Development Steering Group. 2007. "Child Development: Risk Factors for Adverse Outcomes in Developing Countries." *Lancet* 369: 145–57.

Waldfogel, J. 1999. "Early Childhood Interventions and Outcomes." CASE paper 21. Centre for Analysis of Social Exclusion, London School of Economics and Political Science.

Watanabe. K., R. Flores, J. Fujiwara, and L. T-H Tran. 2005. "Early Childhood Development Interventions and Cognitive Development of Young Children in Rural Vietnam." *Nutrition* 135: 1918–1925.

World Bank. ND. World Development Indicators. Online database. World Bank, Washington, DC. Available at: http://go.worldbank.org/SI5SS-GAVZ0.

———. 2004a. "Integrated Child Development Project Implementation Completion Report." Report No 30209. Country Management Unit for Bolivia, Ecuador, and Peru. Human Development Sector Management Unit, Latin America, and the Caribbean Regional Office. World Bank, Washington, DC.

———. 2004b. "Ecuador: Poverty Assessment." World Bank, Washington, DC.

———. 2005. *World Development Report 2006: Equity and Development.* New York: World Bank and Oxford University Press.

———. 2006. *Repositioning Nutrition as Central to Development: A Strategy for Large-Scale Action.* Directions in Development Series. Washington, DC: World Bank.

———. 2006b. "Second Maternal and Child Health and Nutrition Program." Information Completion Report No 36544-AR. World Bank, Washington DC.

———. 2006c. *Mejorar el acceso y la calidad de la educación en la primera infancia en Chile.* Washington, DC: World Bank.

———. 2007. *Methodologies to Evaluate Early Childhood Development Programs.* Doing Impact Evaluation Series, No. 9, Poverty Reduction and Economic Management, Thematic Group on Poverty Analysis, Monitoring and Impact Evaluation. Washington, DC: World Bank.

————. Forthcoming. *Measuring Equality of Opportunities in Latin America and the Caribbean.* Poverty and Gender Unit, Poverty Reduction and Economic Management, Latin America and the Caribbean Region. Washington, DC: World Bank.

World Bank, SERNAM, and Inter-American Development Bank. 2007. *Chile: Country Gender Assessment. Expanding Women's Work Choices to Enhance Chile's Economic Potential.* Report No. 36228-CL. Washington, DC, and Santiago, Chile.

Yoshikawa, H., K. McCartney, R. Myers, K. Bub, J. Lugo-Gil, M. Ramos, and F. Knaul. 2006. "Educación preescolar en México." In F. Reimers, ed., *Aprender Mas y Mejor: Políticas, Programas y Oportunidades de Aprendizaje en Educación Básica en México.* Mexico City: Fondo Cultura y Economia.

Young, M., ed. 2002. *From Early Child Development to Human Development.* Washington, DC: The World Bank. Available at: http://www-wds.worldbank.org/external/default/WDSContentServer/WDSP/IB/2002/04/26/000094946_02041304004942/Rendered/PDF/multi-0page.pdf.

————. 2007. *Early Child Development: From Measurement to Action.* Washington, DC: World Bank.

Zahn-Waxler, C., S. Duggal, and R. Gruber. 2002. "Parental Psychopathology." In M. H. Bornstein, ed., *Handbook of Parenting* (2nd ed.). New Jersey: Erlbaum.

Zaitune, C., and N. Menezes Filho. 2006. "Os Efeitos da Pre-Escola sobre os Salários, a Escolaridade e a Proficiência Escolar." Processed. University of São Paulo, São Paulo, Brazil.

Index

Page numbers followed by b, f, or t refer to boxed text, figures, or tables, respectively.

A

academic performance and educational attainment
   access for indigenous persons, 39
   assessment of development, 14
   characteristics of successful ECD programs, 86, 116–17
   developmental significance, 11, 31–32
   disparities in LAC, *xxiii*
   distribution of wealth and, 20, 37–39
   enrollment rates, 133*f*
   in LAC, 20, 21*f*, 41*t*, 127*t*, 132*f*, 133*f*
   maternal employment and, 11
   national economic performance and, 21*f*
   outcomes of health interventions, 69
   outcomes of integrated multiservice programs, 81–82
   outcomes of nutrition interventions, 61, 64
   outcomes of parenting interventions, 64
   outcomes of preschool programs, 76–79
   right to education, 8
   socioeconomic status and, 32
   successful interventions in developed countries, 46–47
   successful interventions in developing countries, 51–52
   see also parental educational attainment; preprimary education
administration and management of ECD programs, 112, 117–18
Anderson, P., 33
Argentina
   distribution of wealth, *xxiv*
   effectiveness of ECD programs, *xxv*
   housing conditions, 30
   longitudinal studies, 105
   maternal and child health programs, 66–67
   poverty alleviation programs, 39
   preprimary education enrollment, 37
   preprimary education program, 76, 85
   reproductive health, 34
   socioeconomic factors in cognitive development, 32
   underweight children, 26
   vaccination rates, 34
   see also Latin America and the Caribbean
Atención a Crisis (Nicaragua), 83
Atención Integral a la Niñez Comunitaria, 68–69, 112, 140, 151*n*.1
Attanasio, O., 85, 151
Australia, 100

www.ingramcontent.com/pod-product-compliance
Lightning Source LLC
Chambersburg PA
CBHW022357280326
41935CB00007B/212